The Wisdom of the Hikam

# The Wisdom of the Hikam

Propositions from the *Hikam* of Ibn Ata'illah amplified by Ibn 'Ajiba's commentary on them in his *Iqadh al-Himam*

Compiled by
Abdalhaqq Bewley

Copyright © Diwan Press Ltd., 2024 CE/1446 AH

The Wisdom of the Hikam

| | |
|---|---|
| Published by: | Diwan Press Ltd. |
| | 311 Allerton Road |
| | Bradford |
| | BD15 7HA |
| | UK |
| Website: | www.diwanpress.com |
| E-mail: | info@diwanpress.com |

All rights reserved. No part of this publication may be reproduced, stored in any retrieval system or transmitted in any form or by any means, electronic, mechanical, photocopying, recording or otherwise without the prior permission of the publishers.

| | |
|---|---|
| Authors: | Ahmad ibn 'Ata'illah al-Iskanderi and |
| | Ahmad ibn 'Ajiba |
| Compiled by: | Abdalhaqq Bewley |

A catalogue record of this book is available from the British Library.

| | |
|---|---|
| ISBN-13: | 978-1-914397-35-6 (casebound) |
| | 978-1-914397-36-3 (paperback) |
| | 978-1-914397-37-0 (ePub and Kindle) |

# Contents

| | |
|---|---|
| **Foreword** | 1 |
| **Derse 1** | 3 |
| Hikam 1 | |
| **Derse 2** | 10 |
| Hikam 2 | |
| **Derse 3** | 17 |
| Hikam 4 | |
| **Derse 4** | 22 |
| Hikam 5 & 6 | |
| **Derse 5** | 28 |
| Hikam 7 | |
| **Derse 6** | 34 |
| Hikam 8 | |
| **Derse 7** | 40 |
| Hikam 10 | |
| **Derse 8** | 44 |
| Hikam 11 | |
| **Derse 9** | 50 |
| Hikam 13 | |

| | |
|---|---|
| **Derse 10** | **55** |
| Hikam 17 | |
| **Derse 11** | **59** |
| Hikam 18 | |
| **Derse 12** | **62** |
| Hikam 19 | |
| **Derse 13** | **65** |
| Hikam 24 | |
| **Derse 14** | **70** |
| Hikam 25, 26 & 27 | |
| **Derse 15** | **75** |
| Hikam 28, 29 & 30 | |
| **Derse 16** | **82** |
| Hikam 31 | |
| **Derse 17** | **85** |
| Hikam 32 & 33 | |
| **Derse 18** | **90** |
| Hikam 34 & 35 | |
| **Derse 19** | **95** |
| Hikam 38 & 39 | 98 |
| **Derse 20** | **100** |
| Hikam 40 & 41 | |
| **Derse 21** | **105** |
| Hikam 42 | |

# Contents

**Derse 22**      **111**
    Hikam 45

**Derse 23**      **115**
    Hikam 47

**Derse 24**      **120**
    Hikam 48, 49 & 50

**Derse 25**      **127**
    Hikam 60

**Derse 26**      **131**
    Hikam 63

**Derse 27**      **135**
    Hikam 64 & 65

**Derse 28**      **141**
    Hikam 66

**Derse 29**      **146**
    Hikam 73 & 74

**Derse 30**      **151**
    Hikam 75 & 76

**Derse 31**      **156**
    Hikam 78

**Derse 32**      **160**
    Hikam 80

**Derse 33**      **165**
    Hikam 83 & 84

**Derse 34**     **170**
    Hikam 85

**Derse 35**     **175**
    Hikam 86

**Derse 36**     **179**
    Hikam 88

**Derse 37**     **183**
    Hikam 89, 90 & 91

**Derse 38**     **188**
    Hikam 92

**Derse 39**     **192**
    Hikam 93

**Derse 40**     **196**
    Hikam 95 & 96

**Derse 41**     **201**
    Hikam 105 & 106

**Derse 42**     **205**
    Hikam 107

**Derse 43**     **208**
    Hikam 112

**Derse 44**     **213**
    Hikam 114

**Derse 45**     **217**
    Hikam 115 & 116

# Contents

**Derse 46** — **223**
    Hikam 118

**Derse 47** — **228**
    Hikam 119 & 120

**Derse 48** — **233**
    Hikam 121 & 122

**Derse 49** — **238**
    Hikam 123 & 124

**Derse 50** — **243**
    Hikam 127

**Derse 51** — **247**
    Hikam 131, 132 & 133

**Derse 52** — **252**
    Hikam 134 & 135

**Derse 53** — **257**
    Hikam 142, 143, 144 & 145

**Derse 54** — **263**
    Hikam 148, 149 & 150

**Derse 55** — **269**
    Hikam 151 & 152

**Derse 56** — **274**
    Hikam 156

**Derse 57** — **278**
    Hikam 159 & 160

**Derse 58** — 283
Hikam 175, 176 & 177

**Derse 59** — 288
Hikam 187

**Derse 60** — 293
Hikam 192

**Derse 61** — 297
Hikam 194, 195 & 196

**Derse 62** — 302
Hikam 197, 198 & 199

**Derse 63** — 311
Hikam 200, 201 & 202

**Derse 64** — 318
Hikam 203 & 204

**Derse 65** — 323
Hikam 208 & 209

**Derse 66** — 329
Hikam 210

**Derse 67** — 333
Hikam 219 & 220

**Derse 68** — 338
Hikam 221 & 222

**Derse 69** — 344
Hikam 225 & 226

## Contents

**Derse 70**     **349**
     Hikam 228 & 230

**Detailed Contents**     **354**

بسم الله الرحمن الرحيم وصلى الله على سيدنا محمد وآله وصحبه وسلم تسليما

# Foreword

Over a period of several years I have regularly used propositions from the *Hikam* of Shaykh Ahmad ibn Ata'illah al-Iskandari together with the commentary on them from *Iqadh al-Himam* by Shaykh Ahmad ibn 'Ajiba as the basis of short discourses given during weekly gatherings of *dhikr* in Bradford. It is these that make up the text of this volume. It is not a complete translation of the *Hikam*, since only about half of the sentences are included, nor is it a complete translation of Ibn 'Ajiba's commentary on the sentences that are included, since some abridgement has taken place, owing to time constraints, and very occasionally short passages from other sources have been introduced. Nevertheless over time a significant body of work has built up and it seemed worth publishing what there is because, as far as I know, there is as yet no English translation of *Iqadh al-Himam* and there was enough of Ibn 'Ajiba's brilliant and magisterial commentary on the sentences of Shaykh Ibn Ata'illah's *Hikam* available to make publication definitely worthwhile.

It is possible that a translation of the whole of the *Iqadh al-Himam* will be brought out at some point but that is unlikely to happen in the near future. In the meantime it is hoped that this present compilation will give readers access to a substantial portion of the sublime wisdom inherent in Shaykh Ibn Ata'illah's incomparable *Hikam* as expounded and illuminated by the scintillating commentary of Shaykh Ibn 'Ajiba in his *Iqadh al-Himam*.

Abdalhaqq Bewley

# Derse 1

$$\text{مِنْ عَلَامَةِ الِاعْتِمَادِ عَلَى الْعَمَلِ،}$$
$$\text{نُقْصَانُ الرَّجَاءِ عِنْدَ وُجُودِ الزَّلَلِ.}$$

**1: A sure sign of reliance on action is a loss of hope when you slip up**

The word "reliance" means to lean on something and depend on it, while the word "action" refers to a movement of either the body or the heart. If an action accords with the *shari'a*, it is called obedience and if it contravenes the *shari'a*, it is called disobedience. The people of this science divide action into three categories: actions of the *shari'a*, actions of the *tariqa*, and actions of the *haqiqa*; or you might say, actions of Islam, actions of Iman and actions of Ihsan; or actions of worship (*'ibada*), actions of slavehood (*'ubudiyya*) and actions of absolute slavehood (*'ubuda*), which is in fact pure freedom; or actions of the people of the beginning, actions of the people of the middle and actions of the people of the end. *Shari'a* is to worship Allah, *tariqa* is to direct yourself towards Allah, and *haqiqa* is to witness

Allah; or you might say *shari'a* is to put the outward right, *tariqa* is to put the inward right, and *haqiqa* is to put the secret right.

The limbs are put right by three things: repentance (*tawba*), fearful awareness (*taqwa*) and going straight (*istiqama*); the heart is put right by three things: sincerity (*ikhlas*), trueness (*sidq*) and tranquillity (*tuma'nina*); and the secret is put right by three things: watchfulness (*muraqaba*), witnessing (*mushahada*) and direct knowledge of Allah (*ma'rifa*); or you might say, the outward is put right by acting by what is commanded and avoiding what is forbidden; the inward by ridding it of base characteristics and adorning it with noble characteristics; and the secret, which in this instance means the spirit (*ruh*), by humbling and breaking it, until it becomes disciplined and able to take on courtesy (*adab*), humility and good character.

When we talk of actions here we are only referring to those actions that enable the purification of the limbs, heart and spirit to be accomplished and the necessary ones for each of them, in this context, have already been specified. Awareness and gnosis of Allah, on the other hand, are the fruits of purification and inner refinement. As the secret is purified, it fills up with awareness, gnosis and illumination.

It is not valid to go on to a further spiritual station until the previous one has been fully realised. As the Shaykh says elsewhere: "He who has a radiant beginning will have a radiant end." So you should not undertake the actions of *tariqa* until you have fulfilled the actions of *shari'a* and accustomed your limbs to performing them. This is done by sincere repentance through fulfilling all its conditions, by fearful awareness through carrying out all its elements, and by going straight in its fullest sense, that is by following the Messenger ﷺ in his words, actions, and states.

Once the outward has been purified and illuminated by the *shari'a*, you may move from the outward actions of the *shari'a* to the inward actions of the *tariqa*, which involve purifying yourself from the attributes of the normal human condition as will be discussed in due course. When you have freed yourself from these attributes of humanness, you will be adorned with the attributes of spirituality (*ruhaniyya*), which entails maintaining correct *adab* with Allah when His *tajalliyat* – His self-manifestations – arrive. When that happens, the limbs are relieved of their tiredness and all that remains is good *adab*. One of the people of full realisation said, "He who arrives at the reality of Islam will not flag in action; he who arrives at the reality of Iman will not be able to act by other than Allah; and he who arrives at the reality of Ihsan will not be able to turn to anyone except Allah."

In travelling through these stations, the seeker (*murid*) should not rely on himself nor on his own actions, state, or strength, but should rather rely on the bounty of his Lord, His gift of success, and His guidance and direction. Allah says in the Qur'an: *"Your Lord creates and chooses whatever He wills. The choice is not theirs,"* (28:68) and: *"If your Lord had wanted to, He would have made mankind into one community but they persist in their differences, except for those your Lord has mercy on."* (11:118) The Prophet ﷺ said,

"None of you will enter the Garden by virtue of his actions." The [Companions present] asked, "Not even you, Messenger of Allah?" He replied, "Not even me, unless Allah envelops me in His mercy."

The hallmark of reliance on Allah is that you feel no lessening of hope when you commit disobedient actions and no increase of it when you do good actions; or you might say that heedlessness does not augment your fear nor does wakeful awareness augment your hope. For such people, fear and hope are always in equal balance because their fear arises from witnessing the Divine Majesty and their hope from witnessing Divine Beauty. Allah's Majesty and Beauty are unchangeable, never increasing nor decreasing, so what stems from them never changes either, unlike in the case of those who rely on action. When their good actions are few, their hope is diminished and when their good actions are many, their hope is increased. This is because of their associating something else (*shirk*) with their Lord and the sheer fact of their own ignorance. If they were to be annihilated to themselves and attain going on by their Lord, they would be relieved of their toiling and gain gnosis of their Lord.

What is indispensable is a perfect shaykh, who will take you from the toils of your lower self to a place where you will find rest in the witnessing of your Lord. The perfect shaykh is the one who relieves you of toil, not the one who burdens you with it. "He who directs you to action, has tired you out and he who directs you to this world, has defrauded you, but he who directs you to Allah has been true to you," as was confirmed by Shaykh Ibn Mashish ﷺ. Being directed to Allah is being directed to forget the lower self, for when you forget yourself, you remember your Lord. Allah Almighty says: *'Remember your Lord when you forget'* (18:24), i.e. when you forget Him. The cause of tiredness and toil is remembering the lower self and worrying about its concerns and portions; anyone free of that, finds nothing but rest.

The words of Allah: *"We created man in trouble"* (90:4), refer specifically to the people of the veil (*hijab*), or you might say, people whose lower selves are still alive. As for him whose lower self has died, the Almighty says of him: *"If he is one of Those Brought Near, there is solace and sweetness and a Garden of Delight"* (56:88), meaning that he will have the solace of reunion, the sweetness of beauty, and the Garden of the delight of perfection. The Almighty says: *"They will not be affected by any tiredness there"* (15:48) i.e. toil. Rest, however, can only be reached after much toil and victory can only be achieved after hard pursuit of it, for "The Garden is surrounded by things which are hateful to you."

We read in the book *Solving the Riddles*, "Know that you will not attain to the stages of nearness until you have climbed six steep slopes. The first is weaning the limbs from opposing the *shari'a*; the second is weaning the self from its usual comforts; the third is weaning the heart from human frivolities; the fourth is weaning the self from its natural turbidity; the fifth is weaning the spirit from any echoes of sensory experience; the sixth is weaning the intellect from all illusory imaginings. When you reach the top of the first slope you overlook the sources of the wisdom of the heart; from the top of the second you see the secrets of direct Divine knowledge; from the top of the third, you see indicators of the intimate converse of the *malakut*; from the top of the fourth, the shining lights of the higher stages of proximity; from the top of the fifth, the lights of the vision of the landscape of love; and from the top of the sixth, you descend into the meadows of the Holiest Presence, and there you withdraw by the ethereal subtleties of intimacy you witness in them from the gross densities of sensory experience. When Allah desires to single you out and make you one of His select few, He will give you to drink a draught from the cup of His love, a drink that will increase your thirst, a drink whose savour will increase your yearning, whose proximity will intensify your quest, and whose headiness will augment your restlessness."

Some excellent scholars have found difficulty in squaring up Allah's words, *"Enter the Garden for what you did"* (16:32) with the words of the Prophet ﷺ, "None of you will enter the Garden by his actions." The solution to this apparent paradox lies in the fact that the Book and the *Sunna* alternate between the *shari'a* and the *haqiqa*, or you might say between clarifying the *shari'a* aspect of something – its outward appearance – and its *haqiqa* aspect – its inner reality. The same thing may have its *shari'a* aspect defined in one part of the Qur'an and its *haqiqa* aspect in another and the same applies to the *Sunna*. Alternatively, the Qur'an may define the *shari'a* aspect of a particular thing in one place with the *Sunna* defining its *haqiqa* aspect, and vice versa. The Messenger ﷺ acts as an explainer of what Allah reveals, as Allah makes clear when He says: *"We have sent down the Reminder to you so that you can make clear to mankind what has been sent down to them..."* (16:44) So Allah's words: *"Enter the Garden for what you did"* give the *shari'a* aspect for the people governed by Divine Wisdom, who are the people of *shari'a*; while the words of the Prophet ﷺ: "None of you will enter the Garden by his actions" give the *haqiqa* aspect for the people governed by Divine Power, who are the people of *haqiqa*.

Similarly, the words of the Almighty: *"But you will not will unless Allah wills"* (81:29) provide the *haqiqa* aspect, while the words of the Prophet ﷺ: "When one of you does a good action, a good action is written for him," provide the *shari'a* aspect. In short, the *Sunna* qualifies the Qur'an and the Qur'an qualifies the *Sunna*. So everyone must have two eyes: one looking to the *haqiqa* of things and the other to their *shari'a* aspect. If someone finds that the Qur'an talks about the *shari'a* aspect of something in one place, he will know for certain that its *haqiqa* aspect is defined elsewhere in the Qur'an or *Sunna*; and, likewise, if he finds that the *Sunna* talks about the *shari'a* aspect of something in one place, he will know for certain that its *haqiqa* aspect is defined elsewhere in the *Sunna* or the Qur'an. So it is clear that there is no contradiction whatsoever between the *ayat* and the *hadith*.

# Derse 2

إِرَادَتُكَ التَّجْرِيدَ مَعَ إِقَامَةِ اللَّهِ إِيَّاكَ فِي الأَسْبَابِ مِنَ الشَّهْوَةِ الْخَفِيَّةِ، وَإِرَادَتُكَ الأَسْبَابَ مَعَ إِقَامَةِ اللَّهِ إِيَّاكَ فِي التَّجْرِيدِ انْحِطَاطٌ عَنِ الْهِمَّةِ الْعَلِيَّةِ.

**2: Your desire for divestment
when Allah has established you
in the world of means
is a hidden appetite.
Your desire for the world of means
when Allah has established you in divestment
is a fall from high aspiration.**

The word for divestment, *tajrid,* literally means "stripping away and removing" and is used for things like removing a garment or shedding a skin. According to the Sufis there are three types of *tajrid*: divestment of the outward alone, divestment of the inward alone, and divestment of both together. Outward divestment consists of abandoning worldly means and breaking physical habits; inward divestment consists of abandoning psychological attachments and illusory obstacles; and divestment of them both consists of abandoning both inner attachments and physical habits. Or you might say outward divestment is to abandon everything which distracts the limbs from obeying Allah; inward divestment is to abandon everything which distracts the heart from being present with Allah; and divestment of both is devote the heart and its container to Allah alone. Perfect outward divestment constitutes abandoning worldly means and stripping the body of its normal clothing and perfect inward divestment constitutes divesting the heart of every ignoble attribute and adorning it with every noble one. This – perfect divestment – is what the shaykh of our shaykhs, Sidi Abdarrahman al-Majdoub, was referring to in his poem when he wrote:

> O students of theology, here are oceans
> which will leave you dumfounded.
> This is the station of divestment,
> those standing in the presence of their Lord.

Anyone who divests his outward and not his inward, is a liar, like someone who plates base metal with silver – his inward is ugly and his outward pleasing. Anyone who divests his inward and not his outward – if such a thing is really feasible – is good, like someone who plates silver with base metal. Such people, however, are extremely rare since outward attachments usually influence inward ones. When someone's outward is occupied by the sensory, his inward is usually occupied by it as well, since energy cannot go in two different directions at the same time. Anyone who divests both his inward and outward is the epitome of true sincerity, he is that pure gold which befits the treasuries of kings.

Shaykh Abu'l-Hasan ash-Shadhili said, "The *adab* of the divested *faqir* manifests itself in four ways: respect for those old in the path, compassion for those new to the path, humbling the self and not seeking recognition for it. The *adab* of the *faqir* in the world of means also manifests itself in four ways: keeping the company of the godfearing, avoiding the dissolute, doing the prayer in congregation, and bringing comfort to the poor and wretched by giving from what he has received. He should also take on the *adab* of the divested *faqir* since perfection lies in that. Another aspect of the *adab* of someone in the world of means is that he should remain in the world of means, where Allah has established him, until such time as Allah Almighty Himself takes him out of it, either through the instructions of his shaykh, if he has one, or by some other clear indication, such as it becoming almost impossible in every way for him to continue in it. Only then should he move on to divestment."

Desire for divestment, when Allah has established someone in the world of means, is a hidden appetite because the intention of the self in doing that might be to gain rest when it does not have the necessary certainty to endure the privations of poverty. Then when poverty does come, he is shaken and perturbed and returns to the world of means, which is worse for him than if he had never left it in the first place. This is how it reveals itself to be an appetite and it is hidden because outwardly the *faqir* displays seclusion and self-denial, which is a noble and sublime state, while inwardly he conceals the part of him whose intention was to gain respite, honour, *wilaya* or some other benefit, rather than the attainment of true slavehood and the development of certainty. He also shows a lack of *adab* towards Allah by wanting to leave the situation in which Allah has placed him and failing to wait patiently until Allah has granted him permission to do so. The sign of his still being established in the world of means is his continued success in it, its not getting in the way of his practise of the *deen* and the fact that failure to obtain the sufficiency he now has by abandoning the world of means would cause him to look longingly towards creation and have anxiety about provision. Only when these circumstances cease to exist may he move on to divestment.

Shaykh Ibn Ata'illah says in *at-Tanwir*: "What Allah demands of you is that you should remain in the situation in which He has established you until He Himself is the One Who removes you from it, just as He Himself was the One Who placed you there in the first place. It is not a matter of you abandoning the means but of the means abandoning you. One of the people of Allah said, 'I once abandoned a certain type of means but later returned to it. Then the means abandoned me and I never returned to it.'" The *Tanwir* continues, "I went to Shaykh Abu'l-'Abbas al-Mursi when I had resolved to take on divestment, saying to myself, 'How can I possibly reach Allah Almighty in the state I am in at the moment, what with my preoccupation with outward knowledge and the amount of time I spend socialising with other people.' Before I had even opened my mouth to speak, he said to me, 'There was a man who kept my company who spent much of his time engaged in the acquisition of outward knowledge and had become very proficient in it. When he came to taste something of this Path he came to me and said, "Sidi, I have resolved to abandon my present path and devote myself to your company." So I told him, "It is not a matter of that. Rather remain on your present path and then that which Allah has allotted you from us will come to you in its own good time."' Then the shaykh looked at me and said, 'This is the way of true men (*siddiqun*): they never abandon anything until Allah Himself is the One Who removes them from it.' So I left his presence with Allah having cleansed my heart of those thoughts and found respite in submission to Allah Almighty."

Shaykh Ibn Ata'illah continues, "The only reason he forbade him to take on divestment was because his self was greedy for it." When the self is greedy for something, it means that thing is easy for it, and what is easy for it has no good in it. Something is only easy for the self when the self has a share in it. Then he adds, "If he desires to gain benefit, a *murid* should not enter divestment from a position of outward strength until that strength has left him. If divestment takes place when someone is in that state, then weakness will soon follow, succeeded by objectors who come up with arguments which trouble and unsettle him in his resolve. Indeed, it is very possible that, if he is not touched by Divine kindness, he will allow himself once again to mix with people, go back to what he was doing before and will have a negative opinion of the people of divestment, saying to himself, 'There is nothing to what they say. We entered that land along with them and saw that there was nothing there.' The murid who should take on divestment is the one who finds divestment a heavy burden at the outset, because it is very difficult for his *nafs*, as he has it up against a wall with a sword to its throat giving it no room whatsoever to move."

If someone who is in a state of divestment desires to return to the world of means without express permission, that constitutes a fall from high aspiration to low aspiration or a fall from greater *wilaya* to lesser *wilaya*. The shaykh of our shaykhs, Sidi 'Ali ؓ said that his shaykh Sidi al-'Arabi said to him, "My son, if I had come across anything higher, quicker and more beneficial than divestment, I would have told you about it. But with the People of the Path, divestment has the same role as that played in alchemy by the elixir, a *qirat* of which is more valuable than all the gold in the world. That is the importance of divestment in terms of this path."

I heard our shaykh's shaykh ؓ say, "The gnosis of the divested *faqir* is better and his thought processes are clearer because purity comes from purity and turbidity comes from turbidity: purity of the inward comes from purity of the outward and turbidity of the inward comes from turbidity of the outward. Whenever someone increases in the sensory, they decrease in the meaning." Some reports state that taking something of this world diminishes a scholar's rank with Allah, even though he may remain dear to Him. However, a *faqir* who has permission to make use of means is like one who is divested, since for him the means itself have become an instrument of his slavehood. Thus divestment without permission is a form of means and means with permission is a form of divestment. Success is by Allah.

NOTE: All this only applies to those who are travelling on the Path. As for those who have arrived and are firmly established, however, there is nothing to be said since they have been taken out of themselves, have been seized by Allah and move by Him. Allah has taken charge of their affairs, preserved their secrets and guarded their hearts with armies of lights, preventing the darknesses of other-than-Allah from having any effect on them. This is how the relationship between the Companions and means should be understood, may Allah be pleased with them all and benefit us by their *baraka*.

Know that both those involved in the world of means and those in a state of divestment are working for Allah since they are all sincere in their turning to Allah. This is so much the case that one of the people of Allah said, "The likeness of someone in a state of divestment and someone involved in the world of means is that of two slaves belonging to a king. He orders one of them to work and eat that way and the other to remain constantly in his presence, taking his sustenance from what is allotted to the king himself." However, as is well known, the sincere-turning-to-Allah of someone in a state of divestment is stronger because of his lack of impediments and severing of attachments.

# Derse 3

أَرِحْ نَفْسَكَ مِنَ التَّدْبِيرِ.

فَمَا قَامَ بِهِ غَيْرُكَ عَنْكَ لَا تَقُمْ بِهِ لِنَفْسِكَ.

**4: Give yourself a rest from management:
You should not try to do yourself
what someone else is already doing for you.**

In its linguistic usage the word "management" (*tadbir*) means "assessing matters and their possible outcomes". However, in its technical usage – as Shaykh Zarruq says – it is: "The pre-planning of future matters whose occurrence is feared or hoped for, by taking them into your own hands completely without consigning the outcome to Allah. When it is accompanied by consigning the outcome to Allah then, when it is a matter of the Next World, it is good intention, when it is a matter of ordinary bodily needs, it is appetite, and when it is a purely worldly matter, it is wishful thinking."

From this we can see that there are three types of management: blameworthy, desirable, and permissible. The blameworthy type is that which is accompanied by over-certainty as to the outcome and excessive planning, whether it is a matter of the *deen* or this world. This is because of the lack of *adab* inherent in that attitude and the tiredness which swiftly afflicts you when you act on it. There is absolutely no point in taking on for yourself what the Living, Self-Subsistent is doing for you.

People over-concerning themselves with the management of their worldly affairs is blameworthy. This is because Allah has taken on for them the responsibility of this matter. What is meant by this is that people try to ordain for themselves what will happen according to their own desires and fancies. They also plan for what they consider to be best for themselves including spiritual conditions and actions. They even prepare for this and pay great attention to it. What Allah asks of them is that they disentangle their hearts from it and engage in carrying out His worship and the things He really has made them responsible for. This kind of planning is a great drudgery that people burden themselves with. It may be that most of what they intend for themselves doesn't happen. As a result, particularly where spiritual ambitions are concerned, their efforts come to nothing and they completely lose heart and may form a bad opinion of Allah. Then, they may start to neglect their worship, oppose aspects of the *shari'a*, argue about destiny, and waste years of their life. All this tells the intelligent person to leave and avoid this kind of management and cut off its means and causes of existence.

The things you plan by yourself are, as a general rule, not in harmony with the winds of destiny and are often succeeded by worries and troubles. That is why Ahmad ibn Masruq said, "Whoever gives up management achieves rest." Sahl ibn 'Abdullah said, "Leave off management and choice. They cause problems for people in their lives." The Messenger of Allah ﷺ said, "Allah put ease and rest in contentment and certainty." Shaykh ash-Shadhili said, "Do not choose in any of your affairs. Choose not to choose; flee even from that choice; and then flee from your fleeing, and from everything else, to Allah Almighty. *'Your Lord creates and chooses whatever He wills.'* (28:68)" He also said, "If you must manage, then manage not to manage." These statements must be understood as referring to the type of management that is accompanied by over-certainty as to the outcome. If, however, it is accompanied by consigning the outcome to Allah, then it is not blameworthy provided it does not go on too long.

The desirable type of management is planning to carry out the obligations which are your legal responsibility and those supererogatory actions which are recommended for you, while at the same time consigning them to the Divine Will and having regard for the Divine Power. This is what is called right intention. The Prophet ﷺ said, "A believer's intention is better than his action." He ﷺ also said, in a *hadith qudsi*, "When My slave intends to do a good action but does not do it, I assign one full good action to him…"

This is how the words of Shaykh Ibn Ata'illah ﷺ, "What someone else is already doing for you" should be understood, since what they are in effect saying is that there is no harm in your managing things which someone else is not doing for you, that is to say acts of obedience. This is why Ibrahim al-Khawwas ﷺ said, "All of knowledge is contained in two phrases: 'Do not give yourself the responsibility of getting what you already have enough of,' and 'Do not neglect the getting of what you have not yet got enough of.'" The phrase "Do not give yourself the responsibility of getting what you already have enough of" refers to the first blameworthy type of management, and the phrase "Do not neglect the getting of what you have not yet got enough of" refers to the second desirable type of management.

The permissible type of management is the planning which goes with carrying out worldly affairs or meeting ordinary bodily needs while at the same time consigning their final outcome to the Will of Allah and having regard for what emanates from Divine Power, and not relying at all on your own planning. The words of the Prophet ﷺ, "Management is half of livelihood," should be understood in this light, on the condition, of course, that it is not over-indulged in, since the permitted amount of planning is that it should pass through the heart like the wind, entering one side and emerging from the other. This is management by Allah. The sign of its being by Allah is that when the opposite of what is planned emanates from [the realm of] Divine Power, the person concerned feels neither constriction nor perturbation, but rather he is as the one addressed by the poet:

Submit yourself to Salma and go wherever she goes.
Follow the winds of destiny and turn wherever they turn.

Shaykh Ibn Ata'illah says in *at-Tanwir*: "Know that

things are subject to either praise or blame depending on the direction in which they lead you: blameworthy management is what distracts you from Allah, obstructs you from serving Allah and precludes your interaction with Allah; while praiseworthy management is what brings you to near to Allah and makes you the subject of His pleasure."
More on the same subject may be found in his book. What I have said here is what has come to me regarding the subject of the management of affairs. Shaykh Ibn Ata'illah wrote a whole book about it entitled *At-tanwir fi isqat at-tadbir* (Illumination of the Dropping of the Management of Affairs), in which he explains this matter in a masterful way. However, everything he wrote is summed up by what we have said and Allah knows best. When Shaykh Ibn Ata'illah completed the book, he read it out to the perfect wali, Sidi Yaqut al-'Arishi, who said upon hearing it, "Everything you have said can be summed up by the following two verses:

Nothing comes to pass except what He wills.
So jettison your cares and abandon yourself to Him.
Jettison the distractions which preoccupy
your mind and you will find relief and restfulness."

# Derse 4

اجْتِهَادُكَ فِيمَا ضُمِنَ لَكَ وَتَقْصِيرُكَ فِيمَا طُلِبَ مِنْكَ دَلِيلٌ عَلَى انْطِمَاسِ الْبَصِيرَةِ مِنْكَ.

**5: Your earnest striving for what
has already been guaranteed to you
and your falling short in respect of
what is required from you
is clear evidence of the dimming of your inner eye.**

"Earnest striving" is devoting all of one's efforts and energy towards obtaining something, while "falling short" is being remiss about something and letting the opportunity of doing it pass you by. The "inner eye" is the means by which the heart sees in the same way that the outer eye is the means by which the body sees. The inner eye sees meaning while the outer eye sees sensory form; or you might say the inner eye sees spiritual forms and the outer eye sees material forms; or you might say the inner eye sees the beyond-time and the outer eye sees the in-time; or you might say the inner eye sees the Creator and the outer eye sees the creation.

If Allah desires to open someone's inner eye, He occupies their outward with serving Him and their inward with loving Him. As inward love and outward service grow, the light of the inner eye becomes stronger and stronger until it overwhelms the outer eye, so that the light of outward sight is swallowed up by the light of inner sight and the outer eye also starts to see those subtle meanings and timeless lights which are the province of the sight of the inner eye. This is what Shaykh al-Majdhub ﷺ meant when he said:

> My sight was swallowed up by another seeing,
> I became annihilated to everything transitory.
> I achieved realisation, I found no otherness.
> I stayed there, in that state, filled with delight.

If Allah desires disappointment for His slave, however, He occupies a person's outward with serving creation and their inward with loving creation. That continues until the light of their inner eye becomes dimmed. The light of outward sight overwhelms the light of inward sight and they only see and serve what is sensory, with the result that they spend great efforts in getting the provision which has already been allotted to them and guaranteed for them, while at the same time falling short of meeting the obligations required of them. If expended effort is replaced by total preoccupation, and falling short by actual abandonment, then the dimness turns into blindness, which is disbelief itself and we seek refuge with Allah from that ever happening! That is because this world is like the river of Saul: only those who drink from it by merely scooping up a little in their hand are safe – those who slake their thirst in it are certainly not, as Shaykh Zarruq ﷺ said, so understand!

Shaykh Abu'l-hasan ﷺ said, "The inner eye is like the outer eye: the smallest thing falling into it prevents it from being able to see, even if that does not bring about blindness. In the same way, being preoccupied by something disrupts one's ability to see inwardly and muddies one's ability to reflect clearly; wanting it immediately banishes all good; and acting on it causes a portion of people's Islam to leave them and its opposite to come in its place, may Allah protect us! If people continue on this evil path, their Islam gradually fades away. And if this reaches the stage where their love of rank and position, and their preference for this world over the Next, leads them to turn their back on other Muslims and curry favour with the powers that be, then their Islam has left them completely. Do not be fooled by what they outwardly appear to be: the essential life breath of the *deen* is missing from them because the reality of Islam is love of Allah and love of His right-acting slaves."

Going to great lengths to get what is in any case guaranteed is blameworthy, regardless of whether that is by deed, as we have just said, or by word, which is asking for something to happen before its appointed time, either by supplication or some other means. This is what Shaykh Ibn Ata'illah is referring to when he says:

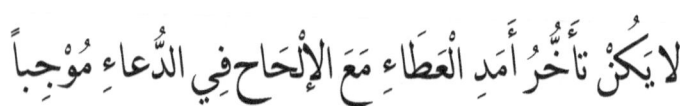

لِيَأْسُكَ. فَهُوَ ضَمِنَ لَكَ الْإِجَابَةَ فِيمَا يَخْتَارُهُ لَكَ لَا فِيمَا تَخْتَارُهُ لِنَفْسِكَ. وَفِي الْوَقْتِ الَّذِي يُرِيدُ لَا فِي الْوَقْتِ الَّذِي تُرِيدُ.

**6: Do not make a delay in His giving you something you have fervently prayed for a cause for despair on your part. He has guaranteed to answer your supplication – but in the way He chooses, not the way you choose, and at the time He wants, not the time you want.**

Doing something "fervently" means doing it over and over again in exactly the same way. "Supplication" is a request made with *adab* on the carpet of slavehood in the presence of Lordship. Something's "cause" is part of what is intrinsic to its existence. "Despair" is the snuffing out of all aspiration and hope.

One of Allah's names is *al-Qayyum*, an intensive form of the word *qiyam* (meaning to stand up, to be existent, to undertake something). Allah continually undertakes the creation of all existence, from His Throne to His earth. He has assigned a fixed lifespan and a pre-ordained end to every manifest form, giving each one a specified shape and an allotted amount of provision. *"When their time comes, they cannot delay it a single hour nor bring it forward."* (7:34) If your heart becomes attached to anything in this world or the Next, revert to what Allah has promised, be content with His knowledge and do not be greedy, for in greed lies exhaustion and abasement. The shaykh of our shaykh, Moulay al-'Arabi ☙, said, "In the case of ordinary people, their needs are satisfied by their desire for them and their pursuit of them. But in our case, our needs are satisfied by our lack of desire (*zuhd*) concerning them and our being distracted by Allah from seeking them."

If you make *du'a* – and it is something which you must do – then let your *du'a* be an act of worship, rather than one of portion seeking. If you turn away from portions, they will pour down upon you. If, however, you are overcome by the impulse to ask, and you ask for something and do not receive it straight away, do not accuse Allah of breaking the promise entailed by His words: *"Call on me and I will answer you,"* (40:60) and never despair of Allah's generosity and support. Allah has guaranteed you an answer according to what He wishes to give you of the good of this world and the good of the Next. It may be that He will delay His response and answer us at a time when it is better and more beneficial for us, granting our request at the time when He wishes, not the time we want. And it may also be that He will postpone His answer until we reach the Abode of Generosity and Permanence, which is *"better and longer lasting"* (87:17). And if what you ask for is not appropriate for you, it may even be that He will withhold it from you altogether out of kindness to you.

In a *hadith*, the Messenger of Allah ☙ said, "When someone makes *du'a* there are only three possible outcomes: their request is granted immediately; its reward is stored up for them; or a comparable evil is averted from them." Shaykh Abu Muhammad 'Abdu'l-'Aziz al-Mahdawi said, "Anyone who does not give up his own choice in his supplication and remain content with whatever Allah has chosen for him will be led on step by step towards destruction, being one of those about whom Allah says, 'Give him what he wants. I dislike the sound of his voice.' But anyone who is content with what Allah chooses for him – rather than what he may have chosen for himself – may be certain that Allah is responding to him in the best possible way, even if he does not get what he actually asked for."

# Derse 5

So Allah will, as has already been mentioned, fulfil His promise and carry out what He has promised to do – but in the way He wishes and at the time He wants – commanding us to have true sincerity and belief in the truth of Allah's promise and forbidding us from having doubt and vacillation. If we do this, the opening of our inner eye will be completed and the lights of our secret made glad. Then Ibn Ata'illah says:

$$\text{لا يُشَكِّكَنَّكَ فِي الْوَعْدِ عَدَمُ وُقُوعِ الْمَوْعُودِ،}$$
$$\text{وَإِنْ تَعَيَّنَ زَمَنُهُ، لِئَلَّا يَكُونَ ذَلِكَ قَدْحاً فِي بَصِيرَتِكَ}$$
$$\text{وَإِخْمَاداً لِنُورِ سَرِيرَتِكَ.}$$

**7: Do not let the fact that
something promised does not happen,
even if its time is specified,
make you doubt Allah's promise.
Doing that will dim your inner eye
and extinguish the light of your secret.**

"Doubt" about a thing is to vacillate backwards and forwards about whether something will or will not happen. The "promise" is the notification that something will definitely come about at an appointed place and time. The something promised is that thing about which notification was given. "Dimming" something means diminishing it and lowering its rank. The "inner eye" is the human faculty which is capable of perceiving the inner meaning of things, while the "secret" is the human faculty which is able to achieve a firm grasp of knowledge and gnosis. Know that the *nafs* (lower self), *'aql* (intellect), *ruh* (spirit) and *sirr* (secret) are one thing but the term used to describe it varies according to the level of perception displayed. When its level of perception is the lower appetites, it is called the *nafs*; when its level of perception is the judgements of the *shari'a* it is called the intellect; when its level of perception is *tajalliyat* and *waridat* it is called the *ruh*; and when its level of perception is unseen realities and fixed states it is called the secret. The locus, however, of all these things is one. "Extinguishing" something is making it disappear after it has appeared.

I say that when Allah promises something by means of Revelation or Divine Inspiration given to a Prophet or *wali*, or by means of a strong *tajalli*, then, *murid*, if you are truly sincere, have no doubt that that promise will be fulfilled. If the time of the promise is left unspecified, then there is a lot of leeway and its fulfilment may come about after a shorter or longer time. But do not doubt that it certainly will occur, even if it does take a very long time. Indeed, it took forty years for the supplication of Musa and Harun ﷺ against Pharaoh [and his people], when they said, *"Our Lord, obliterate their wealth..."* (10:88), to be fulfilled.

If it is tied to a particular time and it does not occur when that time comes about, you must still not doubt the truth of the promise, since that may be due to reasons and unseen circumstances which Allah has concealed from the Prophet or *wali* concerned, so that His Force, Might and Judgement may be made manifest in the way He decides. Reflect, for instance, on the case of Yunus ﷺ whereby he informed his people of the punishment when he himself had been informed of it and then fled from them. That punishment was contingent upon their lack of Islam and so, when they embraced Islam, the punishment was deferred. Or on the case of Nuh ﷺ when he said, *"My son is one of my family and Your promise is surely the truth"* (11:45), having understood Allah's promise to him [to save his family] in a general and literal way. Then Allah said to him, *"He is definitely not one of your family. He is someone whose action was not righteous."* (11:46) In other words, Allah had only promised the salvation of those members of his family who were righteous, even if Nuh ﷺ had understood His promise to be all inclusive, Allah's knowledge being all-encompassing.

It is because of this hidden secret that the Prophets and the great and true men of Allah do not confine their hopes to the literal wording of Allah's promise. Their unsettledness remains and they find no settledness with anything other than Allah. Rather they look to the vastness of Allah's knowledge and the effects of His overwhelming power.

Examples of this can be found in the words of Ibrahim al-Khalil ﷺ mentioned in the Qur'an: *"I have no fear of any partner you ascribe to Him unless My Lord should will such a thing to happen. My Lord encompasses all things in knowledge,"* (6:80) and the words of Shu'ayb ﷺ: *"We could never return to it,"* i.e. to the religion of disbelief, *"unless Allah our Lord so willed. Our Lord encompasses everything in His knowledge."* (7:89)

There is also the case of our own Prophet ﷺ on the Day of Badr when he called on His Lord so earnestly that his cloak fell from his shoulders, saying, "O Allah, Your covenant and promise! O Allah, if this group is destroyed, there will be no one left to worship you after today." Whereupon the Siddiq ﷺ said to him, "Enough, Messenger of Allah. Allah will fulfil His promise to you." So the understanding of the Chosen One ﷺ was more far-reaching because of the fact that he did not stop with the literal wording of the promise whereas the Siddiq ﷺ did. Each of them was correct but the Prophet's understanding was wider reaching and his knowledge more complete. In the case of al-Hudaybiyya, the time of the promise was not specified, since Allah says: *"He knew what you did not know."* (48:27) So when 'Umar ﷺ asked, "Did you not tell us that we would enter Makka?" the Prophet ﷺ answered, "Did I say it would be this year?" When 'Umar replied "No," the Prophet ﷺ said, "You will certainly enter it and do *tawaf* there."

So, my brother, hold fast and affirm the truth of what Allah has promised you, and have a good opinion of Him, His friends, and especially your shaykh. Beware of hidden denial or doubt about Allah's promise, for that that will dim your inner eye, and may even darken it completely, and will also snuff out the light of your secret. You will go right back to square one, losing everything you have gained, and find that everything you have built has been destroyed. Look for the best interpretation and cling to the best conclusion. We have already mentioned the words of the shaykh of our shaykh, Sidi 'Ali al-Jamal ⚘, who said, "With us, when we say something and it comes about, we experience a single joy. But if it does not come about, we experience ten joys." This statement indicates the vastness of his perception and the fully realised nature of his gnosis of Allah.

Allah may also acquaint His friends with the arrival of the decree but not with the kindness accompanying it. When the decree arrives accompanied by kindness, it may be so light and easy that a person may think that it has not happened at all. We ourselves have witnessed this and what we mentioned previously with respect to both ourselves and our shaykhs, and it neither decreased our sincerity nor extinguished the light of our secret. Praise be to our Lord.

NOTE. Our shaykh the faqih and scholar, Sidi at-Tawudi ibn Sawda, found this particular *hikma* problematic and said, "How can it be imagined that the time of something like this can be specified? If the specification is by means of Divine Revelation, Divine Revelation has ceased, and if it is by means of inspiration, then having doubt about it does not necessarily imply the dimming of the inner eye since it is not obligatory to believe in what has come through inspiration." Our reply to this is: "Our words are intended for true *murids* who are travelling the path or who have already arrived. They are required to affirm all that is said by their shaykhs since the shaykhs are the heirs of the Prophets and follow closely in their footsteps. The Prophets received Divine judgements whereas the *awliya'* receive Divine inspiration, because when the heart is purified of its impurities and all that is other-than-Allah, and filled with lights and secrets, only the Truth can appear in it. If they say something containing a promise or threat, the *murid* must believe it. If he has any doubt or hesitation about what Allah has promised on the tongue of his Prophet or shaykh, that will certainly dim the light of his inner eye and extinguish his secret. If the time is not specified, wait for it to occur, even if it takes a long time. If the time is specified and it does not occur, interpret it like the Messengers as being dependent on hidden reasons and preconditions. That is the difference between the *siddiq* and the *saadiq* because the *siddiq* does not hesitate or feel astonishment whereas the *saadiq* first hesitates and then reaches certainty, and if he sees something miraculous, he is astonished and finds it remarkable. Allah knows best."

# Derse 6

إِذَا فَتَحَ لَكَ وِجْهَةً مِنَ التَّعَرُّفِ فَلَا تُبَالِ مَعَهَا إِنْ قَلَّ عَمَلُكَ. فَإِنَّهُ مَا فَتَحَهَا لَكَ إِلَّا وَهُوَ يُرِيدُ أَنْ يَتَعَرَّفَ إِلَيْكَ؛ أَلَمْ تَعْلَمْ أَنَّ التَّعَرُّفَ هُوَ مُورِدُهُ عَلَيْكَ وَالْأَعْمَالُ أَنْتَ مُهْدِيهَا إِلَيْهِ. وَأَيْنَ مَا تُهْدِيهِ إِلَيْهِ مِمَّا هُوَ مُورِدُهُ عَلَيْكَ

**8: If He opens up a way of making Himself known to you, do not let your lack of actions worry you. The only reason He opened up the way for you was to make Himself known to you. Do you not see that He has brought you knowledge of Himself whereas you only present Him with actions. Where is what you present to Him in comparison with what He has brought to you!**

"Opening up" here means preparation and ease. It is usually used for good things. Here it is followed by knowledge of beautiful things and the manner in which they arrive. What is meant by "way" is an opening which enables you to perceive His Presence and the use of the expression "making known" implies a desire for recognition to take place. You say, "Someone made himself known to me," when he sought to make himself known to you. Direct apprehension of this kind makes the reality of the knowledge of what is known firm in the heart so that it cannot leave it.

If Allah reveals Himself to you by His Name, the Majestic, or His Name, the Conqueror, and by that means opens a door and a way to you for you to have direct knowledge of Him, then know that Allah has shown concern for you, has wanted to select you for His nearness, and has chosen you for His Presence. So cling to *adab* with satisfaction and submission. Receive it with joy and happiness. Do not be concerned about any actions you may neglect because of it. It is a means to actions of the heart. He has only opened this door to you because He wants to lift a veil between you and Him. Do you not know that these manifestations of Divine Majesty are what He sends to you to bring you to Him whereas you aspire to reach Him by means of the bodily actions you present to Him. What a vast difference there is between the puny actions and diseased states you present to Him and the Divine gnoses and face-to-face knowledges He brings you.

So, *murid*, be happy about any manifestations of Divine Majesty and revelations of Divine Power which come to you, such as illnesses, times of hunger and hardship, terrors, and all the other things that are heavy on the *nafs* and difficult for it, such as poverty, humiliation, annoyance from others and other things which the *nafs* hates. All the things of this nature which happen to you are, in fact, great blessings and generous gifts which are signs of the strength of your sincerity; and the greater your sincerity the greater the amount of direct Divine knowledge you will have. Those with the greatest affliction are the Prophets, and then the next best people and the next best. When Allah wants to shorten the distance between Himself and His slave, He grants affliction power over him so that when he is purified and cleansed by that, he is ready for the Divine Presence, just as silver and gold are purified by fire so that they are fit for the king's treasury.

Shaykhs and gnostics continue to delight in these blows and to consider them to be gifts. The shaykh of our shaykhs Sidi 'Ali al-'Imrani called them "the Night of Power" and said, "Severe constraint is the Night of Power which is better than a thousand months." That is because of the actions of the heart which the slave harvests from it. An atom's weight of them are like mountains of actions of the limbs. I wrote two lines of poetry about this:

> When a time of need knocks at my door,
> I open the door to it with joy and happiness.
> I tell it, "Welcome and welcome again!
> Your time with me profits me more than the Night of Power!

Know that these manifestations of Majesty are a test from Allah and a gauge of people and the way that silver and gold are distinguished from copper. There are many pretenders who make a display of gnosis and certainty with their tongues. Then when the tempestuous winds of the decree strike them, they are cast into the deserts of despair and denial. If someone claims what he does not have, he will be exposed and disgraced by being tested.

Shaykh Moulay al-'Arabi ﷺ used to say, "The greatest wonder of all is someone who seeks gnosis of Allah and is eager for it, but then, when Allah gives him knowledge, flees from it and denies it." Shaykh al-Buzidi ﷺ said, "These revelations of Majesty fall into three categories. One betokens punishment and expulsion, one discipline and admonition, and the third increase and ascension." As for the category which betokens punishment and expulsion, it is for someone who has bad *adab* towards Allah and so Allah Almighty punishes him by it. He is ignorant of the reality of what is happening and becomes angry, despairs and denies and so that increases him in expulsion and distance from Allah. As for the category which betokens discipline, it is for someone whose *adab* is faulty and so Allah Almighty disciplines him and He teaches him through it and alerts him to his defective *adab* and he ceases his negligence. It is therefore a blessing for him in the form of retribution. As for the category which betokens increase and ascension, it is for someone on whom these manifestations of Majesty descend without reason and so he has gnosis through them and disciplines himself in them and rises to the station of firmness and stability. That is why one of them said, "Firmness is according to the amount of testing."

It has been narrated that Allah Most High inspired to one of His Prophets, "I afflicted my servant with a difficulty, so he prayed to Me. I then delayed the answer [to his prayer], so he complained to Me. So I said, 'O My servant, how can I show mercy to you [by taking away] the very thing through which I'm showing My mercy to you.'" In the hadith of Abu Hurayra ؓ, the Messenger of Allah ﷺ said, "Allah Blessed and High says, 'When I try My believing slave and he does not complain about Me to his bedside visitors, I free him from My affliction and replace his flesh with better flesh and his blood with better blood. Then, he can start performing actions anew.'"

Abu 'Abdullah Muhammad ibn 'Ali al-Tirmidhi said, "I once got sick and when Allah Most High healed me, I compared to myself what Allah had decreed for me (i.e. this illness in this time period) and the larger amount of worship which I could have continued to do in this time period: which of the two would I choose? Then, I realised that Allah Most High's choice was far more beneficial for me. His choice was the illness that He had decreed for me, and there is no blemish in it since it was His action. What a difference there is between being saved by His action with you and trying to save yourself through your own action. When I understood this, I realised that my lack of acts of worship during the time of my illness was nothing compared to what He had given me. So the illness became in my eyes a great blessing.'" So this is the way that Allah made Himself known to al-Tirmidhi.

LESSON. If you want Majesty made easier for you, you must welcome it with its opposite, which is Beauty. It will be transformed into Beauty immediately. The method of doing that is that when Allah manifests Himself by His Name, the Constricter, outwardly, you should meet Him with expansion inwardly. Then it will become expansion. When He manifests Himself by His Name, the Strong, then meet Him with weakness. When He manifests Himself by His Name, the Mighty, meet Him with inward humility. That is how things are met with their opposite. Shaykh Moulay al-'Arabi ؓ says, "These things all have one reality. If you drink it as honey, you find it to be honey. If you drink it as milk, you find it to be milk. If you drink it as colocynth, you will find it to be as bitter as colocynth. Therefore, my brother, drink what is pleasant and do not drink what is ugly."

# Derse 7

الْأَعْمَالُ صُوَرٌ قَائِمَةٌ،
وَأَرْوَاحُهَا وُجُودُ سِرِّ الْإِخْلَاصِ فِيهَا.

**10: Actions are simply set-up images.
Their life-breath is the existence
of the secret of pure sincerity within them**

The word "actions" here refers to movements of both the body and the heart. The "images" are the pictures of the particular activity formed by the mind. The "life-breath" (*ruh*) is the secret of life which is lodged in living creatures. Here it refers to that quality by which perfection in actions is achieved. "Pure sincerity" is when the heart is entirely devoted to the worship of the Lord together with its secret and its core. That is the true sincerity characterised by giving up all claims to personal strength and power, for an action is only made perfect by that, even if it is sound without it. Pure sincerity precludes showing-off and hidden *shirk* while its secret precludes conceit and self-regard. Showing off detracts from the soundness of actions, while conceit detracts only from their perfection.

All actions are shapes and forms. Their life-breath is the existence of sincerity in them. Just as bodies can only subsist if they possess spirits, since otherwise they are dead and prone, so actions of the body and heart only subsist by the existence of sincerity in them. Otherwise they are just set-up images and empty forms worthy of no consideration. The sincerity of every servant is in truth the spirit of their actions and only through the existence of this spirit do those actions become alive, do they bring them nearer to Allah, do they become worthy of acceptance. If this spirit is lacking, their actions die, fall from the rank of being counted, and become mere figurines without life and forms without meaning. Some of the shaykhs have said, "Correct your actions with sincerity and correct your sincerity by giving up any claim to power or strength."

Allah Almighty says: *"They were only ordered to worship Allah, making their deen sincerely His, as people of pure natural faith,"* (98:5) and: *"Worship Allah, making your deen sincerely His."* (39:2) The Messenger of Allah ﷺ reported that Allah says, "I am the furthest removed from anything which is associated with Me." The Messenger of Allah ﷺ also said, "That which I most fear for my community is hidden *shirk*. It lies in showing off." In one version, "Fear this hidden shirk, It creeps like an ant." They asked, "What is hidden *shirk*?" "Showing off," he replied. In another hadith, the Prophet ﷺ was asked about sincerity and said, "Not until I ask Jibril." When he asked him, he said, "Not until I ask the Lord of Might." When he asked Him, he told him, "It is one of My secrets which I have entrusted to the hearts of those of My slaves who love Me. No angel can see it to enable him to record it and no *shaytan* can see it to enable him to corrupt it." One of the people of Allah said, "This refers to station of *ihsan*: which is to worship Allah as if you were seeing Him."

Pure sincerity has three degrees: the degree of the common people, the degree of the elite, and the degree of the elite of the elite. The sincerity of the common people involves the elimination of created beings from their dealings with Allah while at the same time seeking their share of both this world and the Next, such as the preservation of the body, money, expanded provision, palaces and houris. The sincerity of the elite involves seeking their share of the Next world rather than this world. The sincerity of the elite of the elite involves not seeking any share whatsoever. So their worship is in order to fully realise their slavehood and fulfill the demands of their Lord, or out of love and yearning for the vision of His face. As Ibn al-Farid said:

> My request is not for the bliss of the Garden.
> My only desire is to see You.

Another said:

> All of them worship out of fear of the Fire
> and see salvation as a generous prize,
> Or seek to dwell in the Garden
> and relax in meadows and drink of Salsabil.
> I have no opinion of Gardens or the Fire.
> I do not seek any recompense for my love.

Shaykh Abu Talib said, "Sincerity with the sincere is to

eliminate all creatures from one's dealings with the Real. The first of creatures is the self. Sincerity among the lovers is not to do an action for the sake of the self. Otherwise it is affected by looking for recompense or desiring a share for the self. For the people of realisation, sincerity is to eliminate all creatures from dealings with of the Real by not seeing them in respect of actions and by not relying on them or relaxing with them in states."

One of the shaykhs said, "Make your actions sound through sincerity and make your sincerity sound by freeing yourself from any claim to strength and power." One of the people of Allah said, "Sincerity is not achieved until you are nothing in other people's eyes and they are nothing in yours." That is why another said, "Whenever you fall in people's eyes, you become great in the sight of Allah. Whenever you become great in people's eyes, you fall in the sight of Allah." This happens when you take note of them and are watchful of them.

I heard our shaykh say, "As long as the slave continues to be watchful of people and to have awe of them, his sincerity will never be fully realised." He also said, "Watchfulness of Allah will never be combined with watchfulness of creation because it is impossible to see Him and see other-than-Him with Him." The upshot of all this is that it is not possible to ever be free of the self and purified of subtle showing-off without a shaykh. Allah knows best.

# Derse 8

$$\text{اِدْفِنْ وُجُودَكَ فِي أَرْضِ الْخُمُولِ،}$$
$$\text{فَمَا نَبَتَ مِمَّا لَمْ يُدْفَنْ لَا يَتِمُّ نِتَاجُهُ.}$$

**11: Bury your existence in the earth of obscurity. For anything which grows without first being buried will never produce proper fruit.**

"Bury" means cover up and conceal. "Obscurity" means loss of standing in other people's eyes. "Fruit" is a metaphor for the wisdom, gifts and knowledge which the slave harvests from his knowledge of Allah. That happens when his *nafs* dies and his *ruh* comes to life.

*Murid*, conceal your *nafs* and bury it in obscurity until it is intimate with it, happy with it and finds it sweeter than honey, and until self-aggrandisement becomes more bitter than colocynth. If you bury it in the soil of obscurity and its roots spread out in it, then you will pluck its fruits and obtain its harvest, which is the secret of sincerity and realisation of the station of the elite of elite. If you do not bury it in the earth of obscurity and allow it to give itself renown, its tree dies or its fruits drop off before they ripen. When the gnostics harvest from the gardens of gnosis they planted and the treasures of wisdom they buried, and the storehouses of their understanding become full, you will be at their door poor, begging or trying to steal. Sayyiduna 'Isa ﷺ asked his companions, "Where does grain grow?" They replied, "In the earth." He said, "The same applies to wisdom. It only grows in a heart which is like the earth." One of the gnostics said, "If you bury your *nafs* in earth below earth, your heart will rise to heaven above heaven."

Once the Messenger of Allah ﷺ was sitting with al-Aqra' ibn Habis, a great man of the Banu Tamim, when one of the poor Muslims went past. He asked al-Aqra', "What do you say about this one?" He replied, "Messenger of Allah, this is just one of the poor Muslims. If he were to propose marriage, his proposal would not be worth accepting, and if he were to intercede, his intercession would not be granted, and if he were to speak, his words would not be listened to." Then a wealthy man passed by them and the Messenger of Allah asked him, "And what do you say about this one?" He replied, "If he proposed marriage, his proposal would be accepted, if he interceded his intercession would be granted, and if he were to speak, his words would be listened to." The Messenger of Allah ﷺ said, "The former (the poor man) is better than everything the earth contains and better than this last one." There are many *hadiths* and sayings which praise obscurity. Even if it contained nothing but rest and freeing the heart from this world, that would be enough.

One of the wise said, "Obscurity is a blessing but the *nafs* rejects it. Self-aggrandisement is an affliction yet the *nafs* desires it." He also said, "The end of this Path of ours will only be reached by people who sweep rubbish heaps with their spirits."

There is the story of ash-Shushtari with his shaykh. Ash-Shushtari was a government minister and scholar and his father was an amir. When he wanted to set out on the Path of the People (of Sufism), his shaykh told him, "You will not get anywhere until you sell your goods, wear tattered garments, take a banner and enter the market." He did all that and then asked his shaykh, "What should I say in the market?" He said, "Say, 'I begin by mentioning the Beloved.'" So he entered the market, waving his banner and said, "I begin by mentioning the Beloved." He kept that up for three days and then the veils covering his heart were ripped away and he began, in the marketplace, to sing about direct knowledge of Allah.

There is a companion story about a man who was with Abu Yazid al-Bistami. For thirty years the man did not leave his gathering or part from him. He said one day, "Master, for thirty years I have fasted in the day and prayed during the night and abandoned my appetites and yet I have not found in my heart anything at all of what you have talked about. I still, however, believe and affirm all you say." Abu Yazid said to him, "Even if you continue to pray for another thirty years, if you remain as you are now, you will still never find a single atom of it." "Why, master?" he asked. "Because," he replied, "you are veiled from it by your *nafs*." "Is there any remedy for this," the man enquired, "so that the veil can be removed?" "Yes, there is," Abu Yazid replied, "but you will neither accept it nor carry it out." "Yes, I will," he insisted, "I will do what you say." "Go immediately to the barber," Abu Yazid said to him, "and have your hair and beard shaved off. Take off these fine clothes and replace them with a coarse woollen robe. Hang a nosebag round your neck and fill it with walnuts. Then gather some children around you and shout in your loudest voice, 'Children! I will give a nut to whoever gives me a slap!' Then enter the market where you are respected looking like this until everyone who knows you has had a good look." "Abu Yazid!" he exclaimed, "Glory be to Allah! Do you say this to someone like me and think that I will do it!" "Your words, 'Glory be to Allah' are *shirk*." "How can that be?" he asked. "Because," Abu Yazid explained, "you esteem your *nafs* and so it is that that you are really glorifying." "I cannot do this, Abu Yazid, and I will not do it, but direct me to something less than this that I can do." "You must start by doing this," Abu Yazid told him, "so that your love of high standing falls from you and you humble your *nafs*, then after that I will tell you what is appropriate for you." "I cannot do this." "Yet you said that you would both accept and do it. I know for sure that no one can aspire to be privy to the secrets of the unseen which are veiled from the common people until he makes his *nafs* die and breaks the norms within which the common people are enmeshed. Then normal patterns will be broken for him and secrets will appear to him."

There is also the story of Abu 'Imran al-Barda'i with his shaykh Abu 'Abdullah at-Taudi in Fes. He shaved his head, put on a rough robe and went round holding out a loaf of bread, calling out for someone to save him from it. He did all that. And then there is the story of Shaykh 'Abdu'r-Rahman al-Majdhub, who ate figs from people's trees and sang in the markets. We also have the story of the shaykh of our shaykhs, Sidi 'Ali al-'Imrani, and the way he went about ruining his reputation in Fes which is famous. There is also the case of Shaykh Moulay al-'Arabi who wore a sack and gave people water from a waterskin and did other things all of which are well known.

These stories indicate that obscurity is not what the common people understand it to be. It is not staying inside houses or fleeing to mountains. For those with realisation, doing that is, in fact, tantamount to ostentation. Obscurity, as Shaykh Zarruq said, "...is for the *nafs* to fully realise its lowest characteristic and be constantly aware of it. Its lowest characteristic is abasement and all that burdensome for it. So the *faqir* does his best to adopt the attribute of humility and pluck its fruit in order to attain to effective action and the perfection of realisation."

If it is said that doing things like this will mean exposing oneself to people's words and make them fall into slander and backbiting, I reply that it depends on the aim and intention. If someone does any of these things with the aim of killing his *nafs*, achieving sincerity and healing his heart, he will forgive and excuse those who talk about him. In his book, Sidi 'Ali said, "We excuse those who excuse us and also excuse those who do not excuse us." In his *Qawa'id*, Shaykh Zarruq said, "The legal ruling is general for the common people because its aim to establish the outward *shari'a*, raise its standard and make its words victorious while the ruling of *tasawwuf* is for the elite because it concerns the relationship of the slave with his Lord and nothing else. So it is valid for a *faqih* to object to a Sufi but not valid for a Sufi to object to a *faqih*. One must return from *tasawwuf* to *fiqh* in respect of legal judgements but not in respect of inner realities."

# Derse 9

**13a: How can a heart be illuminated
if the images of created things
are imprinted on its mirror?**

The "images" referred to are the things themselves and their representations in the senses and imagination. "Created things" are all types of creatures, small or large. The word "imprinted" means firmly fixed, since if something in imprinted and stamped on something, its image is transferred to it. The word "mirror" used in respect of the heart is a metaphor for the faculty of insight which is the eye of the heart by which the meaning of things, both beautiful and ugly, is perceived.

Allah made the heart of the human being like a polished mirror in which is reflected whatever stands in front of it. It can only face in one direction at a time. When Allah shows concern for one of His slaves, He fills its reflection with the lights of His *Malakut* and the secrets of His *Jabarut* and the heart is not attached to the love of any dark beings or false illusions. So the lights of *iman* and *ihsan* are imprinted on the mirror of his heart and the moons of *tawhid* and suns of direct knowledge of Allah shine in it. That was what ash-Shushtari was alluding to when he said, "Lower the eye and you will see, and your inner world will shine resplendent. Be annihilated to creation and your secrets will appear to you. By polishing the mirror, your denial will be swept away." Then he said, "The starry heavens orbit within in you and shine and sparkle, and the suns and the moons rise and set within you. Polishing the mirror of your heart sweeps away your denial of the Truth to the point that you recognise Allah in everything and your heart becomes the hub of the whole universe of lights and the moons of *tawhid* and suns of gnosis appear in it."

When, by His justice and wisdom, Allah desires to disappoint a person, they occupy themselves with dark phenomena and physical appetites so that it is those things which become imprinted on the mirror of their heart. Because of that they are veiled by that phenomenal darkness and those imaginary forms from the rising of the suns of knowledge of Allah and the lights of *iman*. As the images of created things pile up in them, the light of *iman* is extinguished and the veil thickened. Then you will only be able to see material existence and only reflect on material existence. That can lead to the veil becoming impenetrable and the total extinction of the light of faith to the extent that the heart ceases even to acknowledge the existence of light in its source. That is the station of disbelief – we seek refuge with Allah!

When the heart is less encrusted with rust, however, and the veil is thinner, people are able to affirm the light even though they cannot really see it. This is the station of the common Muslims. They vary in nearness and distance, and strength and weakness of affirmation, each according to his certainty and the amount of his attachment to this world and his state of servitude to, or freedom from, appetite and illusion. In a hadith it says that the hearts rust as iron rusts and that faith wears out as a new garment wears out. In another hadith it says that everything has a polish, and that what polishes the hearts is *dhikru'llah*. The Prophet ﷺ also said, "When someone commits a wrong action, a black spot forms in his heart. If he stops doing it and asks forgiveness, it is polished away. If he repeats it, it grows in the heart until it overwhelms it. That is the rust which Allah mentions: *'No indeed! Rather what they earned has rusted up their hearts.'* (83:14)"

Since you know that the heart can only face one direction at a time, you must realise that when it faces light, it shines and when it faces darkness, it goes dark. So now you will understand the reason for the astonishment of the shaykh when he asked how a heart could shine with the light of faith and *ihsan* when the dark forms of created things are imprinted on its mirror. Two opposites cannot co-exist. Allah Almighty says: *"Allah has not allotted a man two hearts in his breast."* (33:4) So, *faqir*, you only have one heart. When you turn to creatures, you turn away from the Real. When you turn to the Real, you turn away from creatures and travel from the world of the *Mulk* to the *Malakut* and from the *Malakut* to the *Jabarut*. So the Shaykh tells us that as long as our heart remains shackled to this world by our appetites we will never travel to our Lord.

### 13b: And how can it travel to Allah if it is shackled by its appetites?

Travel is getting up and going from one place to another. Here it means moving from looking at creation to witnessing the Creator, or moving from the *Mulk* to the *Malakut*, or moving on from seeing only secondary causes to seeing the Causer of causes, or moving from the realm of heedlessness to the realm of awareness, or from the portions of the *nafs* to the rights of Allah, or from the world of impurities to the world of purity, or from seeing the sensory to witnessing the meaning, or from ignorance to true knowledge, or from the knowledge of certainty to the vision of certainty, or from the vision of certainty to the truth of certainty, or from watchfulness to witnessing, or from the station of the wayfarers to the destination of those who have arrived. Shackles are chains which hinder your movement, and what is meant by "appetites" here is everything that the *nafs* desires and to which it inclines.

Travel and shackles do not go together. As long as the heart feels an overpowering inclination to any of the ephemeral goods of this world, even if they are permitted in the *shari'a*, it is shackled and fettered in its abode and will not be able to travel to the *Malakut* nor will the lights of the *Jabarut* shine on it. So the heart's attachment to its appetites prevents it from rising to Allah since it is occupied with turning towards them. If it is moving swiftly towards Allah, it is still not safe from being tripped up by them because of the fondness the *nafs* has for them. That is why the great men have abandoned them. Shaykh Zarruq said, "Hornets' stings on a wounded body are less pernicious than the sting of appetites inside the heart."

It has already been said that the reality of *tasawwuf* is that you should be with Allah without attachment to anything else. So, my brother, root out all attachments from within yourself and flee from the land of attachments and then the lights of the realities will shine upon you. This is why travelling and *hijra* are confirmed practices for the murid since remaining in this sensory land does not lead to freedom from sensory attachments.

It has been said that the *faqir* is like water. If water remains for a long time in the same place, it becomes stagnant and foul. If it flows, it is sweet. The distance travelled in the meaning corresponds to the distance travelled in the sensory. The heart travels according to how much its container travels. *Hijra* is a *sunna* of the Prophet ﷺ. From the time the Prophet ﷺ emigrated, he never stopped travelling for jihad and the same applied to the Companions ﷺ. Only a few of them remained in their homeland until Allah had conquered all the lands at their hands and guided people by them. May Allah give us the benefit of their blessings. Amin.

# Derse 10

مَا تَرَكَ مِنَ الْجَهْلِ شَيْئاً مَنْ أَرَادَ
أَنْ يَحْدُثَ فِي الْوَقْتِ غَيْرُ مَا أَظْهَرَهُ اللَّهُ فِيهِ.

**17: Anyone who wants something
to take place in any moment
other than what Allah has manifested in it,
has not abandoned ignorance at all.**

Ignorance is the opposite of knowledge, and it is said that, here, it is lack of knowledge of the Goal. There are two categories of it: simple and complex. The simple is that someone is ignorant and knows that he is ignorant. The complex is that he is ignorant of his ignorance. The worst type of ignorance is ignorance and denial of Allah after seeking to know Him.

Part of the *adab* of the people of true knowledge is to affirm that things are as they are supposed to be and to go with them as they unfold. The author of *al-'Ayniyya* said about that:

> If you ascribe beauty to each thing which is ugly,
> the reality of its beauty will come to you swiftly.

Beauty perfects the imperfection of the ugly.
So then there is no imperfection and nothing ugly.

An-Nuri said, "What Allah desires of His creatures is what they are." When Allah establishes someone in a station, then it is obligatory for that person to remain in it with his heart, whatever it is, and he should look to see what Allah will do with him in it. One of them said, "Anyone who deals with creatures according to the *shari'a* has lengthy arguments with them. Anyone who deals with them according to the *haqiqa*, excuses them." It is mandatory to deal with people by the *shari'a* outwardly, and so remind them, and by the reality in the inward, and so excuse them. Anyone who wants something to appear in any moment other than what Allah makes appear in it, either in himself or in someone else, has amassed all ignorance and has not abandoned any of it, since by doing that He is opposing the Decree and contending with the All-Powerful. Allah Almighty says: *"Your Lord is the Doer of what He wills."* (11:107) 'Abdullah ibn Mas'ud and Ibn 'Abbas said, "I would prefer to hold onto a burning coal than to say about something, 'Would that it were not!' or about something which is not, 'Would that it were!'" Abu 'Uthman said, "For forty years Allah has not established me in a state which I disliked nor moved me to another which angered me."

Shaykh 'Ali said in his book, *The Meaning of Man*: "Those who recognise the people of the realities of the outward and do not deny them any of their states will obtain what is in their hands and will not be denied any of their good. Those who recognise the people of the realities of the inward and do not deny them any of their states, will obtain what is in their hands in every case and will not be denied any of their good. The man of Allah combines the good of both groups and keeps company with both of them. Every group takes on its own colouring, as the shaykh of our shaykh, Sidi Ahmad al-Yamani asserted. He did not deny any of the states of creation. He studied with people of the outward in their outward matters and handed them over to them and affirmed them in them, and he studied with the people of the inward in their inward matters and handed them over to them and affirmed them in them. So he got the best of both groups according to the knowledge and wisdom which Allah had given them. It is said that the perfect *wali* changes with all levels and fulfils all desires."

Anyone who reflects on the hadiths of the Prophet will find them to fit in with this attitude because the Prophet ﷺ was the master of the people of knowledge and the model to be copied by all *murids*. He affirmed people in the wisdom in which Allah had established them and encouraged them in it. That is why we find that there are apparently contradictory hadiths, which are, in reality, not contradictory at all. If you examine the hadiths about *dhikr*, you would say there is nothing better than it. If you examine the hadiths about jihad, you would say there is nothing better than it. If you examine the hadiths about the excellence of knowledge, you would say there is nothing better than it. If you examine the hadiths about doing without, and stripping away the means of this world, you would say there is nothing better than it. If you examine the hadiths about earning and serving the family, the same is true.

So the Prophet ﷺ encouraged the wisdom in each course of action, to the extent that you would say that there could be nothing better than it. That was in order that the people of each category would be at rest and so that they would have a clear sign from their Lord with respect to it. He did not command them to move from what they had, since Allah decreed and desired that wisdom for them. So he affirmed them in it and encouraged them in it to the point that anyone who hears the hadiths about it would think that there was nothing better than it. Indeed, there is nothing better than it for its people. In short, the people of Allah do not deny anything and are not ignorant of anything. One of them said, "It is not possible for there to be anything better than what is." What that means is that in the prior knowledge of Allah nothing else was possible and so there could, indeed, be nothing better than it.

# Derse 11

إِحَالَتُكَ الْأَعْمَالَ عَلَى وُجُودِ الْفَرَاغِ مِنْ رُعُونَاتِ النَّفْسِ.

**18: Putting off action until you have free time comes from the stupidity of the lower self.**

One of the signs of real intelligence is to take every opportunity to act and to hasten to act without delay or wishful thinking, since, if you miss the moment, it can never be replaced. In a *hadith*, the Messenger of Allah ﷺ said, "One of the hallmarks of intelligence is to abhor the abode of delusion and turn to the abode of permanence, to take provision for your time in the grave and to prepare for the Day of Gathering." He also said ﷺ, "The clever person is the one who takes account of himself and works for what comes after death. The stupid person is the one who follows his *nafs* and desires and has wishful thinking about Allah." In the Scrolls of Ibrahim ﷺ we find: "The intelligent person should only busy himself with three things: taking provision for the Hereafter, gaining a legitimate livelihood or taking pleasure in something that is not forbidden."

So putting off actions and postponing them to a time when you think your heart or body will be unoccupied is a sign of foolishness and stupidity. It is delusion. What makes you think you will reach that time? Death may come to you unexpectedly at any moment. You assume you will reach that free time but you are never safe from some other pressing concern presenting itself to you. The Prophet ﷺ warned us that there were two blessings from which many people fail to benefit: good health and spare time. Few people who have been provided by Allah with good health and spare time use them profitably. If they fill them up with obedience to their Lord, they will be showing thanks for them and gain great benefit. If they misuse them, they have suffered a clear loss and shown ingratitude for them and that is one of the hallmarks of disappointment.

The ultimate disappointment is that felt when you have very little in your way but still do not advance on the path of Allah. The *faqir* needs to sever his connections and attachments to this world, oppose his desires, set out to serve his Lord and not wait for a future moment, because the *faqir* is the child of the moment. You only find him occupied with thought, investigation, *dhikr*, fruitful discussion or service on the Path which will take him to Allah. I told one of the brothers, "The truthful *faqir* has no thought or concern except about the Divine Presence or what will bring him to the Divine Presence." Allah knows best.

Shaykh Ibn 'Abbad al-Rundi says there are several things connected with the stupidity of postponing action till later on. One is that it shows preference for this world over the Next World. This preference is not one of the states of an intelligent believer and is in conflict with what is demanded of us. Allah says: *"But you prefer the life of the world when the hereafter is better and longer lasting."* (87:16-17) and: *"But those who believe have stronger love for Allah."* (2:165) And there are many other *ayahs* with a similar meaning. A second thing is that if you put off action until a free moment you expect to arrive in the future, all too often that moment never comes. Our worldly activities nearly always tend to increase since so many of them inevitably lead to more of the same. As the poet said:

No one ever manages to fulfil his worldly aims.
For an aim never ends without another one springing up.

A third thing is that when we do succeed in getting some spare time, our determination to do the action we were going to do has frequently diminished and our intention withered away. Finally there is, in the postponement, an element of claiming independence from Allah and seeing the power and strength to act as originating from ourselves. We should rely on Allah making the action easy for us and removing the barriers between that action and ourselves.

The point is that our actions are not isolated, independent units, we are in a constant dynamic relationship with the rest of existence. What we do has an immediate effect on ourselves and what surrounds us and beyond the time/space dimension which we inhabit. So may Allah make us people of right actions which truly change things for the better and open the way for the establishment of His *deen*.

# Derse 12

لَا تَطْلُبْ مِنْهُ أَنْ يُخْرِجَكَ مِنْ حَالَةٍ لِيَسْتَعْمِلَكَ فِيمَا سِوَاهَا. فَلَوْ أَرَادَ لَاسْتَعْمَلَكَ مِنْ غَيْرِ إِخْرَاجٍ.

**19: Don't ask Him to remove you from one state in order to use you in another. If He wanted to, He could use you without removing you.**

Part of the *adab* of the gnostic is to be satisfied with the knowledge of Allah so that he can dispense with other than Him. When Allah establishes him in a state, he does not disdain it and seek to leave it for another state. If Allah had wanted to remove him from that state and to use him in another, He would use him without being asked to remove him. He should remain where the Real has established him until He is the One to remove him as He brought him into it. *"Say: 'My Lord, make my entry sincere and make my leaving sincere.'"* (17:80)

The sincere entry is that you enter it by Allah and the sincere exit is that you leave it by Allah. This is understanding from Allah and it is a sign of realisation of direct knowledge of Allah. If the gnostic of Allah is single, he does not wish to marry. If he is married, he does not wish for divorce. If he is poor, he does not wish for wealth. If he is wealthy, he does not wish for poverty. If he is healthy, he does not wish for illness. If he is ill, he does not wish for health. If he is mighty, he does not wish for abasement and if he is abased, he does not wish for might. If he is constricted, he does not wish for expansion, and if he is expanded, he does not wish for contraction. If he is strong, he does not wish for weakness, and if he is weak, he does not wish for strength. If he is stationary, he does not wish to travel, and if he is travelling, he does not wish to stay. It is like that with the rest of the states. He waits to see what Allah will do and does not look for what he will do by himself to achieve its removal. He is like the corpse in the hands of the washer or like a pen in the fingers, as the author of al-'Ayniyya said:

> I see myself as an instrument and He moves me.
> I am a pen and the decrees are the fingers.

Allah *ta'ala* says: *"Your Lord creates and chooses whatever He wills. The choice is not theirs."* (28:68) He says, *"But you will not will unless Allah wills."* (76:30) Allah revealed to Da'ud, "Da'ud, you will and I will and it is only what I will. If you surrender to Me in what I will, I will bring you what you will. If you do not surrender to Me what I will, I will tire you in what you will and it will only be what I will." The Messenger of Allah ﷺ said to Abu Hurayra, "The pen is dry about what you will meet." In another hadith: "The pens are dry and the scrolls are rolled up." The shaykh of our shaykhs, Sidi Ahmad al-Yamani said when he and his companions were asked about the reality of *wilaya*: "The reality of *wilaya* is that when a person is sitting in the shade, he does not desire to sit in the sun, and when he is sitting in the sun, he does not desire to sit in the shade."

All of this is with choice rather than the necessary matter. We already mentioned what Shaykh Sidi 'Ali said: "One of the attributes of the perfect *wali* is that he only needs the state in which his Master has established him in the moment," i.e. he has no will except what issued from the element of Power and he does not desire other than it. When the gnostic receives a *tajalli* in any of these matters, moving from one state to another, he should be cautious: and patient until he sees that it is from Allah by an outward or inward sign or a physical or spiritual voice. He should pay attention to what he hears. Allah addresses him by whatever means He will. This is a valid and tried business with the gnostics, so that they only move by permission from Allah and His Messenger since there is no separation for the people of gatheredness. May Allah make us among them. Amin. All of this is when the state in which you are is in keeping with the *shari'a*. Otherwise, seek to leave it however possible.

# Derse 13

$$\text{لَا تَسْتَغْرِبْ وُقُوعَ الأَكْدَارِ، مَا دُمْتَ فِي هَذِهِ الدَّارَ،}$$
$$\text{فَإِنَّهَا مَا أَبْرَزَتْ إِلَّا مَا هُوَ مُسْتَحَقٌّ}$$
$$\text{وَصْفِهَا وَوَاجِبُ نَعْتِهَا.}$$

**24: Do not be surprised at the appearance
of worry and sorrow
as long as you are in this world.
It only exhibits what its attributes demand
and its qualities stipulate.**

What is meant here by "attributes" are things which re-occur all the time, such as death, illness and poverty and the "qualities" referred to are those things which only occur occasionally, such as civil war, floods and earthquakes. Part of the *adab* of the *faqir* is not to think that any of the manifestations of the Real in this world are out of place and not to be surprised at any of them, whatever they are, majestic or beautiful. Allah *ta'ala* says: "*You who believe, seek help in steadfastness and the prayer. Allah is with the steadfast. Do not say about those who are killed in the way of Allah that they are dead. On the contrary they are alive but you are not aware of it. We will test you with a certain amount of fear and hunger, and loss of wealth and life and fruits. But give good news to the steadfast: those who, when disaster strikes them, say, 'Truly we belong to Allah and to Him we will return.' Those are the people who will have blessings and mercy from their Lord; they are the ones who are guided."* (2:153-157) And He says: *"And we test you with both good and evil as a trial."* (21:35)

If overwhelming events, sorrows or majestic manifestations occur in this abode, do not consider that to be something strange because the manifestations of this world are mostly majestic, it being the domain of fear and difficulty and the place of separation and departure. The Prophet ﷺ said in one of his *khutbas*: "People! This abode is the abode of destruction, not the abode of stability, and the station of sorrow, not the station of joy. Whoever knows that does not rejoice in its ease nor is he is saddened by its misery. Allah created this world as the domain of affliction and the Next World as the domain of the end result." So Allah made this world a reason for the reward of the Next World, and the reward of the Next World a recompense for the afflictions of this world. He takes in order to give and afflicts in order to reward. This world passes away at great speed and will soon be gone. So beware the sweetness of its suckling because of the bitterness of its weaning. Shun its instant gratification because of its hateful end. Do not strive to cultivate this abode which Allah will soon destroy nor strive to obtain it when Allah desires you to be free of it. If you do you will be in danger of exposing yourselves to His anger and deserving of His punishment.

Al-Junayd said, "I am not dismayed by anything that comes to me from this world because I have adopted a fundamental principle: it is that this world is inevitably the domain of worry, sorrow, affliction and trial. ... One of its characteristics is that it brings me things I hate. If it brings me something I love, that is a bonus. Otherwise, the basic position is the first one." Abu Sulayman ad-Darani said to Ahmad ibn Abi'l-Hawari, "Ahmad, a little hunger, a little nakedness, a little abasement, and a little steadfastness and then the days of this world will come to an end for you."

So do not think that the sorrows and difficulties which come to you and others in this world are out of place as long as you are here. The manifestations of Divine Majesty that occur in it are simply what is characteristic of it, what its intrinsic nature demands. So do not think anything is out of place and do not be surprised at anything that happens. Your duty is to recognise Allah in both Majesty and Beauty, sweetness and bitterness. Recognising Him in Beauty is something the common people do. Recognising Him in Majesty, however, requires stillness, *adab*, contentment, and submission. So the *faqir* should be like the reed. When the onslaught of the flood arrives, it bends and bows its head, and when it has gone, it lifts its head again.

Just as you do not find the normal emergence of impurities from your body to be out of place when they occur, you should not be sad, nor fear, nor be alarmed when inevitable difficulties occur. In the same way you shouldn't be carried away by happy occurrences – the manifestation of Divine Beauty – so as to become over-elated by them. Majesty is bound to Beauty and Beauty is bound to Majesty and they alternate just as day and night alternate. The *faqir* takes on the colour of each of them. He does not find anything out of place and is not overwhelmed by anything that happens since he knows that all that issues from Allah's Power is one.

Ja'far as-Sadiq said, "Anyone who seeks something which has not been created tires himself out and will never attain it." He was asked what this thing was and replied, "Repose in this world." As the poet says:

> You seek repose in the house of fatigue!
> Failed has he who seeks what does not exist.

Ibn Mas'ud said, "The fundamental nature of this world is that it is a cause for disquiet, so whatever happiness comes out of it is an added bonus." Abu Turab said, "O people, you love three things that are not yours to love. You love your *nafs*, but it belongs to its desires. You love your life, but it belongs to Allah. Finally, you love accumulating wealth, but it belongs to your heirs. In addition, you seek two things which are not there to find: repose and happiness. These two things only really exist in the Garden."

Thus, the *faqir* should not to look for repose or strive for happiness in this world. Rather, he should act according to the statement of the Prophet ﷺ narrated by Abu Hurayra: "This world is the prison of the believer." Expecting trials in life makes them easier for us when we actually meet them and gives us consolation when what we desire does not come about. We should confront what does happen to us with patience, contentment, and submission to the Divine Decree. Our lives in this world will come to an end all too soon and then we will, *insha'allah*, receive a copious reward from Allah Most High, containing repose and happiness beyond anything we could possibly imagine. As the Prophet ﷺ told us the Garden is: "What no eye has seen and no ear has heard and no human heart has ever envisaged." Allah Most High is the Giver of success.

# Derse 14

$$\text{مَا تَوَقَّفَ مَطْلَبٌ أَنْتَ طَالِبُهُ بِرَبِّكَ}$$
$$\text{وَلَا تَيَسَّرَ مَطْلَبٌ أَنْتَ طَالِبُهُ بِنَفْسِكَ.}$$

**25: There is no stopping a goal
you seek by your Lord.
There is no easy way to a goal
you seek by yourself.**

When you have a need related to this world or the Next and want it to be satisfied quickly, then seek it by Allah, do not seek it by yourself. If you seek it by Allah, it will be easy for you and it will satisfied quickly. If you seek it by yourself, it will be hard to satisfy it and it will be difficult. What you seek by your Lord is not delayed or withheld but what you seek by yourself is never easy or simple. Indeed, anyone who depends on his own knowledge and intelligence and relies on his own strength and power, Allah lets him fend for himself, abandons him, deprives him of His success, and disregards him.

Allah Almighty says, relating from Musa 🙏: *"Musa said to his people, 'Seek help in Allah and be steadfast. The earth belongs to Allah. He bequeaths it to any of His slaves He wills. *The successful outcome is for the godfearing.'"* (7:128) Whoever seeks help by Allah and perseveres in pursuing his need, will be successful in it and show himself to be one of the godfearing. Allah Almighty says: *"Whoever puts his trust in Allah, He will be enough for him,"* (65:3), in other words take care for him of all that worries him. The Prophet ﷺ told one of his Companions, Suwayd ibn Ghafala, "Do not seek the amirate. If you seek it, it will be on your shoulders. If it comes to you without asking, then you will be helped in it."

The sign of your seeking something by Allah is detachment regarding it and being distracted from it by Allah, knowing that if and when its time comes, it is entirely by the permission of Allah. The sign of seeking by the self is inner greed for whatever it is and bending over backwards to get it. If someone like this meets difficulties in gaining their goal they become constricted and upset. This is how you distinguish between someone who seeks by Allah and someone who seeks by himself. If someone seeks a need by Allah, it is fulfilled in the meaning, even if it is not satisfied in a sensory way. If someone seeks a need by himself, his efforts are disappointed and his time is wasted, even if his desire and need are apparently satisfied.

Shaykh ash-Shadhili said, "When Allah honours a slave in his movements and stillness, He engages him in slavehood to Himself and veils him from the portions of his *nafs* in whatever is decreed for him so he does not turn to them. It is as if he were cut off from them. When Allah abases a slave in his movements and stillness, He engages him in the portions of his *nafs* and veils him from slavehood to Himself, and so he is tossed about in his appetites and true slavehood to Allah is cut off from him. As for the greatest *siddiqiyya* and greatest *awliya*, all portions and rights are the same for them because they are by Allah in whatever they take or leave." Shaykh Zarruq quoted this in one of his commentaries.

There is a difference between actions by Allah and actions for Allah. Action for Allah comes from the people of the words of Allah: *"You alone we worship."* Action by Allah comes from the people of His words: *"You alone we ask for help."* Shaykh Sidi 'Ali said, "The difference between action by Allah and action for Allah is the difference between the dinar and the dirham." Success is by Allah. Whoever knows by Allah, returns to Him in everything and relies on Him in every state. Shaykh Ibn Ata'illah indicates this by saying:

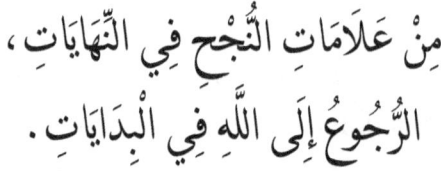

## 26: A sign of success in the end: Turning to Allah in the beginning.

Murid, when you direct your *himma* to seeking something, whatever it is, and want to be successful in it, to obtain what you desire, and for its end to be good and outcome praiseworthy, then return to Allah in the beginning of seeking it and strip away your strength and power. Say, as the Prophet ﷺ said, "If it is from Allah, He will bring it about." So do not be greedy for it and do not be concerned with it. Whatever Allah wills will be and whatever our Lord does not will will not be. As he also said ﷺ, "If men and jinn were to join together to help you with something which Allah had not decreed for you, they would not be able to do that. If they were to join to harm you by anything which Allah had not decreed for you, they would not be able to do that. The pens are dry and the scrolls rolled up."

When you seek something and, in doing it, you depend on Allah and entrust the matter to Allah, you will see what was in the prior knowledge of Allah. The sign of that is success in the end and the achieving of your goal, whether or not it is settled in the sensory, because what you desire is what Allah desires, not what your *nafs* desires. Your portions have been transformed into rights and you only desire what Allah has decided. Only look at what emerges from Allah and you will be annihilated to your portions and appetites.

If you seek something by yourself, relying on your own strength and power, eager to achieve it and striving to obtain it, that is a sign of lack of achieving it and the disappointment of hope in it, even if it is achieved in the sensory. You will have entrusted yourself to that thing and be tired out by it and not be helped in achieving your aim by it. All of this is sound and is a tried and tested outcome experienced by both the common and elite. This is a sentence which completes what preceded it and expands on it. Allah knows best.

Then he completes this matter by outlining a comprehensive principle which affirms everything he has just said.

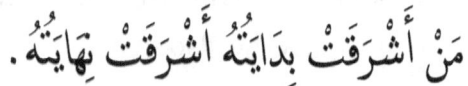

## 27: Whoever has a radiant beginning has a radiant ending.

The radiance of the beginning is entering into it by Allah, seeking it by Allah and relying on Allah while striving in the means to achieving it and showing *adab* towards the Decree. The amount of striving needed is immense because of the immensity of the goal. The subsequent witnessing will be according to the previous striving. Allah ta'ala tells us: *"...that man will have nothing but what he strives for..."* (53:39) And: *"As for those who do jihad in Our Way, We will guide them to Our Paths. Truly Allah is with the good-doers."* (29:69) And: *"Allah's mercy is close to the good-doers."* (7:56)

# Derse 15

$$\text{مَا اسْتُودِعَ فِي غَيْبِ السَّرَائِرِ ظَهَرَ فِي شَهَادَةِ الظَّوَاهِرِ .}$$

**28: What is stored away
in the unseen dimension of the secrets
is bound to appear in the visible world
of outward manifestation.**

Whatever good or evil Allah has stored and placed in people's hearts, or light or darkness, or knowledge or ignorance, or mercy or harshness, or generosity or miserliness, or avarice or open-handedness, or constriction or expansion, or wakefulness or heedlessness, or other praiseworthy or blameworthy qualities, the effect of that is bound to appear on the limbs, in the words and actions of the people concerned. Allah Almighty says: *"You will know them by their mark,"* (2:273) and He says: *"Their mark is on their faces."* (48:29) The Prophet ﷺ said, "If someone conceals a secret, Allah will clothe him in its cloak."

The actions of the limbs proceed from the states of the heart. No one who stores knowledge of his Master in the secret of his unseen will seek anything from anyone else. Anyone who stores ignorance of his Lord in the secret of his unseen will inevitably be connected to what is other than Him. That is how states of the outward come about. They follow the states of the inward. As the Shaykh already said, "Different states have different outcomes. This accounts for the variety of types of action." So outward characteristics indicate inner secrets and words unveil their speaker. Whatever is in you appears on your tongue. Every vessel leaks what is in it. What occurs in people's hearts has its effect on their faces. Allah knows best.

The greatest thing that can be stored in people's secrets is knowledge of Allah. It is of two kinds: knowledge based on evidence and knowledge based on eye-witnessing. He indicates the difference between them by saying:

شَتَّانَ بَيْنَ مَنْ يَسْتَدِلُّ بِهِ أَوْ يَسْتَدِلُّ عَلَيْهِ. الْمُسْتَدِلُّ بِهِ عَرَفَ الْحَقَّ لِأَهْلِهِ، فَأَثْبَتَ الْأَمْرَ مِنْ وُجُودِ أَصْلِهِ. وَالِاسْتِدْلَالُ عَلَيْهِ مِنْ عَدَمِ الْوُصُولِ إِلَيْهِ. وَإِلَّا فَمَتَى غَابَ حَتَّى يُسْتَدَلَّ عَلَيْهِ؟ وَمَتَى بَعُدَ حَتَّى تَكُونَ الْآثَارُ هِيَ الَّتِي تُوصِلُ إِلَيْهِ.

**29: What a difference there is between someone guided by Him, and someone seeking guidance about Him. The one guided by Him has direct knowledge of the Real**

**and verifies the matter from its actual Source.
The one seeking guidance about Him
does so on account of not having reached Him.
Were that not the case, when was He absent
so you would need to seek guidance about Him?
When was He distant
so you would need a trail to lead you to Him?**

Know that when Allah wanted to manifest the secrets of His Essence and the lights of His Attributes, by His Power he made manifest a handful of His pre-eternal light. Divine Power demanded the manifestation of its effect and the witnessing of its lights while Divine Wisdom demanded the lowering of a veil over them and manifestation of its covering curtains. When Power completed its light in the places of manifestation in phenomenal being, then Wisdom lowered the covering cloak of protection over them, and all phenomenal being became lights in a concealing veil.

Then Allah divided creation into two categories and separated them into two groups. One group is singled out for His Power: He made them the people of His *wilaya*, opened the door for them and removed the veil from them, letting them witness the secrets of His Essence and not veiling them from it by the effects of His Power. The other group he allotted for His service and He made them the people of His Wisdom, lowering the veil of illusion over them, making them stop with the outward forms and preventing them from witnessing their inward light. Glory be to the One Who has concealed His secret by His Wisdom and manifested His light by His Power!

The people of love, who are the people of *wilaya* and gnosis among the people of witnessing and eye-witnessing, are guided by light to the existence of the covering veils and so they only see light. They are guided by the Real to the existence of creation and they only find the Real. They are guided by Allah's Power to His Wisdom and they find His Power to be the source of His Wisdom and His Wisdom to be the source of His Power. So by witnessing the Real they withdraw from seeing creation since it is impossible to witness Him and witness something else with Him.

As for the people of service among the people of Wisdom, they seek guidance from the manifestation of the covering veils about the existence of their inner light and from creation about the existence of the Real. They are withdrawn from Him in the state of His Presence and they are veiled from Him by the intensity of His manifestation. One of the people of Allah said, "Allah Almighty affirms the creature for common people and so through it they affirm the Creator. He affirms Himself to the elite and through Him they affirm creation."

What a great difference there is between the one who is guided by Him to the manifestation of His effect and the one who seeks guidance about His existence through the manifestation of His effect! That is because the one who is guided by Him has direct knowledge of the Real, Who alone has true existence: Allah, the Worshipped King. He affirms the true nature of existence, which is its infinite timelessness, from the existence of its Source, the foundational, timeless, pre-eternal *Jabarut*. He realises that in reality existence belongs to Allah alone and he negates the unconditional existence of anything other than Him. He only perceives creation – which might be termed secondary existence – as being entirely dependent on the existence of its timeless Source, so that the branch is directly connected to the root and all becomes *Jabarut*. He only acknowledges the existence of the One Who in reality can alone be described as having it.

As for one who seeks guidance about Allah, this can only be because he is distant from Him in the state of his nearness to Him and absent from Him in the state of his presence with Him. Illusion has made Him appear distant. Lack of true understanding has made Him appear absent. When was He absent from you, so that you would need to seek guidance about Him, since: *"He is nearer to you than your jugular vein"* (50:16). When was He distant from you so that illusory tracks are needed to lead you to Him since: *"He is with you wherever you are"* (57:4). The effect of Divine Power is inseparable from its Source. The attribute is not separate from the described since it only has existence by it and no manifestation except from it.

As we will find later in the *Munajat*: "My God! How can one seek information about You through something which has absolute need of You for its own existence? When were You absent so that You would need evidence to indicate You? When were you distant so that traces would lead to You?" Allah knows best.

Then for those who are guided by Allah, Allah expands for them the arena of knowledges and opens for them the storehouses of understanding, which is not the case for those who seek information about Him. Allah has stinted them in the provision of knowledge by the existence of the veil of illusion. Shaykh Ibn Ata'illah now indicates that by saying:

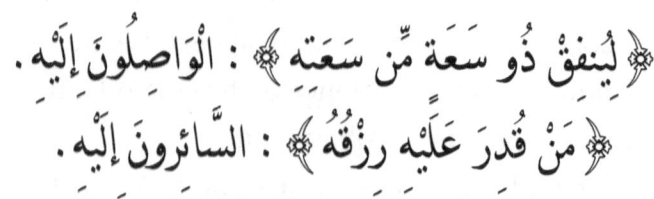

### 30: As for those who have reached Him:
*"He who has plenty should spend out from his plenty."*
### As for those who are travelling to Him:
*"he whose provision is restricted." (65:7)*

As for those who have reached Him, when their spirits escape from the constriction of phenomenal beings to the space of witnessing and eye-witnessing, or you could say, when their spirits rise from the world of forms to the world of spirits, or from the world to the *Mulk* to the world of the *Malakut*, then the arena of the provision of knowledge is expanded for them and the storehouses of understanding are opened to them. They expend jewels of hidden knowledge from the vastness of their wealth and rubies of the protected secret from the storehouses of their treasures. So they have an expanded sphere and ride the steeds of rhetoric and eloquent speech. How swift is the wealth that comes to the one at whom concern is directed! How immense is the opening of the who is attended to! Allah has men such that anyone who looks at them achieves a happiness after which he will never be wretched. They are the people of the secret and the state.

As for those who are travelling to Allah, they remain in the constriction of phenomenal beings and are confined in the world of forms in the prison of illusion. None of the storehouses of understanding are opened to them. They are busy in the *jihad* of themselves and the toil of purifying their hearts, constricted in knowledges and restricted in all forms of understanding. If they find in the journey, they arrive and move from the constriction of beings and travel and prance in the meadows of knowledges, and they win what they hope for and are enriched after they were weary. They return from the path. Or else they fall short and are ruined and lost.

NOTE: If you want the knowledge of tastes to be expanded to you, then disconnect yourself from the matter of provision. As long as you are working for the treasure of others, you will never excavate your own treasure. So disconnect yourself from the material and be in need of Allah and gifts will overflow on you from Allah. *"Sadaqat is for the poor and very poor."* (9:60) If you want expansion of gifts to you, then have sound poverty and need. When opening was delayed for his student Ibn Maymuna, Shaykh ad-Dabbas waited for him and found him reading the *Risala* of al-Qushayri. He told him, "Cast aside your book and dig in the soil of your self and a spring will arise for you. Otherwise leave me." Success is by Allah.

# Derse 16

اِهْتَدَى الرَّاحِلُونَ إِلَيْهِ بِأَنْوَارِ التَّوَجُّهِ،
وَالْوَاصِلُونَ لَهُمْ أَنْوَارُ الْمُوَاجَهَةِ، فَالْأَوَّلُونَ لِلْأَنْوَارِ،
وَهَؤُلَاءِ الْأَنْوَارُ لَهُمْ لِأَنَّهُمْ لِلَّهِ لَا لِشَيْءٍ دُونَهُ
﴿ قُلِ اللَّهُ ثُمَّ ذَرْهُمْ فِي خَوْضِهِمْ يَلْعَبُونَ ﴾ .

**31: Those travelling to Him
are guided by the light of
turning their faces toward Him.
Those who have arrived
have the lights of face-to-face encounter.
The former belong to lights,
but the lights belong to the latter
because they belong to Allah, and are His alone.
Say: 'Allah' then leave them plunging in their games."**

The lights of the "turning of the faces" are the lights of Islam and *iman*, and the lights of "face-to-face encounter" are the lights of *ihsan*. You could say the lights of turning the faces are the lights of outward and inward obedience and the lights of face-to-face encounter are the lights of reflection and looking. Or the lights of turning are the lights of the *shari'a* and *tariqa* and the lights of face-to-face encounter are the lights of the *haqiqa*. Or you could say that the lights of turning are the lights of striving and endurance and the lights of face-to-face encounter are the lights of witnessing and direct speech.

The clarification of that is that Allah Almighty wants to connect His slave to Himself first by the light of the sweetness of outward action, which is the station of Islam, so that he is guided to action and annihilated in it and tastes its sweetness. Then he turns to Him by the light of the sweetness of inward action, which is the station of *iman* with sincerity, truthfulness, tranquillity, intimacy with Allah and being alienated from other than Him, and so he is guided to it and annihilated and tastes its sweetness and is firm in watchfulness. This light is greater than the first and more perfect.

Then he turns to Him with the light of the sweetness of witnessing and it is the action of the *ruh*, and it is the first light of face-to-face encounter. So he is overwhelmed by astonishment, bewilderment and intoxication. When he awakens from his intoxication, becomes sober after his attraction, is firm in witnessing, and recognises the Worshipped King and returns to *baqa'*; then he is for Allah and by Allah. He has no need of the light by his witnessing the light of lights because he has become the light itself and has become a master of the lights after he was mastered by them by his need of them before he reached their Source.

When he arrives, he becomes the slave of Allah, free from what is other than Him. His outward is slavehood and his inward is freedom.

The end result is that as long as the *murid* continues to travel, he is guided by the lights of turning and needs them so that he can travel by them. When he reaches the station of witnessing, he obtains the lights of face-to-face encounter and so he does not need anything because he is for Allah, not for anything less than Him. The travellers are those travelling to lights by their need of them and so they rejoice in them. Those who have arrived have the lights because they are enriched beyond need by Allah. They are for Allah and by Allah, not for anything except Him.

Then the shaykh recited this *ayah* to the Path of the people of indication (*ishara*). "Say, 'Allah' with your heart and your *ruh* and withdraw from other than Him. Then leave people, 'leave them plunging in their games,'" in other words plunging into "other-than-Allah", playing with passion. One of the commentators criticised the Sufis for their citing the *ayah*: *"All the people knew their drinking place,"* (2:60) not understanding what they meant. Shaykh Ibn 'Abbad said, "Do not make the people of the outward an argument against the people of the inward." That is because the sight of the people of the inward is fine and their weaving delicate. Only they understand their indications. May Allah give us the benefit of them and join us to them. Amin.

# Derse 17

$$\text{تَشَوُّفُكَ إِلَى ما بَطَنَ فِيكَ مِنَ الْعُيُوبِ}$$
$$\text{خَيْرٌ مِنْ تَشَوُّفِكَ إِلَى ما حُجِبَ عَنْكَ مِنَ الْغُيُوبِ.}$$

**32: Better to look at the defects hidden inside you than to look for the Unseen Worlds that are veiled from you.**

Your looking at the defects hidden inside yourself, such as envy, pride, love of rank and leadership, anxiety about provision, fear of poverty, seeking to be one of the elite and other such faults, and learning about them and striving to be free of them, is much better for you than looking for things of the Unseen that are veiled from you, such as spiritual states and visions, other people's inner conditions, and the secrets of *tawhid* before being ready for them. The reason for this is that looking at your hidden faults is a way to bringing life to your heart, and the life and sound health of your heart is what is really essential for you because that is what you will need on the Day when the only thing of use to you will be: *"a sound and flawless heart – qalbin salim."* (26:89) It is the key, by Allah, to the everlasting bliss and never-ending delight of the Garden in the Next World. Striving to unveil the Unseen is over and above what is necessary and can be very self-destructive, as it is often connected to arrogance and seeking superiority over other people. As the Shaykh says later: "When someone perceives the secrets of others and does not take on the character of Divine mercy, his perception is just a trial for him and results in bad for him."

Know that there are three types of human defects: defects of the *nafs*, defects of the heart and defects of the *ruh*. The defects of the *nafs* are its attachment to and overindulgence in physical appetites, such as food, drink, and sex, and its over-concern with outward appearance in terms of clothing, means of transport, dwelling places, and other such things. The defects of the heart are its attachment to appetites of the heart, such as social status, reputation, leadership, power, pride, anger, envy and rancour. The defects of the *ruh* are its attachment to inward gifts, like seeking spiritual states, visionary experiences and other things of that nature. Being subject to any of those things detracts from your service to your Lord and prevents you from fulfilling the rights you owe to Him. So your preoccupation with looking at the defects of your *nafs*, heart and *ruh*, and your striving to purify yourself from them, is far better for you than looking for knowledge of the Unseen Worlds which are veiled from you. As Shaykh Muhammad b. al-Habib once said, "One step on the Straight Path is better for you than a thousand visions." Success is by Allah.

Shaykh Ibn Ata'illah follows this by saying:

الْحَقُّ لَيْسَ بِمَحْجُوبٍ، وَإِنَّمَا الْمَحْجُوبُ أَنْتَ عَنِ النَّظَرِ إِلَيْهِ، إِذْ لَوْ حَجَبَهُ شَيْءٌ لَسَتَرَهُ مَا حَجَبَهُ، وَلَوْ كَانَ لَهُ سَاتِرٌ، لَكَانَ لِوُجُودِهِ حَاصِرٌ، وَكُلُّ حَاصِرٍ لِشَيْءٍ، فَهُوَ لَهُ قَاهِرٌ ﴿ وَهُوَ الْقَاهِرُ فَوْقَ عِبَادِهِ ﴾.

**33: The Real is not veiled**
**– it is you that are veiled from seeing Him.**
**If there was anything veiling Him**
**what veiled Him would cover Him.**
**If He was covered,**
**His existence would be contained.**
**If something contains something else,**
**it is master of it.**
**But He is *"the Absolute Master over His slaves."***

A veil is impossible for the Almighty. Nothing veils Him because He is manifest by everything, before everything and after everything. Nothing is with Him nor does anything have real existence except Him. So He is not veiled from you. The thing which veils you is yourself. You are veiled from seeing Him by your reliance on other-than-Him and the attachment of your heart to material things. If your heart were truly engaged in seeking your Lord and had turned away completely from looking at other-than-Him, it would see the light of the Real, shining in the manifestation of created existence, and what was veiled from you by illusion would be open to your witnessing and inner sight.

Everyone has eyes but they do not really see. All of us are in the Divine ocean but very few indeed are aware of it. The Shaykh says later: "It is not the existence of anything with Him that veils you from Allah – since there is nothing with Him – what veils you is the illusion that something exists with Him." That is because if anything physical was veiling Allah, that veil would be covering him. If He were covered by a veil, that would mean that His existence was contained by something else. It is impossible for Him to be covered in any way and therefore contained because anything that contains something else has mastery over it. How could that be when the Almighty says of Himself: *"He is the Absolute Master over His slaves,"* in other words they are in His grasp and under the control of His Power, His Wisdom and His Will. The preposition "over" in this instance designates the elevation of majesty and position, not that of place, as one says, "the sultan is over the wazir" and "the master is over his slave," and "the king is over his subject", and other things which confirm superiority and negate any designation of space, and Allah knows best.

When a person frees themselves from the domination of their human defects, they take on spiritual qualities, such as doing-without, scrupulousness, contentment, humility, forbearance, compassion, generosity, concern for the poor and homeless, the people of Allah and all the Muslims, and other noble qualities of character. When someone takes on these qualities and realises them experientially, after freeing themselves from their opposites, they are then truly sincere slaves of their Lord, free from what is

# 17

other than Him. Then they are really able to respond to His call and be near to His presence. When their Lord says to them, "My slave," and they say to Him, "My Lord!", they are truthful in their response through the reality of their sincere submission.

That does not and cannot happen when people are engrossed in their outward and inward appetites. Then they are in reality a slave to themselves and their appetites. When such people say, "My Lord," they are in fact lying since whoever loves a thing is a slave to that thing and not to Allah. When someone is freed from the bondage of their appetites and desires, they inevitably draw near to the Divine Presence. Indeed they will be inseparable from it since nothing removes us from awareness of the Divine Presence except love for these illusory attachments. When we are freed from them and truly become slaves of Allah, then the veil will be removed from us and we will know with certainty that nothing exists but Him.

# Derse 18

$$\text{اُخْرُجْ مِنْ أَوْصَافِ بَشَرِيَّتِكَ عَنْ كُلِّ وَصْفٍ مُنَاقِضٍ لِعُبُودِيَّتِكَ لِتَكُونَ لِنِدَاءِ الْحَقِّ مُجِيبًا وَمِنْ حَضْرَتِهِ قَرِيبًا.}$$

**34: From the qualities of your humanness,
get rid of every quality incompatible
with your slavehood
so you can respond to the call of the Real
and be near His presence.**

The "qualities of humanness" referred to are the qualities which are incompatible with sincere slavehood. They derive from two matters. The first is the attachment of the heart to animal qualities, which are the appetites of the belly and the genitals, and what follows on from them in respect of love of this world and its ephemeral appetites. The Almighty says: *"To mankind the love of worldly appetites is painted in glowing colours: women and children, and heaped-up mounds of gold and silver, and horses with fine markings and livestock and fertile farmland."* (3:14) The second is taking on satanic qualities, such as pride, envy, rancour, anger, anxiety, frivolity, arrogance, love of rank, leadership, and praise, hardness, coarseness, vulgarity, adulation of the wealthy and contempt for the poor, and other things like fear of poverty, anxiety about provision, avarice, showing-off, haughtiness and innumerable others, so that one of people of Allah said, "The nafs has as many imperfections as Allah has perfections." Shaykh Abu 'Abdu'r-Rahman as-Sulami wrote a lengthy book on the Defects of Self and Its Cures and Shaykh Zarruq wrote about eight hundred verses on this subject. However, if Allah gives someone a shaykh of instruction, they do not need anything except for the ability to listen and act on what they hear.

When a *faqir* frees himself from the domination of his animal qualities, he takes on spiritual qualities, like doing without, scrupulousness, contentment, chastity, freedom from other than Allah, and intimacy with Him. When he frees himself from satanic qualities, he takes on angelic qualities, like humility, sound heartedness, forbearance, tranquillity, gravity, being at peace, easiness, gentleness, obscurity, being content with his knowledge of Allah, compassion, mercy, esteem for the poor and homeless, for the people of Allah and all the Community, generosity, open-handedness, magnanimity, sincerity, truthfulness, watchfulness, witnessing and direct knowledge of his Lord.

When a person takes on these qualities and realises them experientially after freeing himself from their opposites, he is a sincere slave of his Lord, free from what is other than Him. He is then able to respond to His call and be near to His presence. When his Lord says to him, "My slave," and he says to him, "My Lord!", he is truthful in his response through the reality of his sincere slavehood. That cannot happen when he is engrossed in his outward and inward appetites. Then he is in reality a slave to himself and his appetites. When such a person says, "My Lord," he is lying since whoever loves a thing is a slave to that thing and Allah does not want you to be a slave to other than Him. When someone is freed from the bondage of appetites and desires, then he is near to the Presence of Allah. Indeed he will be inseparable from It since nothing removes us from awareness of the Divine Presence except love for these imaginary illusions. When we are freed from them and achieve true slavehood, we will inevitably find ourselves in the Divine Presence.

Know that Allah made these human qualities by which the Presence is veiled a rag with which to wipe away the impurities that keep us from it, such as the self, *shaytan* and this world. Allah made the *nafs* and *shaytan* a rag for the removal of blameworthy actions and made humanness a rag for the erasing of base qualities. For in reality there is nothing but the manifestation of the Real and the *tajalliyat* of the Real. There is only Him, and there is no strength nor power except by Allah. The reason that these defects remain in us is because of our failure to have awareness of them. The reason for that failure is our satisfaction with ourselves. If you were dissatisfied with yourself, you would look for its evil qualities, dig them out and be purified of them. That is why Shaykh Ibn Ata'illah then says:

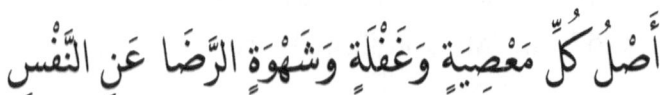

### 35a: The root of every act of rebellion, every appetite and every moment of heedlessness is satisfaction with one's self.

This is because everyone who is satisfied with himself likes its states and covers up its evils as the poet said, "The eye of pleasure is blind to every defect." And then he says:

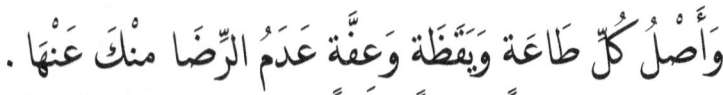

### 35b: The root of every act of obedience and self-restraint and every moment of wakefulness is lack of satisfaction with one's self.

That is because whoever suspects his *nafs* and has a bad opinion of it and looks at it with the eye of anger investigates its defects and extracts its evils. As the poet said, "But the eye of anger reveals bad qualities." Therefore, *murid*, search out your defects and suspect your *nafs* and do not approve of any of its states. When you are pleased with it and admire its states, it will sting you without you being aware of it. It veils you from the Presence while you are looking. Abu Hafs al-Haddad said, "Anyone who does not suspect himself at all times and does not oppose himself in all states and does not drag his self to what it dislikes all the time, is deluded. Anyone who looks at his self and approves of any of it has destroyed it." How could any intelligent person be satisfied with their *nafs*? As we find in Sura Yusuf: "*I do not say that my self was free from blame. The self indeed commands to evil acts – except for those my Lord has mercy on."*(12:53) A poet said about it:

> Be cautious of your self and do not trust its tricks.
> The self is fouler than seventy *shaytans*.

As-Sari as-Saqati said, "Whoever recognises Allah lives. Whoever inclines to this world is fickle. The fool goes to and fro, morning and evening, to no purpose. The intelligent person examines his defects." So, my brother, be concerned with your defects if you want to be faithful to yourself. When you search out the defects of your *nafs* and expose its imperfections, you will be purified, liberated, achieve realisation, and enter the Divine Presence. Sight will be expanded for you and reflection. The shaykh of our shaykh said, "The curse of Allah is on the one to whom the defect of his self is shown and then does not shame him." He often used to advise lack of care about what people think and lack of concern for them since one can only be purified from subtle elements of showing off by ceasing care about how other people see you and you see them.

# Derse 19

لَا تَتَعَدَّ نِيَّةُ هِمَّتِكَ إِلَى غَيْرِهِ، فَالْكَرِيمُ لَا تَتَخَطَّاهُ الآمَالُ.

**38: Do not let the intention of your *himma*
veer to other-than-Him.
Your hopes will never be able to
outstrip the Ever-Generous.**

The "intention of the *himma*" is the goal to which it is directed. The *himma* itself is the energy directed to obtaining your goals. Your "hopes" here are those things which you are aiming to obtain. When your *himma* is connected to something which you want to obtain, then return to Allah and do not direct it towards anything except Him because He is Ever-Generous and His blessings flow constantly night and day. Your hopes will never outstrip the Ever-Generous. He wants to be asked so that He can respond to the request. It has been said in explanation of His Name, the Ever-Generous, that it means that He is the One Who gives when asked and when not asked and does not care how much He gives nor to whom He gives.

When a need is presented to other-than-Him, He is not pleased. When He is treated badly, He pardons. When He reproves, He does not look too deeply. This is part of the perfection of His Generosity and the completeness of His kindness and blessing. Sidi Ibrahim at-Tazi wrote about that in a *qasida*:

> Allah's perfection is the most perfect goodness.
> Allah has perfection without doubt.
> Allah's love is the noblest of any intimacy,
> so do not forget to take on nobility.
> The *dhikr* of Allah, coursing through every limb,
> is more beneficial than slaking burning thirst.
> In truth, there is no existent except Allah,
> so cast aside any tendency to self-esteem.

Since you know of Allah's Generosity, Magnanimity, Perfection and Kindness, do not ask for anything from other than Him when, in fact, doing that is pointless, as Shaykh Ibn Ata'illah then points out when he says:

لَا تَرْفَعَنَّ إِلَى غَيْرِهِ حَاجَةً هُوَ مُورِدُها عَلَيْكَ.

### 39a: Do not ask other-than-Him to relieve you of a need that He Himself brought upon you.

You know that what that is other than the Real is in reality an illusory projection with no actual substance to its existence. So if Allah gives you a need through the existence of poverty, hardship or some other passing thing, take it back to Allah, subject it to the will of Allah, withdraw from it into the remembrance of Allah, and do not turn to other than Him either through affection or flattery. We find in a hadith: "If someone does not ask Allah, Allah is angry with Him." Abu 'Ali ad-Daqqaq said, "The sign of true knowledge is that you look to Allah alone for the fulfilment of all your needs." Or you are absorbed like Musa ﷺ, yearning for the vision of Allah. He said: *"Lord, show me Yourself so that I may look at You!"* (7:143) But one day when he was in real need of immediate help he said: *"My Lord, I am truly in need of any good You have in store for me."* (28:24)

The shaykh then expresses astonishment at people who ask for things from those other than Allah, in spite of their lack of power and their true incapacity, for something that, in reality, He alone can do.

فَكَيْفَ يَرْفَعُ غَيْرُهُ مَا كَانَ هُوَ لَهُ وَاضِعاً

## 39b: How can anyone relieve it other than the One who put it there in the first place?

One aspect of a person's lack of *adab* is that they ask people to relieve them from the effects of Allah's Power when they know of His Kindness and Goodness and the fact that His Kindness is not disconnected from His Power. Shaykh ash-Shadhili said, "I have despaired of me being able to help myself, so how could I not despair of other than me helping me? And given that I hope for Allah's help for other than me, how can I not hope for His help for me myself?" One of the people of Allah said, "I heard a voice saying to me when I was between sleeping and waking: 'Do not display need or it may be doubled for you in recompense for your bad *adab* and going beyond the limits of your slavehood. I have tested you with need so that you will take refuge in Me from it, and pray to Me for it, and rely on Me in it. I have smelted you in the crucible of need so that through it you become pure gold. So do not deviate after the smelting. I have imposed poverty on you and made wealth My domain. If you attribute it to Me, I will let you attain to it. If you attribute it to other than Me, I will cut off My help from you, and will disconnect your means from My means and cast you away from My door. If someone relies on Me, he wins. If someone relies on himself, he is destroyed.'"

Then he clarifies the reason for his astonishment:

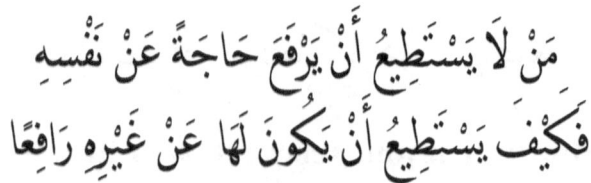

### 39c: If someone is incapable of relieving their own need how can they possibly expect to relieve someone else's?

If someone is unable to put himself right, how does he think he is going to be able to put anybody else right? Both the seeker and sought are weak. One of the people of Allah said, "Whoever relies on other than Allah is in delusion because delusion is that which does not last. Nothing except Him lasts for ever. He is the Eternal, the Timeless who continues and will always continue. His giving and bounty will never cease. So do not rely on anyone or anything whose giving and excellence is not constant and everlasting." As He says: *"What is with you runs out. But what is with Allah goes on forever."* (16:96)

# Derse 20

إِنْ لَمْ تُحَسِّنْ ظَنَّكَ بِهِ لِأَجْلِ وَصْفِهِ،

فَحَسِّنْ ظَنَّكَ بِهِ لِأَجْلِ مُعَامَلَتِهِ مَعَكَ،

فَهَلْ عَوَّدَكَ إِلَّا حَسَنًا؟ وَهَلْ أَسْدَى إِلَيْكَ إِلَّا مِنَنًا؟

**40: If you cannot think well of Him
because of the beauty of His attributes
then think well of Him
because of the way He behaves towards you.
Has He accustomed you to anything but good?
Has He conferred on you anything but favours?**

In respect of having a good opinion of Allah, people fall into two categories: the elite and the common man. In the case of the elite, their good opinion of Allah Almighty stems from their witnessing His beauty and seeing His perfection. So their good opinion of Allah never ceases – no matter whether He directs Beauty or Majesty towards them – because mercy, compassion, generosity and magnanimity are inherent in Him and that never ceases to be the case. When He manifests Himself to them in a majestic or forceful way they know that hidden within that is an aspect of His perfect blessing and encompassing Mercy and so they are dominated by witnessing mercy and beauty and their good opinion of Allah continues in every state.

Where the common people are concerned, however, their good opinion of Allah only stems from witnessing His kindness, good treatment and favour to them. When adversity or a hardship descends on them, they should consider Allah's prior goodness to them and the blessings He has already bestowed on them out of His kindness and favour. They should compare what has now arrived to what has gone before and so receive what comes to them with acceptance and contentment. This feeling may be weak as a result of weak understanding and reflection, or strong as a result of strong understanding and reflection. This is not the case with the first group. That is because in their case their state derives from witnessing Allah's Attributes, which are not subject to alteration, whereas the state of the second group derives from witnessing Allah's action which can and does alter.

So *murid*, if you cannot have a good opinion of Allah through witnessing His eternal attributes of Compassion and Mercy, which do not change, then at least have a good opinion of Him by seeing how He has so often treated you with kindness and favour. Has Allah accustomed you to anything but good and kindness? Has He bestowed on you anything but favour in abundance and manifold blessings? The Messenger of Allah ﷺ said, "Love Allah on account of the blessings he bestows on you and love me on account of your love of Allah." Shaykh ash-Shadhili ☙ said, "We love only Allah." A man said, "Your forebear rejected that, sir, by his words, 'Hearts are disposed to love the one who is good to them.'" Shaykh ash-Shadhili responded, "Since we do not see any good-doer other than Allah, we do not love other than Him."

He also said, "One night I recited, '*I seek refuge with the Lord of people*' until I reached the words, '*...the evil of the whisperer...*' and it was said to me, 'The whisperer comes between you and your Beloved, reminding you of your evil deeds and making you forget your good deeds, insinuating that you have a lot of what belongs to the left and very little of what belongs to the right. This is in order to make you turn from good opinion of Allah and His Generosity to a bad opinion of Allah and His Messenger. So beware of this weak spot. It has captured many worshippers, ascetics and people of obedience and correctness.'"

Since Allah Almighty has only made you used to good and has bestowed so many favours on you, it is astonishing that you should abandon Him and seek other than Him! Shaykh Ibn Ata'illah remarks on that by saying:

الْعَجَبُ كُلُّ الْعَجَبِ مِمَّنْ يَهْرُبُ مِمَّنْ لَا انْفِكَاكَ لَهُ عَنْهُ، وَيَطْلُبُ مَا لَا بَقَاءَ لَهُ مَعَهُ ۞ فَإِنَّهَا لَا تَعْمَى الْأَبْصَارُ وَلَكِنْ تَعْمَى الْقُلُوبُ الَّتِي فِي الصُّدُورِ. ۞

**41: What could be more astonishing than that someone should flee from something they can't escape to search for something that will never last!**
*"It is not the eyes that are blind,
but the hearts in the breasts are blind."* **(22:46)**

What "cannot be escaped" is Allah Almighty and His decree and predetermination. What "will not last" is this world and your own plans and resolutions. So it is indeed amazing you should flee from your Lord, who most certainly cannot be escaped, and turn to seeking other than Him, which most certainly will not last. That must be true because nothing has any existence except what is granted to it by Him nor any continuance except by Him. So why on earth do you try to escape from Him, spending your time failing to seek knowledge of Him, and not draw near to Him by obeying His commands and avoiding His prohibitions. Instead you prefer to seek the fleeting, transitory offerings of this world that are so fickle and impermanent. Even if those things stay with you during your life, they will certainly forsake you at your death. So seek what lasts forever not what will inevitably disappear completely. How excellent is what the poet said:

Oppose this world and you will make sure of being forgiven.
And is it not destined, anyway, to complete annihilation?
Indeed how should this world be viewed
except as a passing shadow,
Which covers you briefly
and then will vanish without a trace.

You could also say that it is totally astonishing that someone should flee from the Power and Decree of Allah, which they cannot possibly escape, and instead put their faith in their own decision-making and choosing when it is abundantly clear that everything we plan and decide for ourselves is irrevocably subject to the Divine Decree. As another poet says:

> How can a building one day reach completion
> if, as you build it, someone else is knocking it down.

All of this is due to the lack of the opening, or indeed the blindness, of the inner eye. That is why Allah tells us that although the physical eye is not blind to the perception of the sensory, because it perceives it and is veiled by it, the eye of the heart is blind to the perception of the meaning – of the reality behind the sensory – and so it too only sees the sensory and loves only it and seeks nothing but it. Shaykh ash-Shadhili said, "The blindness of the inner eye can be seen in three things: allowing the limbs to disobey Allah, greed for the creation of Allah and dissimulation when acting in obedience to Allah." We ask Allah for protection from these things and to open our inner eye. We ask him to grant us guidance in all our affairs and for the gift of states and actions that will make us pleasing to Him.

# Derse 21

لَا تَرْحَلْ مِنْ كَوْنٍ إِلَى كَوْنٍ فَتَكُونَ كَحِمَارِ الرَّحَى؛ يَسِيرُ وَالْمَكَانُ الَّذِي ارْتَحَلَ إِلَيْهِ هُوَ الَّذِي ارْتَحَلَ عَنْهُ. وَلَكِنِ ارْحَلْ مِنَ الأَكْوَانِ إِلَى الْمُكَوِّنِ، ﴿ وَأَنَّ إِلَى رَبِّكَ الْمُنْتَهَى ﴾ .

**42a: Do not travel from created being
to created being.
You will be like the donkey
going around at the mill.
It travels to what it set out from.
Travel from created beings to the Maker of Being.**
*"And the final end is to your Lord."*

Travelling from created being to created being is going from other than Allah to seek other than Allah. That is like someone who is *zahid* in this world, ostensibly devoting himself to Allah but doing so solely out of the desire to relieve himself of responsibility and for this world to come to him on the basis of the words of Prophet ﷺ: "If someone devotes himself to Allah, Allah will spare him every burden and provide for him from where he does not reckon." Or like someone who is *zahid* in this world because he seeks eliteness, or other people's esteem, or power over them, or to put awe of him in their hearts. Or like someone who is *zahid* with the object of being able to perform miracles. Or someone who is *zahid* hoping for palaces and houris in the Next World. All of this is travelling from one created being to another created being. So such a person is like a donkey going round and round at the mill, night and day, never getting anywhere. What he travels from is what he travels to. His *himma* is only for his own self-gratification. He thinks that he is covering a great distance to get to what he aspires to seek but actually he is increased in nothing but loss and exhaustion.

Shaykh ash-Shadhili says, "Stand at one door, not expecting to have doors opened to you, and doors will open to you. Be humble to one Master, not to have necks humbled to you, and necks will be humbled to you. The Almighty says: *'There is nothing that does not have its stores with us...'* (15:21)" So, *murid*, you must take your need to the Glorious King and travel from seeing created beings to seeking the witnessing of the Eternal, or travel from evidence and exposition to the rank of witnessing and eye-witnessing. That is the ultimate goal and the achievement of desire. *"And the final end is to your Lord."*

Do not travel from one created being to another created being, leaving the portions of your self in search the portion of another creature. If you do that you are the same as the donkey going around at the mill which simply goes back to what it has just come from. Being compared to a donkey is evidence of the stupidity and lack of understanding of such a person, since if they possessed any real understanding from Allah, they would travel away from the portions of their own selves and their desires, aiming to reach the presence of their Lord. So, murid, do not travel from one created being to another created being like yourself but rather travel from created beings to the Creator of Being.

Travelling to the Creator is achieved by three things. The first is confining your *himma* to Him, rather than to anything else, until He appears in your heart and you experience no love for other than Him. The second is returning to Him by fulfilling His rights over you while fleeing from self-gratification. The third is constancy in seeking refuge in Him, seeking His help, reliance on Him and submission to whatever He brings. Then the Shaykh indicates how to raise the *himma* to Allah and turn away from what is other than Him by quoting the "Hadith of Emigration" which is found in *Sahih Bukhari*." He says:

وَانْظُرْ إِلَى قَوْلِهِ صَلَّى اللَّهُ عَلَيْهِ وَسَلَّمَ ﴿ فَمَنْ كَانَتْ هِجْرَتُهُ إِلَى اللَّهِ وَرَسُولِهِ فَهِجْرَتُهُ إِلَى اللَّهِ وَرَسُولِهِ، وَمَنْ كَانَتْ هِجْرَتُهُ لِدُنْيَا يُصِيبُهَا أَوِ امْرَأَةٍ يَنْكِحُهَا فَهِجْرَتُهُ إِلَى مَا هَاجَرَ إِلَيْهِ ﴾. فَافْهَمْ قَوْلَهُ صَلَّى اللَّهُ عَلَيْهِ وَسَلَّمَ ﴿ فَهِجْرَتُهُ إِلَى مَا هَاجَرَ إِلَيْهِ ﴾ وَتَأَمَّلْ هَذَا الْأَمْرَ. سَلَامٌ.

**42b: Look at the words of the Prophet ﷺ:**
**"Whoever emigrates to Allah and His Messenger,**
**his emigration is to Allah and His Messenger.**
**Whoever emigrates to something of this world**
**or a woman to marry,**
**his emigration is to what he emigrates to."**
**Understand his words ﷺ:**
**"His emigration is to what he emigrates to."**
**Reflect on this matter**
**if you have any understanding at all!**
**Peace!**

Emigration is moving from one land to another land when someone travels from the land he leaves and settles in the land to which he moves. Here it is one of three matters: traveling from the land of disobedience to the land of obedience; from the land of heedlessness to the land of awareness; or from the land of the world of forms to the land of the world of spirits. Or you could say, from the land of the *mulk* to the land of the *malakut*; or from the land of the sensory to the land of the meaning; or from the land of the knowledge of certainty to the land of the eye of certainty or the truth of certainty. Whoever emigrates from these lands and, by his emigration, is aiming for the pleasure or Allah and His Messenger, or to attain to direct knowledge of Allah and His Messenger, his emigration will bring him to Allah and His Messenger according to his aim and *himma*. But if someone emigrates to get the portions of his self and his desires, then his goal and striving is wasted and the end of his emigration is that for which he emigrates. His emigration will add to the evil consequences of his action.

Therefore, listener, understand his words ﷺ: "His emigration is to what he emigrates to." Reflect on them and put them before your heart and your *nafs*. Look to see whether there remains inside of you any attraction to that from which you emigrated or whether there is still a portion of that "otherness" to which you have emigrated, which is other than the pleasure of Allah and His Messenger, or the knowledge of Allah and His Messenger ﷺ. Allah is jealous and does not want anyone who seeks Him to seek another along with Him. The one who has anything of his own portion and desire remaining in him will not reach Allah. Ash-Shushtari said:

If you desire Our union, then your death is a precondition. Union is not obtained by anyone who has leftovers in him.

He also said:

> No one gains union with Me
> who has anything left inside him.

I heard our shaykh al-Yazidi say, "If you want to see whether your *nafs* has or has not travelled from this world to the world of the *Malakut*, then present to it the things which it desires, and to which it inclines, one after another. If you find that it has truly travelled away from them and love for them has left your heart and it does not turn to any of them, then rejoice, for you have indeed travelled with your spirit to the world of the *Malakut*. If you find that it relies on or inclines towards love of anything of this world, then strive against it and bring it out from it entirely until you have truly travelled to your Lord."

The Shaykh ends with the word "Peace" because the travel referred to is the journey of the heart from witnessing creation to witnessing the Creator and it is what the heart experiences when it reaches its desired destination: *"Salamun, qawlan min rabbin rahim: 'Peace': a word from a Merciful Lord."*

# Derse 22

مَا قَلَّ عَمَلٌ بَرَزَ مِنْ قَلْبٍ زَاهِدٍ،
وَلَا كَثُرَ عَمَلٌ بَرَزَ مِنْ قَلْبٍ رَاغِبٍ.

**45: No amount of action stemming from the heart
of a *zahid* can ever be called small.
No amount of action stemming from the heart
of someone enmeshed in desire
can ever be called large.**

*Zuhd* with regard to something is to remove love of it from the heart and to be cool towards it. With some people it is to dislike anything that distracts them from Allah and keeps them from experiencing the Presence of Allah. A primary aspect of it is connected to property. The sign of someone being *zahid* is that, if gold or dust, silver or stone, wealth or poverty, are either given to them or denied to them, it is the same to them. A secondary aspect of it is connected to rank and reputation, in which case might and abasement, public acclamation and obscurity, praise and blame, rising and falling in rank, are the same to the person concerned. A still further aspect of it is connected to spiritual states, *karamat*, and high spiritual standing. In that case the sign of *zuhd* is that hope and fear, strength and weakness, expansion and contraction are the same. They deal with the one state in exactly the same way as they deal with the other state and they accept the one in the same way they accept the other. Finally perfect *zuhd* is detachment from all created existence and comes about through witnessing the Maker of Being and His command.

When the murid achieves these stations of *zuhd*, or most of them, then all his actions are huge in meaning in the sight of Allah, even if they may seem small in the eyes of other people. This is the meaning the words of the Prophet ﷺ, "A little action in the *Sunna* is better than a lot of action in innovation." What innovation could be greater and worse than love of this world and devotion to it with the heart and body. That did not exist in the time of the Prophet ﷺ nor in the time of the Companions ﷺ. Then after them people who loved this world appeared and built palaces and became proud and adorned themselves. This is the real innovation. The actions of such people are small in meaning even if they are large in number, because what is taken into account is what is in the heart, not the amount of physical effort expended. What is important is the submission of the *ruh*.

The worship of the *zahid* is by Allah and for Allah but the worship of the one enmeshed in desire is by the self and for the self. The worship of the *zahid* is alive and everlasting whereas the worship of the one enmeshed in desire is dead and short-lived. The worship of the *zahid* is always connected and continuing whereas the worship of the one enmeshed in desire is always cut off and blocked. This is why one of the people of Allah said, "The worship of the wealthy is like someone praying on a dunghill."

So the worship of the *zahid*, even if it is little in the sensory, is a lot in the meaning, and the worship of the one enmeshed in desire is little in meaning, even if it seems a lot in the sensory. A metaphor illustrating this is two men who give presents to a king. One of them gives him a small, flawless ruby of enormous value while the other gives him sixty empty boxes. There is no doubt that the king will accept the ruby and honour the one who gave it to him, whereas he will reject the boxes and be angry with the one who gave them to him since he has made a mockery the king by doing that. He wanted to enhance his reputation by the size of his gift but it was of no use to him at all. I heard our shaykh say, "Someone whose heart is full of desire for this world does not really do *dhikr*, even if he says, 'Allah, Allah' with his tongue all the time, since the tongue alone counts for nothing. Someone freed from attachment to this world is always doing *dhikr*, even he only does a little *dhikr* with his tongue."

Sayyiduna 'Ali ﷺ said, "You should be far more concerned about whether an action is accepted than about the action itself. No action is small when it is done with *taqwa*. How can an action which is accepted by Allah be considered small?" Ibn Mas'ud ﷺ said, "Two *rak'ats* from someone free of love of this world done with true knowledge are better and more beloved to Allah than the abundant worship of someone for whom it is just a matter of strenuous effort, even if such a person were to carry on doing it until the end of time." One of the *Salaf* said, "You are not less than the Companions of Muhammad ﷺ in terms of the amount of prayer and fasting you do, but they were far greater in terms of their lack of attachment to this world."

It is said that Sayyiduna 'Isa ﷺ passed by a man who was sleeping while other people were praying. He said to him, "Get up and pray with the people." He said, "I have prayed." 'Isa asked him, "What was your prayer?" He replied, "I left this world to its people." He told him, "Carry on sleeping. That is an excellent kind of prayer!" A man said to Shaykh Abu'l-Hasan, "How is it that people hold you in such high regard when I do not see you doing much in the way of *'ibada*." He replied, "It is on account of my holding to something that Allah imposed on His Messenger." "What was that?" he asked. Shaykh Shadhili replied, "Turning from you and your love of this world."

Shaykh Zarruq said, "The people of *zuhd* gain three great benefits from their *zuhd*. The first is freedom of the heart from occupations and distractions. The second is its witnessing to the sincerity of their love for Allah since this world attracts love and is only repudiated for something one loves more. The third is because it is an indication of direct knowledge of Allah and reliance on Him." One of the people of Allah said, "A thousand words from an impure heart achieve nothing whatsoever but one word from a purified heart achieves a thousand things."

# Derse 23

لَا تَتْرُكِ الذِّكْرَ لِعَدَمِ حُضُورِكَ مَعَ اللَّهِ فِيهِ ، لِأَنَّ غَفْلَتَكَ عَنْ وُجُودِ ذِكْرِهِ أَشَدُّ مِنْ غَفْلَتِكَ فِي وُجُودِ ذِكْرِهِ. فَعَسَى أَنْ يَرْفَعَكَ مِنْ ذِكْرٍ مَعَ وُجُودِ غَفْلَةٍ إِلَى ذِكْرٍ مَعَ وُجُودِ يَقَظَةٍ، وَمِنْ ذِكْرٍ مَعَ وُجُودِ يَقَظَةٍ إِلَى ذِكْرٍ مَعَ وُجُودِ حُضُورٍ، وَمِنْ ذِكْرٍ مَعَ وُجُودِ حُضُورٍ إِلَى ذِكْرٍ مَعَ وُجُودِ غَيْبَةٍ عَمَّا سِوَى المَذْكُورِ، ﴿ وَمَا ذَلِكَ عَلَى اللَّهِ بِعَزِيزٍ ﴾ .

47: Do not give up *dhikr* of Allah
because you are not present with Allah in it.
It is worse to forget to do *dhikr* of Him
than to be inattentive while doing *dhikr* of Him.
He might raise you up from *dhikr* with heedlessness
to *dhikr* with concentration,
and from *dhikr* with concentration
to *dhikr* with presence,
and from *dhikr* with presence
to *dhikr* with withdrawal from all that is other than Him.
"That is not difficult for Allah."

*Dhikr* is a strong pillar on the Path of the People. It is the best of actions. Allah Almighty says: *"Remember Me and I will remember you."* (2:151) He also says: *"You who believe, remember Allah a lot."* (33:41) A lot of *dhikr* means never forgetting Allah. Ibn 'Abbas said, "Every act of worship which Allah ordained has a specific time, and there are excuses for those who perform them outside their time – except for *dhikr*. Allah did not appoint any particular time for it. He says: 'Remember Allah a lot,' (33:41) and He says: 'When you have finished the prayer, then remember Allah, standing, sitting and lying on your sides.' (4:103)"

A man said, "Messenger of Allah, I find the practices of Islam a lot, so tell me something I can do by which I can make up for what I miss, and be brief." He ﷺ replied, "Let your tongue be moist with *dhikru'llah*." The Prophet ﷺ also said, "Shall I tell you of the best and purest of your actions in the sight of your Lord, the highest of your degrees and what is better for you than spending gold and silver, and better for you than meeting your enemy and your striking their necks and their striking your necks." They asked, "What is that, Messenger of Allah?" He said, *"Dhikru'llah."*

'Ali said, "I asked, 'Messenger of Allah, which path is the nearest one to Allah, the easiest for the slaves of Allah and the best in the sight of Allah Almighty.' He replied, "Ali, you must be constant in *dhikru'llah*."' 'Ali said to him, "Everyone has to do *dhikru'llah*." The Prophet ﷺ continued, "The Last Hour will not come until there does not remain of the face of the earth anyone who says, 'Allah'." 'Ali said to him, "How should I do *dhikr*, Messenger of Allah?" He ﷺ

said to him, "Close your eyes and listen to me and then say the same thing while I am listening to you." The Prophet ﷺ said, "There is no god but Allah" three times with his eyes closed, and then 'Ali said it in the same way. He taught this to al-Hasan al-Basri and then al-Hasan taught al-Habib al-'Ajami and Habib passed it to Da'ud at-Ta'i and Da'ud to Mar'uf al-Karkhi and then Mar'uf to as-Sari as-Saqati and as-Sari to al-Junayd, and then it moved through the masters of teaching.

No one reaches Allah except by way of *dhikr*. The slave's obligation, therefore, is to occupy his time with it and to expend great effort in doing it. Whoever is given *dhikr*, is given true life. Whoever abandons it, is dismissed. So all *murids* should cling to *dhikr* in every state and not abandon *dhikr* on the tongue just because their heart is not present in it. You should remember Allah with your tongue, even if you are heedless with your heart. Your neglect of the activity of *dhikr* of Allah is worse than your heedlessness while you are doing it, because your neglecting to do *dhikr* of Him is turning away from Him completely, while your doing *dhikr* of Him, even if heedlessly, is turning towards Him in a certain way.

By remembering Allah the tongue is adorned with obedience to Allah. When *dhikr* is absent it is much easier for you to turn to disobedience. One of people of Allah was asked, "Why should we do *dhikr* with our tongues when our hearts are heedless?" He replied, "Thank Allah for your success in doing *dhikr* with the tongue. If it were busy with something other than *dhikr*, where would you be then?"

So everyone should cling to the *dhikr* of the tongue until Allah opens to them the *dhikr* of the inner heart. It may well be that Allah Almighty will move you from *dhikr* with heedlessness to dhikr with concentration – in other words to being awake to the meanings of the *dhikr* when you are busy with it. And Then He may move you from *dhikr* with concentration to *dhikr* that brings you to the Presence of the One you are invoking so that your heart is made tranquil by *dhikru'llah* and you are present with your heart and remembrance of Him is constant. This is the *dhikr* of the elite. The first is the *dhikr* of the common people.

If you are constant in this *dhikr* of Presence, that will raise you to *dhikr* by which you withdraw from all that is other than the One you are remembering – *dhikr* in which your heart is immersed in light. Then the nearness of the light of the One remembered may become overwhelming and the one doing the *dhikr* will be drowned in that light until they withdraw from all that is other than Allah. Then the one doing the *dhikr* becomes remembered, the seeker becomes the sought and the one seeking arrival the one made to arrive. That is not difficult for Allah. So the one who was in the lowest degrees may rise to the highest ranks where the tongue is still and the *dhikr* moves to the inner heart.

In fact, where the people of this station are concerned, the *dhikr* of the tongue itself may actually become heedlessness, because the *dhikr* of the tongue demands the independent existence of those who do it, while, in this case, the one doing *dhikr* is effaced in the station of direct eye-witnessing. Shaykh ash-Shadhili said, "The reality of *dhikr* is being cut off from the *dhikr* by the One being remembered and from everything other than Him by His words: *'Remember the Name of your Lord and devote yourself to Him completely.'* (73:7)" Al-Qushayri said, "*Dhikr* is the gradual entry of the one doing the *dhikr* into the Presence of the One being remembered."

*Dhikr* is the cause of the life of the heart and leaving it is the cause of its death. Corroboration of this is found in the hadith: "The metaphor of the one who remembers his Lord and the one who does not remember his Lord is that of the living and the dead."

# Derse 24

$$\text{مِنْ عَلَامَاتِ مَوْتِ الْقَلْبِ عَدَمُ الْحُزْنِ عَلَى مَا فَاتَكَ مِنَ الْمُوَافِقَاتِ، وَتَرْكُ النَّدَمِ عَلَى مَافَعَلْتَهُ مِنْ وُجُودِ الزَّلَّاتِ.}$$

**48: A sign of the death of the heart:
lack of sadness about chances for good you have missed,
and lack of regret about mistakes you have made.**

Three things cause the death of the heart: love of this world, neglect of *dhikru'llah,* and allowing the limbs to commit acts of disobedience. Three things result in the life of the heart: lack of attachment to this world, occupation with *dhikru'llah,* and the company of the *awliya'* of Allah. And there are three signs of the heart's death: lack of sorrow at missing acts of obedience, lack of regret for mistakes committed and keeping the company of people whose hearts are dead. That is because the appearance of obedience from a person is a sign of ultimate happiness and the appearance of disobedience is a sign of ultimate wretchedness. If the heart is alive with *ma'rifa* and *iman,* it is pained by things that will make it wretched and joyful about what will make it happy. Or you could say that acts of obedience appearing from the slave are an indication of the pleasure of his Lord and the appearance of acts of disobedience an indication of His anger.

The living heart senses what pleases its Master and rejoices, and senses what angers Him and grieves. The dead heart does not sense anything. It is the same to it whether it obeys or disobeys. It does not rejoice in obedience and right action nor is it sad about a mistake or disobedience; in that respect it is, indeed, just like a corpse. There is a hadith from the Messenger of Allah ﷺ saying, "Anyone who is delighted by his good actions and grieved by his evil deeds is a believer." 'Abdullah ibn Mas'ud said, "A believer sees his wrong actions as if they were a mountain which he fears will fall on him. A wrongdoer sees his wrong actions as flies which land on his nose and which he lightly swats away." But the slave must not spend too much time looking at these indications of wrong action and then lose hope and have a bad opinion of his Lord, as Shaykh Ibn Ata'llah then indicates by his words:

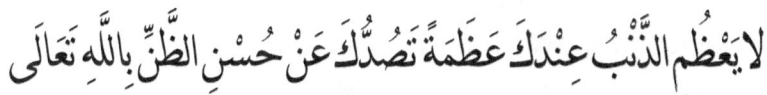

### 49: Do not become so overwhelmed by your wrong action that it stops you having a good opinion of Allah.

In respect of fear and hope, people fall into three categories: the people of the beginning, who should be dominated by fear; the people of the middle, who should have a balance between fear and hope; and the people of the end, who are dominated by hope. When the people of the beginning are dominated by fear, they strive to perform good actions and refrain from making mistakes. In that way they gain success. Allah says of them in *Surat al-'Ankabut*: *"As for those who do jihad in Our Way, We will guide them to Our paths."* (29:69) The people of the middle direct their worship to purification of their inward, and so their worship is of the heart. If they were dominated by fear, they would return to the worship of the limbs when what is desired of them is the worship of the inward with the hope of arrival and fear of Allah's immense power. So their fear and hope are balanced.

As for those who have arrived, they do not see themselves as having either action or non-action. They look at the management of the Real and what flows from the Decree and meet it with acceptance and pleasure. If it is obedience, they thank Allah and bear witness to the favour of Allah. If it is disobedience, they apologise, show *adab* and do not stop with their selves since they hold that they have no real existence. They watch for what emerges from the realm of Power and expect Allah's forbearance, pardon, goodness and kindness more than they expect His force and blame. May Allah have mercy on Imam ash-Shafi'i who said:

<blockquote>
When my heart is hard
and my circumstances are constricted,
I make my hope a ladder to reach Your pardon.
My wrong actions seem immense to me but in relation
to Your pardon, my Lord, Your pardon is far greater.
</blockquote>

> You continue to possess generosity, great favour and grace,
> showing generosity, pardon and nobility.
> Would that I knew whether
> I will go to the Garden and rejoice
> or go to Hellfire, full of regret.

Allah Almighty says: "*Say: 'My slaves who have transgressed against yourselves, do not despair of the mercy of Allah. Truly Allah forgives all wrong actions. He is Ever-Forgiving, the Most Merciful.'*" (39:50)

Reflect on the case of the man who killed ninety-nine people and then asked a monk, "Is repentance possible for me?" The monk replied to him, "No. It is not," and so he killed him, completing the hundred. Then he went to a man of knowledge and asked him the same question and he said to him, "Who can come between you and it? Go to a certain town. There are people in it who worship Allah. Stay among them until you die." Halfway there, he died and the angels of mercy and the angels of punishment quarrelled over who should take him. So Allah told them to measure the distance between the town he left and the town to which he was going and that he would belong to the people of whichever of them was closer. Then Allah inspired the town to which he was going to come nearer and the town from which he left to go further away. In this way he was found to be nearer to the town to which he was going and the angels of mercy took him. The hadith is found in the two *Sahih* collections.

Shaykh Abu'l-'Abbas al-Mursi said, "When the common people are frightened, they fear. When they are made hopeful, they hope. When the elite are frightened, they hope, and when they are given hope, they fear." Shaykh ibn Ata'illah said in his *Lata'if al-Minan*: "The meaning of these words of the shaykh is that the common people stop with the outward. So when they are frightened, they fear since they cannot pass beyond their fear by means of the light of understanding which the people of Allah possess. When the people of Allah are frightened, they hope, knowing that beyond their fear are the attributes of the One they hope for and that no one should despair of Allah's mercy nor give up hope of His grace. They therefore aspire to the qualities of His generosity, knowing that what frightens them is only in order to gather them to Him and return them to Him. When they are made hopeful, they fear His hidden Will, which is beyond their hope, and fear that the hope they feel is in order to test their intellects to see whether they will stop at hope or penetrate to what is hidden in His Will. That is why their hope provokes their fear."

Al-Junayd visited Shaykh as-Sari as-Saqati and found him in a state of contraction. He asked, "What is wrong, shaykh? Why are you in contraction?" He replied, "A young man came to me and asked me, 'What is the reality of *tawba*?' I told him, 'Not to forget your wrong action.' The young man said, 'No, on the contrary, *tawba* is to forget your wrong action.' Then he left me." Al-Junayd continued, "I said, 'What the young man said is correct, because I was in a veiled state and, when Allah moved me to witnessing Him, I found that remembering the veil was itself a veil.'" As-Sari was describing the people at the beginning of the path while al-Junayd was describing the people at its end. Each is correct, and Allah knows best.

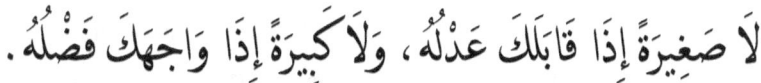

## 50: There is no minor wrong action when you are confronted by His justice. There is no major wrong action when you are faced by His bounty.

A minor wrong action is one which about which there is no threat in the Qur'an or in hadith, and a major wrong action is the one about which there is the threat of punishment or *hadd* in the Qur'an or in the *Sunna*. Other things are said as well. This is all by seeing the outward of the matter. As for what is in the sight of Allah in the Unseen, and by looking at His Forbearance and Justice, it is different to what is supposed. The Almighty says: "*What confronts them from Allah will be something they did not reckon with.*" (39:47) So in the case of whoever is already the object of Divine concern, the wrong action does not harm him. Those are those whose evil deeds Allah transforms into good deeds.

Even if actions are signs, they vary in some stations, and so it is mandatory to have equal hope and fear in some stations and to submit to Allah at all times. Allah says: "*The words of your Lord are perfect in truthfulness and justice. No one can change His words.*" (6:116) When Allah confronts you with His Justice and Majesty, there is no minor wrong action; your minor wrong actions become major ones. When Allah meets you with His Gracious Favour, Generosity, Goodness and Beauty, there is no major wrong action; your major wrong actions become minor ones.

Yahya ibn Mu'adh ar-Razi said, "When they obtain His Favour, no evil deed remains for them. When His Justice is placed on them, no good deed remains for them." It is said that if the hope and fear of a believer are weighed, neither of them outweighs the other. Rather the believer is like a bird with two wings. Shaykh Zarruq said something to that effect. There is the hadith of the man who had ninety-nine scrolls of bad actions, each scroll stretching as far as the eye could see. Then a card the size of a finger nail was produced which contained the words: "There is no god but Allah." Those scrolls were outweighed, indicating the immensity of His Forbearance and Mercy and the comprehensiveness of His Generosity and Grace.

# Derse 25

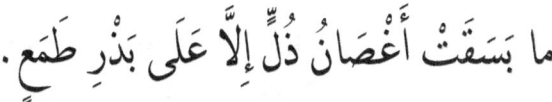

## 60: It is only their growth from the seed of covetousness that makes the branches of abasement high

"Covetousness" is the attachment of the heart to what is in the hands of other people and the longing of the heart for something other than Allah. A covetous person abandons a mighty Lord to chain himself to a lowly slave and so he becomes low like him. He fails to raise his aspiration to the One Who is truly Rich and Noble and lowers his aspiration to the base and blameworthy. Allah provides for the slave according to his aspiration. Someone who is a slave of Allah is free from what is other than Him whereas the covetous person becomes the slave of creatures and the slave of his *nafs* and its desires. This is because, whenever you love something and desire it, you become its slave. Whenever, however, you turn your back on something and remove your aspiration from it, you are free of it.

We read in *at-Tanwir*: "O slave, be like Ibrahim! Your father Ibrahim ﷺ said, *'I do not love what sets.'* (6:77) All that is other than Allah sets, either actually or potentially.

The Almighty says: *'The religion of your forefather Ibrahim.'* (22:76) So it is incumbent on us to follow the religion of Ibrahim. Part of the religion of Ibrahim is not to invest your hopes in created things. On the day when he was shot out of the catapult into the fire, Jibril ﷺ came to him and asked, 'Is there anything you need?' He replied, 'As for anything from you, no. As for something from Allah, yes.' He said, 'Then ask Him for it.' He said, 'His knowledge of my state spares me from having to ask.' So look at how Ibrahim removed his hopes from creation and placed them in the True King. He saw that Allah was nearer to Him than Jibril and even than his own *du'a*. His perfect reliance on Allah was expressed on another occasion in *Surat ash-Shu'ara* when he said: *'They are all my enemies – except for the Lord of all the worlds...'* (26:77)"

Shaykh Abu'l-Hasan said, "I have despaired of my being able to benefit myself, so how can I not despair of anyone else being able to benefit me? I have the hope that Allah will benefit others besides me, so how can I not have that same hope for myself? This is the alchemy and the elixir by means of which one obtains wealth with no poverty in it and might with no abasement in it and spending which does not run out. It is the alchemy of the people of understanding of Allah."

Elucidating this further he said, "A man used to keep my company and was a burden to me. I was frank with him and said, 'My son, tell me what you want and I will give it to you. Then cease to keep my company.' He said, 'Sir, I am told that you know about alchemy and so I have kept company with you to learn it from you.' I said to him, 'You have spoken the truth, and whoever told you that spoke the truth, but I suspect that you will not accept that knowledge from me.' He replied, 'Of course I will accept it!' I said, 'I have studied people and found them to fall into two categories: enemies and friends. I looked at my enemies and knew that they would not even be able to pierce me with a thorn if Allah did not will that to happen to me. So I ceased to bother about them. Then I attached myself to my friends and saw that they too could not help me with anything which Allah had not willed for me either. So I completely turned away from everyone and attached myself to Allah.'" He said on another occasion when he was asked about alchemy, "Expel the creation from your heart and have no hope of your Lord giving you anything other than what He has already allotted to you."

A person's understanding is not indicated by the abundance of his knowledge nor by his persistence in obtaining it. His light and understanding is indicated by his being truly dependent on his Lord, his being gathered to Him with his heart, his being on guard against the slavery of covetousness, and his being adorned with the robe of scrupulousness. It is by that that actions are made good and states are purified. The Almighty says: "*We made everything on earth adornment for it so that we could test them to see whose actions are the best.*" (18:7) Good actions come from having understanding from Allah, the result of which is what we mentioned: being independent of other than Allah, finding Him to be enough for you, relying on Him, presenting your needs to Him, and remaining constantly before Him. All of that is the fruit of understanding from Allah.

So, murid, you must remove your expectations from other people and not abase yourself to them for the sake of provision. Your allotment of provision was already decided before you even came into this world and its manifestation was already confirmed. Listen to what one of the shaykhs said, "O man, whatever is decreed for you to chew will be chewed, so eat it." Abu Bakr al-Warraq said, "If covetousness were to be asked, 'Who is your father?' it would say, 'Doubt about what has been decreed.' If it were asked, 'What is your trade?' it would reply, 'Bringing humiliation.' If it were asked, 'What is your end?' it would reply, 'Deprivation.'"

In short, love of things and desire for them is the cause of abasement, humiliation and enslavement to other people. Not desiring things and not having any aspiration for them brings with it might, freedom and true honour. How excellent is what the poet said:

> I saw that contentment is the nucleus of wealth
> and so I clung to its coat-tails.
> Doing that invested me in a robe of honour
> which was not made ragged by the passage of time.
> I became wealthy without dirhams,
> ennobled above people as a king is ennobled.

This is the greatest wealth and elixir of all elixirs.

# Derse 26

$$\text{مَنْ لَمْ يُقْبِلْ عَلَى اللَّهِ بِمُلَاطَفَاتِ الْإِحْسَانِ}$$
$$\text{قِيدَ إِلَيْهِ بِسَلَاسِلِ الْامْتِحَانِ.}$$

**63: Whoever does not advance to Allah by means of the caresses of kindness is shackled to Him by the chains of trial.**

Allah has divided His slaves into three categories: the people of the left, the people of the right and the forerunners. There is no discussion about the people of the left since they do not turn to Allah at all. The people of the right turn to Him in a way but they have no pre-eminence in that they are content with the outward *shari'a*, not travelling on the Path nor seeking the *haqiqa*. They stay with outward proofs and evidence and do not rise to the station of witnessing and direct knowledge. There is also no discussion about them. As for the forerunners, they turn to Allah and direct themselves towards Him, seeking direct knowledge of Him. They, in turn, are divided into two groups. One group turn to Allah through the caresses of His kindness and out of gratitude for His blessing and grace. They are the people of the Station of

Gratitude. The other group turn to Allah through the fetters of trial and by means of various afflictions and tests. They are the people of the Station of Steadfastness.

The people of the first station turn to Allah willingly and the people of the second station turn to Allah unwillingly. The Almighty says: *"Everyone in heaven and earth prostrates to Allah willingly or unwillingly..."* (13:16) Abu Madyan said, "The *sunna* of Allah is to invite His slaves to obey Him by giving them ample provision and constant preservation so that they turn to Him by His blessing. If they do not do that, then He tests them with good and bad times so that hopefully such treatment will bring them to turn to Him. That is because what is desired is for His slaves to turn to Him, either willingly or unwillingly."

So in the case of some people Allah expands blessings to them, averts affliction and retribution from them, endows them with good health, and provides them with wealth and well-being so that they come to Him in that way. They keep those things out of their hearts and have them solely in their hands. They are, however, very few in number. Allah says: *"But very few of My slaves are thankful."* (34:13) A hadith is related about such people: "This world is an excellent mount for the believer. On it he reaches good and by it he is saved from evil," or words to that effect.

Many people, however, are supported by Allah with blessings and He increases them in wealth and well-being and averts difficulties from them but then those things distract them from turning to Him and prevent them from travelling to His Presence. So He then strips them of those things and strikes them with afflictions and trials and they then turn to Allah by means of the chains of those trials. About such people the Prophet ﷺ said, "Your Lord marvels at a people who are driven to the Garden in chains."

Allah, however, praises equally both the wealthy who are thankful and the steadfast who are poor, saying about Sulayman: *"We gave Da'ud Sulayman. What an excellent slave! He truly turned to his Lord."* (38:29) and about Ayyub: *"We found him steadfast. What an excellent slave! He truly turned to his Lord."* (38:43) So the truth is that the steadfast poor and the thankful rich are in fact the same because they both know that wealth is by Allah. When someone's heart is rich in Allah, they are thankful and wealthy no matter how much or little they have. If a person's hand is full of wealth but their heart is empty of gratitude to Allah, that is real poverty. But if someone's heart is rich in Allah whereas their hand is empty, they are in a real sense truly wealthy.

There is also a third, very rare, possibility, and that is for the hand to be full to overflowing and at the same time for the heart to be rich in Allah, entirely dependent on Him. Illustrating this one of the shaykhs said, "There was a shaykh in Morocco who was one of those who do without this world, one of the people of earnestness and striving. His only livelihood was fish he caught from the sea. He gave away part of his catch as *sadaqa* and lived on the rest. One of the murids of this shaykh wanted to travel to Fez and his shaykh told him, 'When you get there, go and see my brother so-and-so, give him my greetings and ask him to make *du'a* for me. He is one of the *awliya'* of Allah.' The murid said, 'So I travelled to Fez and asked about that man and was directed to a house which was like a palace a king might live in. I was amazed at that. I asked for him and was told that he was visiting the sultan. My astonishment increased. After a time he arrived on the finest horse dressed in sumptuous clothing, looking just like a king. My astonishment increased still further to the point that I wanted to leave straight away and not meet with him at all. I said to myself, however, "I cannot go against the shaykh's instructions." So I asked permission to enter and, on being given permission, went into the house. It was full of servants and fine furnishings. I was taken to the owner and said to him, "Your brother so-and-so greets you." He said to me, "You have come from him?" "Yes," I said. He said, "When you get back say to him from me: 'How great is your preoccupation with this world! How much you turn to it! When will your desire for it cease?'" I said to myself, "By Allah, this is unbelievable; how can he possibly say that!" When I returned to my shaykh, he asked, "Did you meet with our brother?" "Yes," I replied. He asked, "And what did he say to you?" "Nothing," I replied. He insisted, "He must have had something to say to me." So I repeated to him what he had said. After weeping for a long time he said, "My brother spoke the truth. Allah has expunged this world from his heart and put it in his hand while I have removed it from my hand but still have it in my heart!"'" That is from the *Lata'if al-Minan*.

So the states of the *awliya'* are not determined by poverty or wealth because *wilaya* is a matter of the heart which is only known by the one who has it. May Allah, by His unending Generosity, place us among those who are truly content with Him no matter what our outward circumstances are.

# Derse 27

$$\text{مَنْ لَمْ يَشْكُرِ النَّعَمَ فَقَدْ تَعَرَّضَ لِزَوَالِهَا،}$$
$$\text{وَمَنْ شَكَرَهَا فَقَدْ قَيَّدَهَا بِعِقَالِهَا.}$$

**64: Whoever is not grateful for blessings is in grave danger of them disappearing. Whoever is grateful for them ties them up with their own tether.**

The statements of the wise agree on this. Gratitude secures what is already there and captures what is lacking. But someone who receives a gift and is not grateful for it, will be unwittingly stripped of it. Those who are grateful for the blessings they receive "tie them up with their own tether". Those who are ungrateful for them are "in grave danger of them disappearing". Allah says: *"Allah never changes a people's state until they change what is in themselves."* (13:12) meaning that Allah does not change a blessing possessed by people until their gratitude for it changes and that change is marked by their turning to acts of disobedience and disbelief. That is why Imam Junayd ؓ said, "Gratitude is that you do not disobey Allah in the presence of His blessings." It is said that gratitude is the heart's delight with the Giver of the Blessing Himself, not on account of His blessing, and that extends to the limbs so that they busy themselves with obeying His commands and recoiling from His prohibitions.

We read in *Lata'if al-Minan*: "There are three types of gratitude: gratitude of the tongue, gratitude of the limbs and gratitude of the heart. The gratitude of the tongue is to speak about Allah's blessings. The Almighty says: '*As for the blessing of your Lord, speak out.*' (93:11) The gratitude of the limbs is to obey Allah. Allah says: '*Work, family of Da'ud, in gratitude.*' (34:13) The gratitude of the heart is to acknowledge that every blessing to you, or indeed to anyone else, is a gift from Allah. Allah says: '*Any blessing you have is from Allah.*' (16:53) Relating to the first type are the words of the Prophet ﷺ, 'Speaking of blessings is gratitude.' Illustrating the second is that the Prophet ﷺ stood in prayer until his feet became swollen. When he was asked: 'Why do you do that when Allah has forgiven you your past and any future wrong actions?' He replied, 'Should I not be a grateful slave?'"

Know that people fall into three levels in respect of gratitude: the common people, the elite, and the elite of the elite. The gratitude of the common people is for blessings alone. The gratitude of the elite is for both blessings and difficulties. The gratitude of the elite of the elite is their withdrawal from either blessing or difficulty by their witnessing of the Giver of Blessing. And the blessings for which for which one must be grateful are also divided into three: those relating to this world, such as health, well-being, and lawful wealth; those relating to the *deen*, such as knowledge, right action, *taqwa* and gnosis; and those related to the Next World, such as the reward for just a few actions with an endless abundance of gifts. The most glorious of blessings for which we owe gratitude are the blessings of Islam, *Iman* and *Ihsan*. Gratitude for them is in our belief and awareness that they are a pure gift from Allah, arriving without any intermediary and not in any way through our own strength or power. Allah says: *"However, Allah has given you love of faith and made it pleasing to your hearts and has made kufr, deviance and disobedience hateful to you."* (49:7) Then He says about that: *"It is great favour from Allah and a blessing."* (49:8)

Abu Talib al-Makki said, "If our hearts were to be directed into doubt and misguidance rather than good intentions and right action, what could we do about it, what could we rely on, where could we find peace, what could we hope for?" Acknowledging this is showing gratitude for the blessing of *iman*. Ignorance of it is showing great disrespect towards the blessing of *iman*. If you think that *iman* is an intellectual acquisition or that it is possible to obtain it through one's own capacity or strength, that is in fact a denial of the blessing of it. It is feared that anyone who is does that will have his *iman* stripped away because he has exchanged gratitude for the blessing of *iman* for its opposite, ingratitude for it, the Arabic for which is *kufr*.

If people neglect to be grateful for the blessings they have but the appearance of them remains with them, they should not be deceived by that. It may be in order to lead them on, as the shaykh indicates by his words:

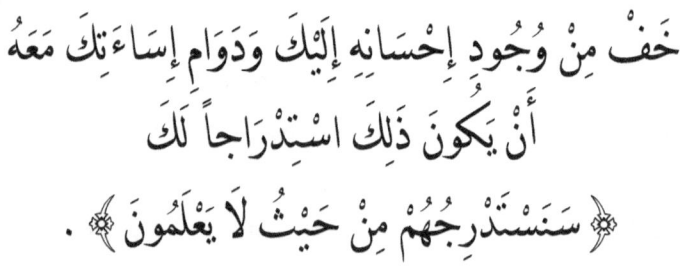

## 65: Have fear that the fact that He remains good to you when you are acting badly towards Him might be to lure you on.
### "We shall lure them, step by step, into destruction, from where they do not know." (7:182)

"Luring on (*istadraja*)" in this context is to conceal affliction in blessing. The one who lures someone on is the one who takes a blessing away from someone little by little while they are unaware of it, as in Allah's words: *"We shall lead them, step by step, into destruction from where they do not know,"* (7:182) meaning, "We will take away their blessings until We drag them into retribution without them being aware that that is happening."

Shaykh Zarruq said, "O murid, fear lest the constant kindness of Allah shows to you by endowing you with health, leisure, ample provision and constant physical or spiritual support, while you are behaving badly towards Him through your distraction, falling short, and lack of gratitude to Him, is in reality your being lured on by Him to your destruction." Ibn 'Ata' said that when such people commit an error, Allah renews His blessing to them and makes them forget to ask forgiveness for that error. Allah says in *Surat al-'Araf*: "*I will give them more time*," (7:183) – in other words support them with well-being and other blessings – "*until We suddenly seize them.*" And He says: "*When they forgot what they had been reminded of, We opened up for them the doors to everything, until, when they were exulting in what they had been given, We suddenly seized them and at once they were in despair.*" (6:45)

The *sunna* of Allah in His creation is to send to people those who will remind them of Allah and direct them to Allah. When they turn away from them and reject them, He increases them in material blessings until they are satiated and exult in them. Then He destroys them suddenly so that that their punishment will be all the harsher. Allah says elsewhere: "*Those who disbelieve should not imagine that the extra time We grant to them is good for them. We only allow them more time so that they will increase in evildoing. They will have a humiliating punishment.*" (3:178) It is, therefore, mandatory for anyone who is aware of a physical blessing, inward or outward, or a spiritual blessing he has received, that he should acknowledge it fully and hasten to be grateful for it in speech, belief and action.

Gratitude in speech is praise and thanking Allah with the tongue. Gratitude in belief is witnessing the Giver of the blessing in the blessing and ascribing it to Him alone, disavowing the means in the heart while thanking the means on the tongue, because, "Whoever does not thank people has not thanked Allah." Your thanking people is gratitude to Allah. When you say to someone, "May Allah repay you well," you have done your duty by them. Gratitude in action is to engage your limbs in obedience to Allah and to avoid His prohibitions, as we said earlier. If we do not fulfil this obligation – that of showing gratitude to Allah – it is feared that our *iman* will be gradually stripped away from us and we will be lured on little by little into destruction.

# Derse 28

مِنْ جَهْلِ الْمُرِيدِ أَنْ يُسِيءَ الْأَدَبَ فَتُؤَخَّرُ الْعُقُوبَةُ عَنْهُ، فَيَقُولُ: لَوْ كَانَ هَذَا سُوءُ أَدَبٍ لَقَطَعَ الْإِمْدَادَ، وَأَوْجَبَ الْإِبْعَادَ، فَقَدْ يَقْطَعُ الْمَدَدَ عَنْهُ مِنْ حَيْثُ لَا يَشْعُرُ، وَلَوْ لَمْ يَكُنْ إِلَّا مَنْعَ الْمَزِيدِ، وَقَدْ يُقَامُ مَقَامَ الْبُعْدِ وَهُوَ لَا يَدْرِي، وَلَوْ لَمْ يَكُنْ إِلَّا أَنْ يُخَلِّيَكَ وَمَا تُرِيدُ.

**66: It is ignorance on the part of a *murid* with bad *adab*
to then say, if punishment is delayed,
"If this were really bad *adab*,
He would have cut off help to me or banished me."
Help can be cut off while one is unaware of it
– by stopping any increase
– or by letting you do what you like.**

One of the well-established commands for the true *murid* is that he should have *adab* with Allah in everything and cling to exalting Him in everything and maintain respect for Him in everything. If he fails in any of these matters and has bad *adab* with his Lord, he should hurry to repent and apologise with abasement and contrition. If he then puts off repentance until later, help will be cut off from him and exile and distancing are inevitable for him, even though he may not immediately be aware of it happening.

Because of that he deludes himself and says, "If this really were bad *adab*, then help would have been cut off from me." This is terrible ignorance on his part which will lead to ruin if he does not receive kindness from the Lord of the worlds. Help may well be cut off from him while he is unaware of it. An example of that is trees which are by water. If the water is cut off from them, the effect of that does not show up on them for quite a long a time, but then they gradually dry up. The heart of the murid is like that. He is not aware of help being cut off until some time has passed. Even if the punishment is only that of being denied advancement on the path, that is more than enough, because if someone is not in increase, then they are in decrease.

When Allah is concerned for a slave and wants to make them reach His Presence, He disarranges everything their *nafs* relies on and upsets them, to the point that He makes them despair of this world and no longer rely on anything in it. Then He chooses them for His Presence and selects them for His love. An illustration of that is the story of Musa when Allah removed from him his reliance on his staff. Allah asked him: *"What is that in your right hand, Musa?" He said, "It is my staff. I lean on it and beat down leaves for my sheep with it and have other uses for it." He said, "Throw it down. Musa." He threw it down and suddenly it was a slithering snake.* (20:17-19) When he fled from it and completely despaired of it, Allah said to him: *"Take hold of it and have no fear."* Because it was never going harm him provided that he was acting by Allah. In a similar way it is said to the *faqir*, "What is that in your right hand, *faqir*?" He says, "It is this world on which I rely and by which I achieve my goals." Then he is told, "Cast it from your hand." It is in reality a slithering snake which has bitten him while he was not aware. When he despairs of it and truly trusts in Allah, he is told, "Take hold of it and do not fear because now you are taking it by Allah, not by yourself." Allah knows best.

Where common people are concerned, *adab* with Allah is to obey His commands and avoid His prohibitions. *Adab* with His Messenger ﷺ is to follow the *Sunna* and avoid the people of innovation. If such people fall short in respect of Allah's commands and ignore His prohibitions, they will certainly be punished sooner or later both in the sensory and the meaning. In the case of the elite, *adab* with Allah is to do much *dhikr* of Him and to be aware of His Presence and to love Him more than anything else. Shaykh Zarruq added, "…and it also entails keeping within His limits, being true to contracts, clinging to Allah, being content with what happens, and expending effort in His way." Their *adab* with His Messenger ﷺ entails following his guidance and taking on his noble qualities. If they fall short in their *dhikr* of Allah, or their hearts wander indiscriminately, or their love inclines to something other than Allah, or they fall short in respect of any of the things that were just mentioned, they also will be punished in both the sensory and the meaning.

With respect to the elite of the elite, who are those who have arrived, their *adab* with Allah is to have humility in every situation, to have respect for everything, constant recognition of the manifestation of Allah's Majesty and Beauty, and to see beyond secondary causes. Their *adab* with His Messenger ﷺ is to have realisation of his true worth, respect for his community, and to witness his light. Abu'l-'Abbas al-Mursi said to Shaykh Ibn Ata'illah, "For thirty years the Messenger of Allah ﷺ has not been absent from me for the blink of an eye. If he were absent from me, I would not count myself to be one of the Muslims." If a gnostic falls short in *adab* in any way, then he too is punished in the sensory or in the meaning but generally he wakes up straight away and immediately puts right any failure. Allah says of them: *"As for those who have taqwa, when they are bothered by visitors from Shaytan, they remember and immediately see clearly."* (7:201)

Part of the *adab* of *fuqara* towards the *fuqara* is seeing good in them and believing in their goodness. The *fuqara* should not deprecate anyone, even if they see in them something which seems outwardly to be a defect. A believer looks for excuses. The *fuqara* should look for seventy excuses. If you see that person continuing to manifest that imperfection, you should look for that defect in yourself. The believer is the mirror of his brother. What the looker sees is in fact their own reflection. The people of purity only witness purity and the people who are mixed only witness mixture.

## 28

The people of perfection only witness perfection and the people of imperfection only witness imperfection. Always remember the hadith in which the Prophet ﷺ said, "There is nothing better than two traits: having a good opinion of Allah and a good opinion of the slaves of Allah. There is nothing worse than two traits: having a bad opinion of Allah and a bad opinion of the slaves of Allah." Success is by Allah.

# Derse 29

إِذَا أَرَدْتَ أَنْ تَعْرِفَ قَدْرَكَ عِنْدَهُ فَانْظُرْ فِى مَاذَا يُقِيمُكَ.

**73: If you want to know your worth with Him look at where He has put you.**

Allah, by His wisdom, has divided His creation into two categories: the wretched and the happy. And He has also divided those who are happy into two groups: the people of distance and the people of nearness, or the Companions of the Right and those who are brought near, who are the Forerunners. If you want to learn whether you are one of the people of wretchedness or the people of happiness, look into your heart. If you affirm the existence of your Lord and unify Him in His kingdom and obey the one who made Him known to you – His Messenger ﷺ – then you are one of those for whom the best has been decreed. If you deny or doubt your Lord, or associate others with Him in your belief, and do not obey the one who acquainted you with Him ﷺ, then you are one of the people of wretchedness.

If you find that you are one of the people of happiness and want to know whether you are one of the people of nearness or the people of distance, then look again. If you are one of those who finds evidence for Him in His secondary effects, then you are one of the people of distance among the Companions of the Right. If you are one of those finds evidence for everything else by Him, then you are one of the Forerunners, one of those who are brought near.

If you find that you are one of the Companions of the Right and want to learn your worth with Him and whether you are one of the honoured or one of the abased, look again. If you obey His commands, avoid His prohibitions and hasten to please Him and love His *awliya'* and those He loves, then you are one of the honoured and esteemed. If you disdain His commands, are easy about His prohibitions, lax in obeying Him, violate His sanctity, and are hostile to His *awliya'*, then, by Allah, you are one of those condemned, deprived and outcast unless you are taken in hand by the concern of the Lord of the worlds.

If you are one of the people of nearness and have reached the station of witnessing, you will be among those who do not see other than Him. If you affirm the means (*wasita*), confirm His Wisdom (*hikma*) and give everything with a due its due, then you are one of the perfect ones who are brought near. If you negate Wisdom and withdraw from the means, then you are intoxicated (*madhjub*) and overcome. So you are deficient in that respect. In that case, unless you become sober, you will leave the path unless your hand is taken by a shaykh who has arrived or a perfect gnostic.

There is another criterion by which you will recognise where you are in respect of nearness and distance. If you find a teaching shaykh whose lights Allah unveils to you and acquaints you with the special qualities of his secret, then you are absolutely one of the people of nearness by action or potential by the words of the Shaykh: "Glory be to the One Who made guidance to His *awliya'* guidance to Himself, only allowing them to be reached by those He wants to make reach Him." If you do not find a teaching shaykh and are deluded by the words of someone who says that they do not exist, then you are definitely one of the Companions of the Right among the common Muslims. This is the usual case, and the aberrant case has no judgement. Allah knows best.

In a hadith the Prophet ﷺ said, "Allah, the Blessed and Exalted, says, 'I am Allah. There is no god but Me. I created good and evil, so happiness to the one whom I created for good and at whose hands I make good occur. Woe to the one whom I created for evil and at whose hands I made evil occur." In another hadith: "Whoever wants to know where he is with Allah should look where Allah is with him." In one variant, "Whoever wants to know his place with Allah should look at the place Allah has in his heart." Allah puts the slave where the slave puts Him in himself. Allah Almighty says: *"As for him who gives out and has taqwa and confirms the Good, We will pave his way to the Ease."* (92:5-7) Allah knows best.

مَتَى رَزَقَكَ الطَّاعَةَ وَالْغِنَى بِهِ عَنْهَا،
فَاعْلَمْ أَنَّهُ قَدْ أَسْبَغَ عَلَيْكَ نِعَمَهُ ظَاهِرَةً وَبَاطِنَةً.

## 74: When He gives you obedience and unconsciousness of it through Him, know that He has showered His blessings upon you, outwardly and inwardly.

When you have outward obedience to Him and are inwardly free of other than Him, He has given you full measure and granted you inward and outward blessings. This is the mark of the Forerunners, who are wealthy by Allah and poor in relation to other than Him. They have no need of other than the One they worship so that they do not see the worship they do. Their worship is by Allah, for Allah, and from Allah, showing thankfulness for the blessing they have received and fulfilling the duties of slavehood. In a hadith, the Messenger of Allah ﷺ said, "The slaves who are most beloved of Allah are the hidden, independent, godfearing ones," or words to that effect and in another hadith he said ﷺ, "Wealth does not consist in having a lot of goods. Wealth consists in the wealth (independence) of the self." That is wealth in Allah and that is the true blessing.

Their outward blessing is the adornment of their limbs by the *shari'a* and their inward blessing is the shining of their secrets by the *haqiqa*. It is said that their outward blessings are contentment and well-being and their inward blessings are guidance and gnosis. It is said that the outward blessing is the body having rest from opposition to His commands and the inward blessing is safety from contending with His judgements. The reality of the blessing is that it is something which does not cause any pain and is not followed by any regret. It is said that the greatest blessing of all is to stop seeing the *nafs*. It is said that the blessing is what connects you to the realities and purifies you of attachments to creatures. Success is by Allah.

# Derse 30

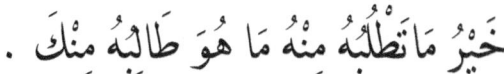

### 75: The best thing you can ask for from Him is what He asks for from you.

What Allah asks for from us is rectitude, both outward and inward. True rectitude consists in the attainment of complete obedience to Allah outwardly and the realisation of complete gnosis of Allah inwardly. Or you could say that what He asks from us is for us to make our outward limbs correct by means of the *shari'a* and to make our hearts and inward secrets correct by means of the *haqiqa*. Or you could say that what He asks from us is, on the one hand, for us to obey His commands and avoid His prohibitions, and, on the other, for us to do a lot of dhikr and submit to His overwhelming Power.

In the case of the people of Allah, perfection is when the depth of their knowledge of Allah frees them from the need to ask for anything. If they do ask, what they ask for from their Lord is what He is asking for from them. In a hadith it says that Allah will not ask created beings about His Essence and Attributes, nor will He ask them about His decree and judgement. What He will ask them about are His commands and prohibitions. This is because obedience to Allah's commands and prohibitions are an aspect of people's earning and responsibility, while knowledge of the Essence and the Attributes and satisfaction with, and submission to, the Divine Decree are part of the reward for actions and the result of obedience to Allah.

When someone does what Allah commands him to do, He gives them knowledge of Him. This common knowledge is evidential knowledge. But when someone's thirst for knowledge of Allah is intense, He takes them to someone who will take him by the hand and show him the way to the knowledge of the elite: direct knowledge of Him.

One of the people of Allah said, "When you feel a need for something, let Allah take care of it." In other words do not look towards it in such a way that you are veiled from Allah by it, so that it comes between you and Allah. The Almighty says: *"Do not covet what Allah has given to some of you in preference to others – men have a portion of what they acquire and women have a portion of what they acquire; but ask Allah for His bounty."* (4:32) Allah's bounty is wealth in Him and independence from other than Him. One of the supplications of Imam al-Junayd was: "O Allah, every request I make to You comes from Your command to me to ask. So make my asking You a request for what You love. Do not make me one of those who look towards what they ask for and rely on other than You in their asking."

So the best thing to ask for is the ability to perform the obligations due from you to Him. Then you are asking Him for what He asks from you: obedience and rectitude. Do not ask him for things which may not be decreed for you and therefore be denied them before you even ask. That is a sign of delusion, as Shaykh Ibn Ata'illah then indicates by his words:

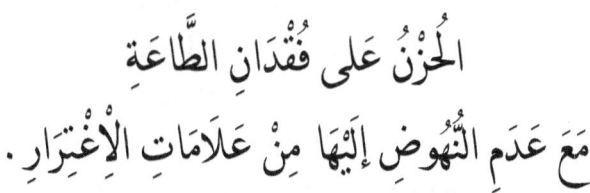

## 76: Sorrow over loss of obedience while failing to bring it about is a sign of delusion

"Sorrow" is feeling sad about something. If you do not have something and regret not having it, or feel pain about something you have been denied and cannot have, you feel sorrow about your lack of that thing. If you then put in place the means to acquire it, that is known as the sorrow of the truthful. Abu 'Ali ad-Daqqaq said about this kind of sorrow, "Someone experiencing sorrow travels in a month a distance another person would not cover in years." If, however, you do not set about putting in place the means to acquire it, then it is called the sorrow of the liars. So if you are sad about not having obedience and then do everything you can to attain it, that is the sorrow of the truthful. If you do not do that, it is the sorrow of the liars. Rabi'a al-'Adawiyya heard a man say, "O my sorrow!" She said to him, "Say rather: 'What a tiny little sorrow!' If your sorrow had been true, you would not able to breathe." Abu Sulayman ad-Darani said, "Weeping is not about tears coming out of your eyes. Real weeping is to put right the matter which is causing you to weep." It is said: "Do not let a man's weeping delude you. The brothers of Yusuf came to their father in evening weeping when they had done what they did." That kind of sorrow is a sign of being deluded. "Delusion" is to affirm the reality of something that has no reality.

There are three types of sorrow: that of liars, that of the truthful, and that of real travellers. The sorrow of liars is the kind of sorrow we just talked about which does not lead to determination to do anything about it. The sorrow of the truthful is sorrow accompanied by effort, striving, acting on it, and taking the time needed to do what is necessary to overcome it. The sorrow of real travellers is very short-lived since nothing can stop them doing what is needed, nothing can hold them back. As for those who have arrived, as Allah tells us a dozen times in His Book: *"They feel no fear and they know no sorrow."* And He tells us that they say: *"Praise be to Allah Who has removed all sadness from us!"* (35:34) Weeping has no place in this station since there is no sorrow in the Garden. Abu Bakr as-Siddiq saw some people reciting and weeping. He said, "That is how we were and then our hearts became more resilient." What he meant by resilience was firmness in *adab* and concealment. At the start of the Path the heart is very soft and deeply affected by admonitions and greatly moved by states. When the *faqir* progresses the heart becomes firmer and is not affected in the same way. It becomes like a firm mountain; but bear in mind the *ayah*: "*You will see the mountains you reckoned to be solid going past like clouds.*" (27:90)

Shaykh Abu'l-Hasan ash-Shadhili ﷺ said, "If someone is unable to compel his *nafs* to obey him in undertaking acts of obedience and finds himself sinking into the quagmire of his appetites, there are two things he must do. The first is cling to consciousness of the fact that Allah has given him the priceless gift of guiding him to Islam and *iman* and constantly thank Allah for that in order to make sure that it does not slip from his grasp. The second is that he must continue to earnestly implore Allah, hoping for a response, saying, 'O Lord! Rescue me! Rescue me!' If he neglects to do either of these two things he is lost." Success is by Allah.

# Derse 31

**78: Hope goes hand in hand with action. Otherwise it is just wishful thinking.**

Defining "hope", one of the people of knowledge said, "Hope (*raja'*) is the attachment of the heart to something desired which can be obtained in the future through engaging in actions which will bring it about." A more compact expression is: "Hope is desire accompanied by working for what is desired in order to obtain it." On the other hand "wishful thinking" is craving something without that being accompanied by the action needed to bring it about. Shaykh Zarruq said that if this lack of action is accompanied by a real resolve to have the thing, then it is a kind of fantasy planning and a lot worse.

If someone desires to obtain tangible blessings, such as palaces and houris in the Garden, he must strive for them, obey Allah and hasten to perform supererogatory good actions. Otherwise his hope is nothing more than foolishness and delusion. Ma'ruf al-Karkhi said, "Seeking the Garden without action is a wrong action and hoping for intercession without any basis for it is a form of delusion. The hope of gaining Allah's mercy on the part of someone who does not obey Him is ignorance and stupidity." To claim that hope is valid in this situation is like a poverty-stricken person claiming they are wealthy or that fire can be kindled from seawater.

True hope lies in the real attainment of knowledge and the opening of the storehouses of understanding. And in order for that to happen you must study, read, sit with people who are known to combine knowledge and action, and concentrate on having *taqwa* and scrupulousness. The Almighty says: *"Have taqwa of Allah and Allah will give you knowledge."* (2:281) If someone does this, they are a true seeker and will achieve what they hope for. Otherwise they are impostors and will remain ignorant. One of the people of realisation said, "Whoever gives his all for knowledge, will take it all. Whoever does not give his all will not take any of it let alone all of it."

In a hadith, the Prophet ﷺ said, "Knowledge is only gained by teaching, and forbearance is only gained by taking on forbearance. Whoever seeks good will be given it and whoever is on guard against evil, will be protected from it." What *taqwa* imparts is an understanding which is in harmony with the Book and *Sunna*, expands the hearts and augments what is grasped. Anyone who hopes to reach a high station and realise the stages and delights of the lovers and the tasting of the people of direct knowledge, must keep the company of the great among the People of Allah – the people of the secret – bowing their heads, sacrificing their selves and taking on what they are instructed to do with humility, brokenness and contrition. If you cannot find such a person, you should be sincere in your search, for the secret of Allah is all in the sincerity of your search. You should spend your time in remembrance of Allah and cling to silence, retreat and have a good opinion of Allah and the slaves of Allah. If you do that Allah will take you to someone whose hand you can take. As Allah tells us in *Surat al-An'am*: "*If Allah knows of any good in your hearts, He will give you something better than what has been taken from you...*" (8:70)

We read in *The Book of Rules*: "Rule: Seeking something in the right way and with a proper aim is most likely to bring about its attainment." It is confirmed that the realities of the sciences of Sufism are special divine gifts which are not obtained by the normal methods of study. So one must employ the correct methodology which consists of three things. The first is acting by what you know to the greatest possible extent. The second is entrusting yourself to Allah according to the degree of your aspiration. The third is reflecting on the meanings of things while holding to the core of the *Sunnah*. Then understanding will unfold, error will be corrected, and opening will be facilitated. Al-Junayd indicated that when he said, "We did not take Sufism from chitchat, quarrelling and argumentation. We took it from hunger, sleeplessness and clinging to action."

In a report, the Prophet ﷺ said, "If anyone acts by what he knows, Allah will give him a knowledge which he did not know." Abu Sulayman ad-Darani said, "When people truly abandon wrong action, they rove about in the *malakut* and return with rare knowledges without any scholar having taught them to them." If someone wants to gain knowledge of these matters and starts employing the means to acquire them, that is the sign that they will have success in their quest and that their hope is genuine. If someone desires them without making any effort to gain the means to obtain them, it is just wishful thinking on their part, in other words nothing but delusion and stupidity. Al-Hasan said, "Slaves of Allah, be fearful and on guard against wishful thinking. It is the pit of the stupid into which they fall. By Allah, Allah gives no slave good in this world or the Next by means of wishful thinking." The Prophet ﷺ said, "The intelligent person is the one who humbles himself and works for what is after death and the feeble-minded person is the one who allows his lower self to follow its desires and then indulges in wishful thinking about Allah."

# Derse 32

بَسَطَكَ كَيْ لَا يُبْقِيَكَ مَعَ القَبْضِ، وَقَبَضَكَ كَيْ لَا يَتْرُكَكَ مَعَ البَسْطِ، وَأَخْرَجَكَ عَنْهُمَا كَيْ لَا تَكُونَ لِشَيْءٍ دُونَهُ.

**80: He expands you so as not to keep you in contraction. He contracts you so as not to leave you in expansion. He withdraws you from both so that you do not belong to anything but Him.**

Expansion is joy which descends on the hearts or spirits, either because of the nearness of witnessing the Beloved, or witnessing His Beauty, or the lifting of the veil from the Attributes of His Perfection and the manifestation of His Essence, or without any apparent reason. Contraction is sadness and constriction which descends on the heart because of failing to attain to something desired, not reaching a goal, or without any apparent reason. They alternate for the traveller on the Path as night follows day. The common people are contracted when they are overpowered by fear and expanded when they are overwhelmed by hope. The elite are expanded when they receive a manifestation of an attribute of Divine Beauty and contracted when they receive a manifestation of an attribute of Divine Majesty. In the case of the elite of the elite, Divine Beauty and Divine Majesty are the same for them. They are not changed by what happens because they are by Allah and for Allah and see nothing other than Him. So the first two are dominated by their states but the elite of the elite have mastery over their states.

When contraction takes hold of you and fear has control over you and you are under its power and accustomed to it, Allah brings you out of it into expansion so that your heart is not burned up and your body melted by it. When expansion comes over you and you rejoice in it and are familiar with Allah's Beauty, then He contracts you so as not to leave you in expansion, since that might cause you to have bad *adab* and be drawn into perdition, because very few people are able to maintain their *adab* in expansion. So He makes you travel between witnessing His Majesty and His Beauty. When you witness the effect of the attribute of His Majesty, you are contracted and when you witness the effect of the attribute of His Beauty, you are expanded.

Then, if He wills, He opens the door for you and removes the veil between Himself and you. When that happens you withdraw from the effects of Majesty and Beauty by witnessing Allah Himself. Then His Majesty does not veil you from His Beauty nor His Beauty from His Majesty; His Essence does not bar you from His Attributes nor His Attributes from His Essence. You witness His Beauty in His Majesty and His Majesty in His Beauty; and you witness His Essence in His Attributes and His Attributes in His Essence.

He brings you out of witnessing the effect of Majesty and Beauty so that you are the slave of Allah in every state. He brings you out of everything so that you are free of everything and a slave to Him alone in everything.

Know that *adab* is necessary in both contraction and expansion. If there is bad *adab* in them, the person concerned will be shown the door or thrown to the wolves. The *adab* of contraction involves maintaining peace of mind, sobriety and calmness in the face of whatever difficulty has been decreed, and turning in it to Allah, the All-Powerful. Contraction resembles the night and expansion the day. The night is a time of sleep, peace, and stillness. So, *murid*, be steadfast and calm in the darkness of the night of contraction until the sunlight of the day of expansion shines on you. Day must follow night as night must follow day: *"He merges night into day and merges day into night."* (57:6) This is the *adab* for contraction which does not have a known cause. If it has a known cause, then refer in it to the Causer of all causes. That is the Ever-Generous Ever-Giving. Has He accustomed you to anything other than good? Has He given you anything other than His favour? Any difficulty is always a precursor of something beneficial. He tells us in His Book: *"For truly with hardship comes ease, truly with hardship comes ease."* (94:5-6) The One Who sent down the sickness is the One Who sends you the remedy. If you are suffering hardship, submit it to Allah, then you will find rest. In short, the reason for your contraction is your looking at others and neglecting your Lord.

As for the people of purity, they only witness purity. That is why the Prophet ﷺ said, "If someone is afflicted by a worry or sorrow and says, 'Allah! Allah! I do not associate anything with Him,' then Allah will remove his worry and sorrow," or words to that effect. The hadith is *sahih*. Look at how the Prophet ﷺ directed the one who is contracted to the remedy for it, which is affirming *tawhid* and withdrawing from *shirk*. He ﷺ directed us with his words, but what is implied is their meaning. It is as if he were saying, "Recognise Allah and affirm His Oneness and your contraction will be transformed into expansion and your difficulty replaced by blessing."

The *adab* of expansion is restraining the limbs from excess, especially the tongue. When the *nafs* is joyous, it is reckless, impetuous and mercurial. Sometimes it utters words without proper consideration and falls into the danger of being cut off because of bad *adab*. That is why people's feet slip when they are in a state of expansion. When you sense expansion, you should curb yourself with the bridle of reticence and rein yourself in; you should wear the adornment of tranquillity and gravity and should withdraw as much as possible. The metaphor of a *faqir* in the state of expansion and impetuosity is that of a pot boiling on the stove. If it is left to boil untended, the savoury liquid will disappear and only burnt dregs remain. If the fire is turned down, the savoury liquid will remain and grow in flavour. It is the same with the *faqir* in a state of impetuosity and expansion. Their light is strong and their heart concentrated. If they are agitated and overstep, their strength will be followed by a negative reaction and be replaced by weakness. That is only as a result of their bad *adab*, and Allah knows best. It is for this reason that the people of Allah fear expansion more than contraction.

# Derse 33

رُبَّمَا أَعْطَاكَ فَمَنَعَكَ، وَرُبَّمَا مَنَعَكَ فَأَعْطَاكَ.

**83: It may be that in giving to you He deprives you, and it may be that in depriving you He gives to you.**

Generally, when something is given to the *nafs* in its commanding and blaming stages, it expands and, when it is deprived, it contracts. This is because its pleasure and appetite lies in receiving what it wants and, when it is deprived, it feels cut off and abandoned and is contracted by that. That is because of its ignorance of its Lord and lack of understanding. If it possessed understanding from Allah, it would know that deprival is the same as giving and giving is the same as deprival, as will be made clear. So, faqir, understand your Lord and do not question Him regarding the way He cares for you.

He may give you what your *nafs* desires and by doing that deprive you of His closeness. He may deprive you of what your *nafs* desires and by doing that bring you closer to Him. He may give you the best and most beautiful things of this world and yet deprive you of the beauty and radiance of His Presence. But He may deprive you of the adornment of this world and let you witness of the beauty of His Presence. He may give you physical nourishment and deprive you of spiritual nourishment but He may deprive you of physical nourishment and give you spiritual nourishment instead. He may make you accepted by creatures and deprive you of acceptance by Him or deprive you of acceptance by creatures and grant you intimacy with Him.

He may give you a great fund of knowledge and yet by that veil you from witnessing the All-Knowing. He may, though, deprive you of a lot of knowledges and yet grant you intimacy with the All-Knowing and then you will encompass everything known and unknown. He may grant you the might of this world and deprive you of the might of the Next World, or He may grant you the might of Next World and deprive you of the might of this one. He may give you disposal of the *Mulk* and deprive you of access to the *Malakut*, or deprive you of disposal of the *Mulk* and give you access to the *Malakut*. He might grant you the lights of the *Malakut* and deprive you of rising to the sea of the *Jabarut*, or He might veil you to the lights of the *Malakut* and grant you admission to the ocean of the *Jabarut*.

Shaykh al-Akbar Ibn al-'Arabi al-Hatimi said, "When you are deprived, that is His giving. When you are given to, that is His deprival. So choose renouncement over acquisition." His evidence is the words of the Almighty: *"It may be that you hate something when it is good for you."* (2:214) When you understand this, you know that, in reality, deprival is giving, as the Shaykh makes clear when he says:

مَتَى فَتَحَ لَكَ بَابَ الفَهْمِ فِي المَنْعِ، عَادَ الْمَنْعُ عَيْنَ الْعَطَاءِ .

## 84: When He opens for you the door of understanding what deprivation really is, you will see that deprivation is in fact the very source of giving.

O slave, when you have some understanding of Allah through catching a glimpse of His boundless mercy, kindness, generosity and the all-encompassing nature of His knowledge, you will realise that, if you ask Him for something, are concerned with something, or need something, and He denies it to you, He only does that that out of mercy and kindness to you, since you are not being deprived by someone who is miserly, incapable, ignorant or negligent. His depriving you is an aspect of His good guardianship of you and part of His blessing to you and will lead to the best result for you.

As mentioned earlier, Allah tells us in *Surah al-Baqara*: *"It may be that you hate something when it is good for you and it may be that you love something when it is bad for you. Allah knows and you do not know."* (2:214) It may very well be that we plan to do something we think will be good for us when in fact it will be bad for us. Benefits may accrue from what seem to be hardships and hardships from what seem to be benefits. There may be blessings in apparent afflictions and afflictions in apparent blessings. We may gain good at the hands of our enemies and harm at the hands of those who love us. So when the door of Divine understanding is opened for you in deprival and you know the good contained in it, deprival becomes in your case the same as giving. An illustration of that is a child who sees a sweet. Its father knows there is poison in it, so when the child tries to get it, his father stops it. The child cries because it doesn't understand why. If the child had known what was in the sweet, it wouldn't have wanted it and would have understood that its father's action was motivated by nothing but love.

The same applies to those who desire this world, leadership or something else, which in fact will be harmful to them, and who are then prevented by Allah from getting what they want. That is in reality an example of His mercy to them and concern for them. People who truly understand Allah, surrender the matter to Him and do not question Him in respect of what He decides and judges. Those who lack understanding of Allah, feel aggrieved, and sometimes even angry, when things do not go the way they want them to. When the secret of the matter is later laid bare, they may then realise the good there was in it for them but will have forfeited any reward for patience, because the Prophet ﷺ said, "Patience is at the first blow."

Look at the case of a man of Allah Who lived in the desert. One day his donkey, dog and rooster died. His family came to him when the donkey died and said, "Our donkey has died!" "Good," he replied. Then they said, "The dog has died." "Good," he said. Then they said to him, "The rooster has died." "Good," he said. So the people of the house got angry and said, "What kind of good is this! Our assets are disappearing before our eyes!" It so happened that some bandits attacked that tribe that night and carried off everything they had. To find their tents, they relied on the braying of the donkeys, the barking of dogs, and the crowing of the roosters so his tent was untouched, there being nothing to reveal it to them. See how Allah protects His friends and how excellent His management of them is. See how that *wali* understood straight away the secret in what had happened. This is understanding of Allah. May Allah provide us with an ample portion of it! Ash-Shibli said, "The Sufis are children under the guardianship of Allah." He meant that Allah has undertaken to preserve the Sufis and manage their affairs according to their best interests and does not leave them to their own devices. Allah knows best.

# Derse 34

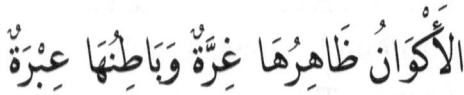

**85a: Material existence: Its outward is deception; its inward is instruction.**

The outward aspect of material existence is deception for two reasons. The first is the physical attractiveness that Allah has placed in it: the beauty of nature and what people desire in terms of food, drink, clothing, means of transport, marriage partners, houses, gardens, and fertile land, as well as all kinds of wealth, children, friends, communities, and other things which human beings delight in having. So most people devote their time to these things and work to have them night and day throughout their lives until the destroyer of all pleasures reaches them. Then grief and regret overcome them but they are of no use when the pens have written and the ink is dry. Such people leave this world without provision or preparation and will find themselves far removed from Allah.

It is for this reason that Allah cautions us against being deluded by, and halting at, the outward. He says: *"To mankind the love of worldly appetites is painted in glowing colours: women and children, and heaped up mounds of gold and silver, and horses with fine markings, and livestock and fertile farmland."* (3:14). Then in the next *ayah* He says: *"Say, Shall I tell you of something better than that?' Those who have taqwa will have Gardens with their Lord, with rivers flowing under them, remaining in them timelessly, for ever, and purified wives, and the Pleasure of Allah. Allah sees His slaves."* (3:15) He also says: *"We made everything on the earth adornment for it so that We could test them to see whose actions are the best..."* (18:7) to test to see which of them will be the most wary of it. He said to His Prophet ﷺ: *"Do not direct your eyes longingly to what We have given certain of them to enjoy the flower of the life of this world, so that We can test them by it."* (20:129-130)

The Messenger of Allah ﷺ was asked about *"the friends of Allah Who will feel no fear and will know no sorrow."* He said, "They are those who look at the inward aspect of this world when most people look at its outward. They are concerned with the future life after this world while most people are concerned with immediate gratification..." 'Ali said in something he wrote to Salman al-Farisi, "The metaphor of this world is that of a snake. It is soft to the touch but its venom is deadly. Turn away from it, and from what you like about it, since it will not be with you for long, and stop worrying about it since it is certain that you will leave it."

Allah made the outward form of these material beings – the things of this world – a temptation and a trial, and their inward an instruction. Those who halt at their outward appearance are deluded; those who penetrate to their inward meaning are accepted by Allah. The people of heedlessness and falsehood stop with the immediate pleasures and outward attractiveness of material existence and so are deluded by its deceptive allurement until the time that it is suddenly snatched away. The people of wakefulness and resolve, however, penetrate to its inward meaning and recognise the speed with which it will depart and how short a time it will last. They therefore occupy themselves with gathering provision for and preparing for what will certainly follow it. They are the ones who will *"feel no fear and know no sorrow"*.

Allah made the outward forms of material beings a screen which covers His secret and manifests His Wisdom. Or you could say that the outward form of material beings is darkness and their inward is light. Whoever stops with the darkness is veiled and whoever penetrates to witnessing the light has true knowledge. Or you could say that the outward of material beings is sensory and their inward is meaning. Or you could say that the outward of material beings is *mulk* and their inward is *malakut*. The Shaykh then talks about the one who halts at the outward form of things and the one who penetrates to their inward reality, saying:

فَالنَّفْسُ تَنْظُرُ إِلَى ظَاهِرِ غِرَّتِهَا،
وَالْقَلْبُ يَنْظُرُ إِلَى بَاطِنِ عِبْرَتِهَا.

## 85b: The *nafs* looks at their outward deception, while the heart looks at their inward instruction.

When the *nafs* looks to the outward form of created existence for its instruction, it will be deluded by the satisfaction of appetites and desires that that makes possible. The only way it can be shifted from that is by anxious yearning, unsettling fear, or divine concern shown through a shaykh who possess the elixir that brings about the transmutation of the heart. Or, on rare occasions, it can come out of nowhere. Allah possesses immense favour. The heart, however, looks at the inward meaning of created forms for instruction because of the light of true knowledge it possesses, which enables it to separate truth from falsehood and distinguish between what is beneficial and what is harmful. This is the fruit of *taqwa* and purification. Or you could say that, because of its inner sight, the heart penetrates through to the inner meaning, whereas the physical eye only sees the sensory outward.

In short, people who are subject to their lower *nafs* halt at the outward form of material existence. They are deluded by its immediacy and have little or no concern with their inevitable departure from it. So they are veiled from their urgent need for preparatory action and deluded by wishful thinking and unrealistic hopes. The people whose hearts have been brought to life, however, do not stop at the outward form of material existence. They penetrate to its inward meaning and are concerned with their inevitable destiny. They are not deluded by the immediacy of material existence and put effort and diligence into preparing themselves and getting ready for the inescapable journey they know is coming.

The people of spirits and secrets, on the other hand, do not stop with the outward appearance of material beings, nor do they concern themselves with their inward meaning. They occupy themselves with the purification of their hearts in order to open themselves to true awareness of the Knower of the outward and inward of all things and make themselves fit for His Presence and the vision of His Face: *"Such people are the party of Allah. Truly it is the party of Allah Who are successful."* (58:22) And: *"Those are the Ones Brought Near in Gardens of Delight"* (56:13-14). They will be: *"on seats of honour in the presence of an All-Powerful King."* (54:55) By His Magnanimity, Favour, Generosity, and Mercy may Allah place us among them.

# Derse 35

$$إِذَا أَرَدْتَ أَنْ يَكُونَ لَكَ عِزٌّ لَا يَفْنَى،$$
$$فَلَا تَسْتَعِزَّنَّ بِعِزٍّ يَفْنَى.$$

**86: If you want the kind of might
that will never vanish
don't give might to something that inevitably will.**

The might that does not vanish is might by Allah and the true independence gained by obedience to Allah; or that gained by nearness to those who have been given might by Allah. Might by Allah is earned by esteeming Him and exalting Him, awe of Him, love for Him, direct knowledge of Him, good *adab* with Him in everything and in every state, and by being content with His decrees, humble in the face of the force of His Majesty, having modesty and fear of Him, and by abasement and contrition before Him. I heard our shaykh say that Abu'l-Hasan ash-Shadhili said, "By Allah, I have not seen any might except in abasement." The might gained by nearness to those whose have been given might by Allah is through keeping their company, esteeming them, serving them, and maintaining good *adab* with them. This is, in truth, being exalted by Allah since they are the means of access to Him.

If anyone achieves this kind of might, they have gained a might which will never vanish and it will attach to them, their children, and their children's children until the Day of Rising. The Almighty says: *"If anyone wants might, all might belongs to Allah."* (35:10) He also says: *"And those who make Allah their friend, and His Messenger and those who believe: it is the party of Allah Who are the victorious!"* (5:58) What is meant by *"those who believe"* here are the *awliya'*, the people of perfect faith. Allah says: *"But all might belongs to Allah and to His Messenger and the believers. But the hypocrites do not know this."* (63:8)

When someone has achieved might by Allah, no one can abase them. Look at the case of the man who ordered Harun ar-Rashid to act correctly and made him angry by doing that. He gave the order: "Tie him to an ill-tempered donkey so that it kicks him to death." But it did not do anything to him. Then he said, "Lock him up and brick him into his cell." They did that and he was seen in the garden outside. He was brought and Harun asked, "Who let you out of the prison?" "The One Who admitted me into the garden," he replied. "And who admitted you into the garden?" he asked. "The One Who let me out of the prison," he replied. So Harun knew that he would not be able to abase him and commanded that he be saddled on a mount and a call given before him: "Harun wanted to abase a slave whom Allah had exalted and was unable to do it."

The might that will vanish is the kind of might gained

through something created, like the might of unjust rulers and those attached to them, which is reckoned according to the great number of their followers, armies, riches and power. Or might gained through wealth, rank, leadership and other things which are inevitably cut off and die out. If anyone achieves might in this way, his might will disappear and his abasement follow. Might achieved through creation is always followed by abasement, sooner or later. Look at the case of the man who was arrogant in the Haram and afterwards was found begging from people, saying, "I was proud in a place where people should be humble and I am now in a situation where everyone is over me."

In His book Allah calls attention to both cases. He says to the one who achieves might by means of something created: *"Look at your god to which you devoted so much time. We will burn it up and then scatter it as dust into the sea."* (20:95) So, *murid*, if you want to have the kind of might that will not end, then seek might by Allah, by obeying Him and by nearness to the *awliya'* of Allah; do not seek might through something created which will definitely come to an end. If someone seeks might through someone who will die, his might will die along with that person. Allah says: *"Do they hope to find power and strength with them? Power and strength belong entirely to Allah."* (4:138) Abu'l-'Abbas al-Mursi said, "I see that true might lies only in removing your aspiration from created things."

NOTE AND GUIDANCE. Know that the reason for the might which Allah gives his *awliya'* is His love for them.

So might is the result of Divine love. In the *Sahih* the Messenger of Allah ﷺ is reported as saying, "When Allah Almighty loves a slave, He calls out to Jibril, 'Allah Almighty loves so-and-so, so love him!' and Jibril loves him. Then a call goes out among the people of heaven, 'Allah Almighty loves so-and-so, so love him!' and the people of heaven love him. Then acceptance is placed in the earth for him and the people of earth love him." In one variant, "Acceptance of him is cast into the water, so that people drink it in and all love him," or words to that effect. The reason for Allah's love of the slave is their doing without in this world. In the hadith reported by at-Tirmidhi, the Messenger of Allah ﷺ said, "Do without this world and Allah will love you. Do without what people have and people will love you."

You should also know that this might that Allah gives to His *awliya'* does not occur during the early stages of their journey. This is so that creation does not tempt them away from reaching the Truth. Part Allah's kindness to them is that He makes people averse to them or gives them power over them so that they are freed from bondage to created things and achieve arrival and fixity (*tamkin*). Then, if He so wishes, He makes their might appear so that people benefit from them and by them He guides whomever He wishes of His creation. But if He so wills, He conceals them and withholds their might until they come before Him and then it is known and their position manifest in an abode which will never come to an end.

# Derse 36

اَلْعَطَاءُ مِنَ الْخَلْقِ حِرْمَانٌ، وَالْمَنْعُ مِنَ اللَّهِ إِحْسَانٌ.

**88: A gift from a creature is really deprivation while deprivation from Allah is really kindness.**

Gifts from creatures are deprivation in three ways. The first way you are deprived is by the feeling of elation such gifts often give you and the feeding of your appetites and desires that that entails. In that lies the death and hardening of the heart. The second way you are deprived is by the lowering of your degree and the detraction from your rank and station that that can bring about. That is why the great men of Allah give up their appetites, heeding Allah's words in *Surat al-Ahqaf*: *"You dissipated the good things you had in your worldly life and enjoyed yourself in it."* (46:20) So the people of the Path resist asking people for things because their lower selves have died and their hearts are alive. If you have a lot of gifts from creation, then your *nafs* rejoices and is comfortable and takes much longer to die, which is not the case when it is confronted by deprival. Then it dies quickly because it has no portion in deprival. For instance, jihad in which no booty is gained is greater than jihad which results in booty as we know from a sound hadith in which the Messenger of Allah ﷺ said, "If a group go out on an expedition in the way of Allah and fight and take booty they get two-thirds of their reward in this world but if no booty is taken, then they get their true reward in full."

The third kind of deprival is reliance on those who give the gifts and the heart's inclining to love for them. The self is naturally disposed to love those who are good to it and so it becomes dependent on them and is a captive in their hands. 'Ali advised, "Do not put a benefactor in between you and Allah and so as to make you feel indebted to other than the One Who has really blessed you." He said in a poem:

> By my life, if someone gives you a blessing
> for which you stretch out your hand, he is your master.
> When you are in need of someone,
> he is then truly your master and you are his captive.
> So live in contentment. Contentment is noble wealth.
> This is all I have to say.

The shaykh of our shaykhs and foundation of our Path after our Prophet ﷺ, Moulay 'Abdu's-Salam ibn Mashish said to Abu'l-Hasan ash-Shadhili ﷺ, "Abu'l-Hasan, run away from people who try to do you good faster than you run away from those who try to do you harm. The former are likely to afflict you in your heart but the latter will only afflict you in your body. It is better that you be afflicted in your body than in your heart. It is much better for you that an enemy should convey you to your Lord than that someone you love should bar your way to Him." It is for this reason that the Prophet ﷺ said, "When anyone does you a favour, repay him for it," in other words, remove your indebtedness to him and your responsibility to him. Allah knows best.

Deprivation from Allah is really kindness to you for two reasons. One was already mentioned: Allah does not deprive you out of miserliness or powerlessness but, on the contrary, He only does so out of His real concern for you. It is very possible for you to want something which is not appropriate for your state at that moment and so He holds it back from you until a moment which is better and more appropriate for you, or He stores it up for you until a day in which you really are in need of it. The second way deprivation from Allah is really kindness is because it keeps you constantly standing at His door and seeking refuge in His presence. Doing that invests you with great honour and elevates your worth in His eyes. We read in a *hadith qudsi*, "When a righteous person makes supplication, Allah Almighty says to His angels, 'Leave him in need. I love to hear his voice.' When a wrong-acting person makes supplication, He says to the angels, 'Fulfil his need. I dislike hearing his voice,'" or words to that effect.

NOTE: What the shaykh mentions with regard to gifts from creatures constituting deprivation only applies to those travelling on the Path and to worshippers. As for those who have reached the goal and are established with Allah, Allah protects them and makes them withdraw from witnessing creation. So they act by Allah, take by

Allah and refuse by Allah and do not see other than Allah in existence. They only see the gift as coming from Allah and they never see creation without witnessing it as the unfolding of Divine Wisdom. Success is by Allah. There is no power nor strength except by Allah.

# Derse 37

$$\text{جَلَّ رَبُّنَا أَنْ يُعَامِلَهُ الْعَبْدُ نَقْدًا فَيُجَازِيَهِ نَسِيئَةً.}$$

**89: Our Lord is far too majestic,
when a slave deals with Him in cash,
to pay him on credit.**

Cash is immediate and credit is deferred. An aspect of generous behaviour is that when someone buys something, they pay for it in cash and then add something extra out of kindness and as a gift. As Allah tells us He has bought from us our selves and our property and repays us with the Garden: *"Allah has bought from the believers their selves and their wealth in return for the Garden."* (9:111) So if anyone sells his self and property to Allah and pays in cash by surrendering at once to Him, Allah will repay him immediately with the garden of direct knowledge Himself and add to that later on the Garden of Delight, as well as various other blessings, such as continual witnessing of His Presence, and the vision of His Noble Face.

Our Lord is too majestic and sublime to have His slave deal with Him in cash, – in other words pay Him straight away what he owes – and then to pay him on credit – in other words delay His reward to him. He is bound to pay him immediately what is appropriate for him in this world and store up for him what is appropriate for him in the Next World. Allah hastens to him several things in this world. One is that He repels harmful things from him and brings him benefits and prosperity by His words: *"He takes care of the righteous."* (7:196) Allah also says: *"Whoever shows fear of Allah – He will give him a way out and provide for him from where he does not expect."* (65:2-3) And the Almighty further says: *"Yes, the friends of Allah will feel no fear and will know no sorrow,"* (10:62) and that may even pass on to their descendants.

Another thing is the lights which shine on him and the unveiling of secrets to his heart. They are the lights of turning towards Allah and the lights of direct encounter. Allah says: *"O you who believe! If you show fear of Allah, He will give you discrimination,"* (8:29), that is a light by which the believer is enabled to distinguish truth from falsehood. And He says: *"Show fear of Allah and Allah will give you knowledge"* (2:281), so that is the light of knowledge. And He also says: *"Allah is the Protector of those who believe. He brings them out of the darkness into the light."* (2:256) He brings them out of the darkness of *kufr* into the light of *iman*, out of the darkness of disobedience into the light of obedience, out the darkness of distraction into the light of remembrance, out of the darkness of the sensory into the light of the meaning, and out of the darkness of creation into the light of its Creator. Another thing is that it makes you worthy to stand before Allah, as the shaykh makes clear when he says:

$$\text{كَفَى مِنْ جَزَائِهِ إِيَّاكَ عَلَى الطَّاعَةِ أَنْ رَضِيَكَ لَهَا أَهْلاً.}$$

## 90: It is enough repayment for your obedience that He has considered you worthy of it.

The King only summons to His service those whom He wants to honour and only admits to His presence those He wants to exalt; only the people of excellence and nobility are attached to Him. He says: *"Were it not for Allah's favour upon you and His mercy, none of you would ever have been purified."* (24:21) Success in having obedience is the most tremendous gift and also, at the same time, its own greatest reward, because it achieves three things for those who have it. The first is ensuring, in one way or another, a robust connection to their Lord; the second is some form of direct access to Him; and the third is to completely establish in them the full picture of slavehood. Allah knows best.

Yet another reward is the intimacy and nearness which comes to their hearts during their actions of obedience. It is that which the Shaykh mentions next:

$$\text{كَفَى الْعَامِلِينَ جَزَاءً مَا هُوَ فَاتِحُهُ عَلَى قُلُوبِهِمْ فِي طَاعَتِهِ،}$$
$$\text{وَمَا هُوَ مُورِدُهُ عَلَيْهِمْ مِنْ وُجُودِ مُؤَانَسَتِهِ.}$$

## 91: Enough of a reward for the actively obedient is what He discloses to their hearts in their obedience to Him and the intimacy with Himself He brings to them.

Three things are disclosed to people's hearts through their actions of obedience to Allah: presence (*muhadara*) watchfulness (*muraqaba*) or witnessing (*mushahada*). Presence (*muhadara*) is for the seekers, watchfulness for the travellers and witnessing for those who have arrived. Presence is for the common people, watchfulness for the elite and witnessing for the elite of the elite. They are all aspects of true humility, of disappearing in the Presence of Allah.

Shaykh Zarruq said, "There are three things which someone experiences in the state of obedience. The first is real intimacy with Allah, including the gentleness and the true humility it brings with it. The second is being approved of by Allah in His Presence, which brings about a sweetness by which everything else is forgotten. The third is obtaining understanding, increase of knowledge and direct inspiration, which entirely eclipses every other type of knowledge." One of the *arifin* said about this knowledge, "There is a Garden in this world such that anyone who enters it does not yearn for the Garden of the Next World nor for anything else at all." He was asked, "What is it?" "Direct knowledge of Allah," he replied. Another said, "The approval of the Beloved and the intimate conversation with Him of the one who is given nearness to Him in this world are not actually part of this world; they are in reality part of the Garden which Allah manifests in this world."

This intimacy of obedience is of three types: the intimacy of *dhikr*, which is for the people of annihilation in action, the intimacy of nearness, which is for the people of annihilation in the Attributes, and the intimacy of witnessing, which is for the people of annihilation in the Essence. The first is for the people of Islam; the second for the people of *iman*; and the third for the people of *ihsan*. One of the people of Allah said, "There is no act of obedience that does not have an insurmountable obstacle in front of it which has to be overcome. If you are steadfast in the face of the difficulty it presents, you will reach rest and ease." So our struggle against the *nafs*, our opposition to our desires and then, by Allah's blessing, our steadfastness in turning away from this world will definitely be followed by pleasure and bliss: the pleasure of obedience we have described and the indescribable bliss of direct knowledge of Allah.

# Derse 38

مَنْ عَبَدَهُ لِشَىْءٍ يَرْجُوهُ مِنْهُ، أَوْ لِيَدْفَعَ بِطَاعَتِهِ وُرُودَ الْعُقُوبَةِ عَنْهُ، فَمَا قَامَ بِحَقِّ أَوْصَافِهِ.

**92: Whoever worships Him for something they hope for from Him or in order to ward off the arrival of punishment by their obedience to Him has not given His Attributes what they truly deserve.**

In the worship of Allah, people fall into three groups with respect to their sincerity. One group worship Allah out of fear of His punishment, sooner or later, or desire for His mercy and preservation, sooner or later. They are the common Muslims. The Prophet ﷺ said, "If it were not for the Fire, no one would have prostrated to Allah." Another group worship Allah out of love for His Essence and yearning to meet Him, not out of desire for His Garden or preservation, nor out of fear of His Fire and punishment. They are the passionate lovers among the travellers. The third group worship Allah purely to undertake the duties of slavehood and to show *adab* towards the boundless magnificence of Divine Lordship. They are the people with direct knowledge and love of Allah. The worship of the first group is by themselves for themselves. The worship of the second is by themselves for Allah. The worship of the third group is by Allah for Allah and from Allah to Allah.

Anyone who worships Allah for something he hopes for in this world or the Next or, by obeying Him, to prevent punishment reaching him in this world or the Next, has not undertaken what is demanded by the Attributes of Divine Lordship, which are Immensity, Greatness, Might, Wealth and all the qualities of perfection and attributes of Majesty and Beauty. This is because the Attributes of Lordship – Immensity and Majesty – demand humble slavehood accompanied by complete contrition and abasement. Do you not see that, even if there were no Garden or Fire, Allah would still be worthy of worship, because the One, the All-Conquering is worthy of worship in any case? Do you not think that the One Who has blessed us by bringing us into being and continually sustaining us is absolutely entitled to the gratitude of all His creatures?

A true slave does not serve his Master for the sake of gifts or presents. He serves Him simply because of the fact of his slavehood to Him and, in turn, his Master undertakes to support him and provide for him. Would Allah bring you into existence and then deny you His overwhelming Generosity? Would He admit you into His house and then deny you His bounteous hospitality? If you believe that, you have a bad opinion of the Generous Lord. He endowed you with His favour and provision while you were still in your mother's womb. Then, when He brought you out into the world, He spread out His generosity in front of you and let you go in it wherever you wanted and do in it whatever you desired. Found written on a stone in the Ka'ba were the words:

> Remember My kindness to you when you were a drop of sperm and do not forget My fashioning of you in the womb. Rely on Me in all your affairs. I will be enough for you in the face of anything you fear. Surrender the whole affair to Me and know that I will direct My judgements and do whatever I wish.

You should be ashamed before Allah if you seek a wage for the worship that the One, the All-Gracious has Himself bestowed upon you! Remember the words of the Almighty: *"Praise be to Allah Who has guided us to this! We would not have been guided, had Allah not guided us."* (7:42) And He says: *"Your Lord creates and chooses whatever He wills."* (28:68) And He says: *"But you will not will unless Allah wills."* (76:30) The Messenger of Allah ﷺ said, "None of you should be like a bad slave so that he only acts when he is afraid, nor like a bad employee who only works when he is paid a wage." 'Umar said, "What an excellent slave Suhayb is! Even if he had no fear of Allah, he would still not disobey Him." And in the reports of Da'ud we find: "Allah revealed to me: Is there anyone who will worship Me, not for a reward, but simply to give Lordship its due?"

When you raise your *himma* above seeking things for yourself, then things will be poured out on you. It says in one report that Allah will preserve people's children and grandchildren by the act of obedience of their grandparents and its evidence for this is Allah's words about the two orphans in *Surat al-Kahf*: "*Their father was one of the righteous.*" (18:82) Allah guarded the treasure of those two children on account of the righteousness of their father and made sure his fortune reached them. They were protected because their father was someone who had abandoned his affair to Allah. Sa'id ibn al-Musayyab told his child, "I make the prayer long for your sake." By which he meant, "I worship Allah sincerely so that He will look after you." So the support and help of Allah, which is His gentleness and kindness, is given, in any case, to those who obey Allah without expecting anything in return and even extends beyond them to those around them.

# Derse 39

مَتَى أَعْطَاكَ أَشْهَدَكَ بِرَّهُ، وَمَتَى مَنَعَكَ أَشْهَدَكَ قَهْرَهُ،
فَهُوَ فِي كُلِّ ذَلِكَ مُتَعَرِّفٌ إِلَيْكَ،
وَمُقْبِلٌ بِوُجُودِ لُطْفِهِ عَلَيْكَ.

**93: When He gives to you,
He is showing you His goodness.
When He deprives you,
He is showing you His irresistible force.
In both cases He is making Himself known to you
And drawing you near by His graciousness to you.**

The Names of Allah Almighty include the Gracious (*Latif*) and the Most Merciful (*Rahim*). He is gracious to His slaves and merciful to His creation at every moment and in every state, whether He gives to them or deprives them, and whether He expands them or contracts them. If He gives to them or expands them, He makes them witness His kindness and goodness and they recognise that He is Gracious to His slaves, Gentle to His creation, Generous, Magnanimous, and Beneficent, and so their love for Him grows and their yearning and longing for Him increase. Their thankfulness increases and so their blessings increase. This entails immeasurable kindness, beneficence, generosity and grace.

If He deprives them or contracts them, He makes them witness His force and grandeur and so they know that He is a Majestic, Great, Immense, Conqueror. So they fear His Power and melt out of fear of Him and are humble under His irresistible force. Consequently their worship of Him continues, their wrong actions diminish, their evil qualities are effaced and their errors disappear. So on the Day of Rising they will come wiped-clean, purified, radiant and joyful, since Allah will not combine two fears or two securities for His slave. If you fear Him in this world, He will give you security on the Day of Rising. If you feel safe from Him in this world, you are deluded and will fear Him on the Day of Rising, as stated in *hadith*.

Therefore do not doubt your Lord in either deprival or giving. When He gives to you, He makes you witness His Kindness, Mercy and Generosity and you recognise that He is Kind, Generous, Compassionate and Merciful and you rely on His generosity and magnanimity and not that of anyone else. You are freed from the shackles of greed, and sorrow and anxiety are removed from you. You also take on the character of generosity, mercy and beneficence. Allah loves His slaves to take on His qualities. The hadith says: "Take on the qualities of the All-Merciful." 'A'isha said, "The character of the Messenger of Allah ﷺ was the Qur'an," and the Qur'an contains the qualities of the All-Merciful. So it is as if she was saying that his character was that of the All-Merciful. She herself, however, was diffident in the face of the Divine Presence and showed *adab* towards Divine Lordship.

When He deprives you or contracts you, He makes you witness His Force and Majesty and so you recognise that He has overwhelming Power and your fear becomes great, and awe and diffidence before Him strong. This causes Allah to exalt you, honour you, preserve you and be shy before you as you are shy before Him. Allah positions His slave according to his position with Him and the slave obeys his Lord according to his recognition of Him and fear of Him.

In all of that – giving and deprival, contraction and expansion – the Almighty is making Himself known to you, enabling you to recognise Him through His Names and Attributes. There is not one of His Names that does not necessarily manifest its own innate quality in His creation. So His Name, the Generous, *al-Karim*, inevitably shows itself in all types of giving and beneficence and it is manifest as such in His creation. His Name, the Withholder, *al-Mani'*, inevitably shows itself in every kind of deprival and it also is manifest as such in His creatures. His Name, the Avenger, *al-Muntaqim*, becomes manifest in what happens to some people who oppose Him. His Name, the All-Conquering, *al-Qahhar*, is manifested in his overpowering of people in whatever way He wills, whether through deprival or through other people and is also manifest to His creatures in the inevitability of their death. That is part of what His Name, the All-Conquering, entails. It is the same with every

Divine Name. They ineluctably manifest themselves in existence and all of them are manifest in the human race.

When you realise this reality with regard to your own experience of being given to and being deprived, then you will also realise that Allah is, in every case, showing you His Gentleness and Kindness since it is He Who is making Himself known to you in everything that happens and turning towards you in every situation. This is summed up in the advice of the shaykh of our Path, the Qutb, Moulay Abdassalam ibn Mashish who said, "Be content with what Allah has allotted to you. When that results in what pleases you, which in that case is a manifestation of Allah's Beauty, thank Allah for it. When it results in hardship, which is then a manifestation of His Majesty, be steadfast in it."

So you should make every effort to recognise Him in every situation and acknowledge His favour to you, whether it is showing itself to you in a beautiful or majestic form. You should turn to Him with your entire being in everything that happens to you and submit both spiritually and physically to His inexorable Power. Then you will be truly His slave and He will truly be your Lord. Allah knows best.

# Derse 40

$$\text{رُبَّمَا فَتَحَ لَكَ بَابَ الطَّاعَةِ وَمَا فَتَحَ لَكَ بابَ الْقَبُولِ}$$

**95a: He may well open the door of obedience for you and yet not open the door of acceptance.**

There is no point in obedience when it is not accompanied by acceptance, because the whole point of obedience is to gain the love and acceptance of the One you are obeying. When that happens Allah turns towards those who obey Him, removes the veil from their hearts and allows them to sit on the carpet of love. If He opens the door of obedience to you and that remains the limit of your aspiration; and you do not pluck its fruits and taste the sweetness of intimacy with Allah; and you do not find yourself free from the need for other than Him; and you do not find contentment in your knowledge of Him; and you are not completely satisfied with what He has allotted to you; then, murid, do not be deluded by the fact that He has opened the door of obedience to you and made you a worshipper of Him.

If He has opened the door of worship to you and denied you arrival through it, it is because you rely on it, depend on it, have become familiar with it and because the performance of the act of worship distracts you from the sweetness of witnessing the One Who has blessed you with it. You have taken the act of worship as an end in itself. That is why one of them said, "Beware of the enjoyment of acts of obedience. It is a deadly poison because it holds the one who has it in the station of worship and bars them from the station of love. What a great difference there is between the one whom He occupies with worshipping Him and the one He chooses for His love and selects for His Presence." It is, in fact, sometimes better for the slave to commit a wrong action than to have this sort of obedience as Shaykh Ibn Ata'illah points out in his following words when he says:

وَرُبَّمَا قَضَى عَلَيْكَ بِالذَّنْبِ فَكَانَ سَبَبَاً فِي الوُصُولِ .

## 95b: He may well decree wrong action for you and yet it becomes a means of arrival.

When someone is travelling to His Master, aiming to reach the Presence of his Beloved and to gain His Good-pleasure, they sometimes become weary or bored or lazy. Then Allah gives a wrong action power over them, or their *nafs* gets the better of them, and they slip up. When they recover from their lapse, however, their striving on the path becomes greater. They wake up from their heedlessness and overcome their laziness. Their desire for the Presence of their Lord is increased, leading them to withdraw from other-than-Him and raise their aspiration to the manifestation of the Truth and the secrets of the Divine Essence. A metaphor for that is someone who is travelling and falls asleep. Then he falls off his horse and hits his head on a rock. When he gets up, the jolt he has received has completely banished his tiredness and he continues his journey wide awake and far more aware of what he is doing and where he is going.

We read in a hadith, "How many a wrong action has made a person enter the Garden!" They asked, "How can that be, Messenger of Allah?" He replied ﷺ, "They continue to repent and flee from it in fear of their Lord until they die and enter the Garden," or words to that effect. In another hadith reported by Abu Hurayra the Messenger of Allah ﷺ is reported as saying, "By the One in whose hand my soul is, if you had not sinned, Allah would have removed you and brought other people who did and who then asked for forgiveness so that He could forgive them." And the Prophet ﷺ, said about certain acts of obedience, "Many a faster only has hunger from his fast and many a person who prays at night only has lack of sleep from his standing in prayer." So the Shaykh then says:

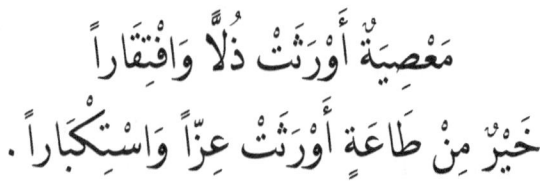

**96: Disobedience that instils abasement and utter poverty is better than obedience that instils self-importance and pride.**

## 40

Disobedience that brings about contrition is better than obedience which causes pride because what is desired from obedience is humility, submission, abasement and contrition. If acts of obedience lack these things and are instead characterised by their opposites, then acts of disobedience that bring about these qualities are better than them since, when they are present, the form of obedience or disobedience which brought them about is immaterial. What is important is what results from them. Allah does not look at your forms or your actions. He looks at your hearts.

The true fruits of obedience are abasement and contrition, and the fruits of disobedience are normally arrogance and hardness. If the fruits are reversed, the realities are also reversed. So obedience turns into disobedience and disobedience into obedience. That is why al-Muhasabi said, "What Allah desires of His slaves is their hearts. So if a scholar or worshipper is proud and haughty, whereas an ignorant or disobedient person is abased out of fear of Allah, the latter is in reality more obedient to Allah than former." Shaykh Abu'l-'Abbas al-Mursi said, "Every act of bad *adab* which results in good *adab* is not in fact bad *adab*." He was dominated by witnessing the vastness of Allah's mercy and would treat people according to their rank with Allah. So someone known for right action might visit him and he would ignore them, while someone known for the opposite might come in and he would honour them. That was because the former came with pride in his actions while the latter, in spite of his wrongdoing, was in a state of abasement and opposition to them.

Shaykh Ibn Ata'illah says in *Lata'if al-Minan*: "Abu Yazid said, 'I heard a voice in my secret saying: "My storehouses are overflowing with worship. If you truly desire Me, you must have abasement and utter poverty."'" The Messenger of Allah ﷺ said, "If you do not commit wrong actions, I fear for you what is worse than that: arrogance." This is in the two *Sahih* collections. The shaykh of our shaykhs said, "An act of disobedience to Allah is a thousand times better than acts of obedience stemming from the *nafs*." The words of the shaykh mean that when someone commits a wrong action, which the decree leads him to commit in spite of himself, and then he regrets that and is really contrite, that is better for him than a thousand acts of obedience which he witnesses as coming from himself and on account of which he considers himself better than his fellow slaves of Allah.

# Derse 41

$$\text{لِيُخَفِّفْ أَلَمَ الْبَلَاءِ عَلَيْكَ عِلْمُكَ بِأَنَّهُ سُبْحَانَهُ هُوَ الْمُبْلِي لَكَ. فَالَّذِي وَاجَهَتْكَ مِنْهُ الْأَقْدَارُ هُوَ الَّذِي عَوَّدَكَ حُسْنَ الاخْتِيَارِ.}$$

**105: Let the pain of affliction be lessened for you by your knowledge that it is Allah Who is testing you. For the One Who confronts you with decrees is He Who has accustomed you to His best choice for you.**

When you suffer an affliction, or a trial befalls you in in your body, family or wealth, remember the One Who brought it upon you. You know that Mercy and Compassion are two of His essential characteristics and have been manifest in the love and kindness He has shown you throughout your life. If you do that you will understand the blessing which the difficulty you are experiencing contains and the great generosity and magnanimity which will succeed it, even if that has no outward manifestation and only consists in purifying you from wrong actions, cleansing you of faults and bringing you near to the Presence of the Knower of the Worlds. Are you accustomed to anything from Him other than the best? Have you seen from Him anything except extreme kindness and grace? The One Who confronts you with decrees is the same One who has accustomed you to excellent choice. The One Who confronts you with the judgements of His Power is the same One who has accustomed you to His overwhelming goodness and kindness. The One Who confronts you with outward trials is the same One who has bestowed on you inward gifts and favours.

Imam al-Junayd said, "Once, while I was sleeping, my uncle as-Sari woke me up and said to me, 'Junayd! I dreamt that I was standing before Allah and He said to me, "Sari, I created creation and all of them asked for My love. Then I created this world and nine-tenths of them fled from me and just a tenth remained with Me. I created the Fire and nine-tenths of the tenth fled and a tenth of the tenth remained with Me. Then I imposed on them an atom's weight of affliction and nine-tenths of the tenth of the tenth fled from Me. I said to those who remained with Me, "You did not want this world nor did you flee from the Fire. What do you want?" They replied, "You know what we want." I said, "I will release such affliction on you according to the number of your breaths that even the firm mountains could not bear it. Will you still be steadfast then?" They said, "If You are the One Who afflicts, then do whatever You wish." Those are truly My slaves.'"

The Shaykh says in *at-Tanwir*, "The opening of the gate of understanding helped them to bear the difficulty of the decree." If you wish, you could say that the *waridat* of the blessing involved made them strong enough to bear the affliction, or you could say that the witnessing of His good choice makes them strong enough to bear His decrees, or if you wish, their knowledge of the existence of His knowledge of them made it possible for them endure the existence of His judgement, or if you wish, His manifestation to them of His perfect Beauty made them endure the Majesty of His actions, or if you wish, their knowledge that steadfastness brings about delight allowed them to endure the adversity of His decree, or if you wish you could say that their knowledge of the kindness and gentleness He has, in reality, placed in hardship enabled them to bear with equanimity any difficulty He has ordained for them. Shaykh Ibn Ata'illah speaks of this in his next words when he says:

مَنْ ظَنَّ انْفِكَاكَ لُطْفِهِ عَنْ قَدَرِهِ فَذَلِكَ لِقُصُورِ نَظَرِهِ .

**106: Anyone who thinks that His pervading gentleness is in any way separate from His Decree that is due to great short-sightedness on his part.**

An aspect of the immense kindness and goodness of Allah is that His gentleness is not separate from His Decree. A decree only descends when it is preceded and accompanied by gentleness. This is borne out by both transmission and reason. As for reason, it is clear that there is no affliction which befalls a slave without there being something much worse that Allah could, if He so desired, inflict. So when you are suffering an affliction, bear in mind those who are suffering a greater affliction than you. How many a human beings are suffering from terrible illnesses! How many are languishing in awful situations with no one to care for them! How many are blind or incapacitated or in anguish, and we might go on and on *ad infinitum* with examples of that. We ask Allah for the gift from Him of constant well-being in both the worlds!

As for transmission, many *hadiths* and *ayahs* of the Qur'an announce the reward for bearing illness, pain and hardship with patient endurance and praise those who are steadfast. For instance, Allah says: *"The steadfast will be paid their wages in full without any reckoning"* (39:10) And: *"Allah is with the steadfast."* (2:152) And: *"We will test you with a certain amount of fear and hunger and loss of wealth and life and fruits. But give good news to the steadfast."* (2:154) The Prophet ﷺ said, "No fatigue, illness, anxiety, sorrow, harm or sadness afflicts any Muslim, even to the extent of a thorn pricking him, without Allah wiping out his mistakes by it." And there are many *hadiths* about fever, stating, for instance, that an hour of fever is expiation for a year's wrong action, and other things are said. Shaykh Ibn 'Abbad related an unequivocal statement in confirmation of this, and whoever desires multiplication of rewards, removal of veils and contentment with the decree should read it. What we have mentioned is enough, Allah willing.

# Derse 42

$$\text{لَا يُخَافُ عَلَيْكَ أَنْ تَلْتَبِسَ الطُّرُقُ عَلَيْكَ؛}$$
$$\text{وَإِنَّمَا يُخَافُ عَلَيْكَ مِنْ غَلَبَةِ الْهَوَى عَلَيْكَ.}$$

**107: What is feared for you is not that
the Path will be unclear to you.
What is feared for you is that
lower desires will overpower you.**

There is no doubt that Allah has made clear for us the path of arrival on the tongue of His Messenger ﷺ. He made clear to us the guideposts of the *shari'a*, the lighthouse of the *tariqa* and the lights of the *haqiqa*. He assigned for us the laws of Islam, the pillars of *Iman* and the station of *Ihsan*. There is nothing which will bring us near to Allah that the Prophet ﷺ did not direct us to, and there is nothing which will distance us from Him that he did not warn us about. He did not spare any effort in guiding people and making the correct path known. He did not return to Allah Almighty until he had left people with the upright *deen*, the Straight Way and the radiant path from which only someone blind could go astray. Allah says: *"Today I have perfected your deen for you and completed My blessing upon you and am pleased with Islam as a deen for you."* (5:4) And He says: *"There is no compulsion where the deen is concerned. Right guidance has become clearly distinct from error."* (2:255) The Prophet ﷺ said, "I have left you the generous *Hanafiyya*." One variant has, "the radiant religion. Its day is like its night," or words to that effect. Ahmad ibn Hadarawyh al-Balkhi said, "The path is clear, the proof evident and the caller has been heard. There can be no confusion after this except for people who are blind."

Therefore, *murid*, is not feared that the Path which will take you to Allah will be unclear for you because it is very clear indeed. What is feared for you is that lower desires will overwhelm you and make you blind and deaf to it. When lower desires take control, they make one deaf. So it is not feared that guidance will be unclear for you. What is feared for you is that you will follow your lower desires. It is not feared that the truth will be unclear for you. What is feared for you is base character. Allah tells us: *"If you obeyed most of those on earth, they would misguide you from Allah's Way."* (6:117) So it is not feared that you will not have people of Allah to guide you. What is feared for you is that you will turn to other people who will cut you off from the Path. It is not feared that the people of true sincerity will be hidden from you. What is feared for you is lack of true sincerity in yourself. Allah says: *"Being true to Allah would be better for them."* (47:22)

By Allah, the only thing that veils the people of truth from you is your own lack of truth. If you had had a good opinion of Allah and the friends of Allah, Allah would have removed the veil between you and Him, and you would have found them so near to you that you would not have to travel to them.

# Derse 43

لَا يَسْتَحْقِرُ الْوِرْدَ إِلَّا جَهُولٌ. الْوَارِدُ يُوجَدُ فِي الدَّارِ الْآخِرَةِ، وَالْوِرْدُ يَنْطَوِي بِانْطِوَاءِ هَذِهِ الدَّارِ. وَأَوْلَى مَا يُعْتَنَى بِهِ مَا لَا يُخْلَفُ وُجُودُهُ. الْوِرْدُ هُوَ طَالِبُهُ مِنْكَ، وَالْوَارِدُ أَنْتَ تَطْلُبُهُ مِنْهُ. وَأَيْنَ مَا هُوَ طَالِبُهُ مِنْكَ مِمَّا هُوَ مَطْلَبُكَ مِنْهُ.

112: **Only an ignorant man disparages the *wird*.**
**The *warid* will be there in the Next World**
**But the *wird* necessarily ends with this one.**
**It is better to concern yourself**
**with something that cannot be replaced.**
**The *wird* is what He asks of you.**
**The *warid* is what You seek from Him.**
**Where is what He asks of you**
**over against what you seek from Him?**

The word *wird* literally means a drinking place. The Almighty says: *"What an evil watering-hole to be led down* to." (11:97) In technical terms it denotes what a shaykh gives his student to carry out in the form of *dhikr*s and other acts of worship. The literal meaning of the word *warid* is arrival and that which arrives. In technical usage it denotes whatever divine inspirations Allah breathes into the hearts of His friends. Sometimes that will bewilder them or make them withdraw from their senses. Such inspirations are always sudden and do not last long for the person concerned.

There are three categories of *wird*. The first is the *wird* of ordinary worshippers; the second, the *wird* of travellers on the Path; and the third, the *wird* of the people of arrival. The *wird* of the first group, consists in spending their time in different types of worship, such as *dhikr*, prayer and fasting. The *wird* of the travellers on the path is to abandon preoccupation with this world and part with sensory attachments, and to purify the heart from distraction and defects and adorn it with virtues after it has been emptied of vices. Such people apply themselves to a particular *dhikr*, specified by their shaykh, and confine themselves to that along with the concentration of the heart on the presence of their Lord. The *wird* of those who have arrived is their complete elimination of their lower desires and their total absorption in love of their Lord. Their existence is reflection and contemplation of the Divine Presence.

Anyone who is established by his Lord in a particular *wird* should cling to it, not go beyond it and not disdain anyone else for what they may or may not do. People of knowledge do not disdain anything. They deal with everything according to its station and affirm everything in its proper place. The reward and fruit of every *wird* will become apparent in the Next World. Allah says: *"This is your Garden which you have inherited for what you did."* (7:42)

The true slave of Allah devotes himself to those duties of slavehood for which he is responsible, undertaking the right due to his Lord. By continuing in that he attains the pleasure of the Living, the Self-Subsistent. Thus the most fitting thing with which a human being can be concerned is that whose existence will be cut off when they die, in other words their *wird*. We must take advantage of its existence as long as we are in this worldly realm because there will be no possibility of action after we leave it. The Next World is the abode of repayment. This world is the abode of action without repayment and the Next is the abode of repayment without action. We must, therefore, take every advantage of our lives before they end. Each time we fail to do that is a missed opportunity that can never be regained. It states in a hadith that every moment you experience in which you do not remember Allah will be a cause of regret for you on the Day of Rising, realising, of course, that there are many different ways of doing *dhikr*: each according to his state. Al-Hasan said, "I have met people who were more solicitous of their moments than they are of their dinars and dirhams."

So, in short, concern with the *wird* is better and more profitable than concern with the *warid* because the *wird* is one of the tasks of slavehood and it continues as long as the slave remains in this abode. Just as the rights of lordship do not end, so, also, the duties of slavehood do not end. An-

Naqshbandi said, "This is why the master of this station ﷺ did not stop worshipping until his feet were swollen. He was asked, 'Why do you do this when Allah has forgiven you any past or future wrong actions?' He replied ﷺ, 'Should I not be a grateful slave?' This is the path of the group of al-Junayd. He did not cease his doing his *wird* even on his deathbed. He was asked why and said, 'Who could be more in need of it than I, at the time when these pages of mine are being rolled up?' He, with all his greatness, did not stop, so what can be said about us in our condition?"

Abu'l-Hasan ad-Darraj says, "Al-Junayd often talked of the people of Allah and the *wirds* and acts of worship which they continue to perform after the great gifts which Allah has given them. He said, 'For the people of Allah, acts of worship are better than the crowns which sit on the heads of kings.'" A man saw al-Junayd with a *tasbih* in his hand and said to him, "In spite of your high station, you have a *tasbih* in your hand?" "Yes," he replied, "we will never abandon that which was the means of our arrival at what we have reached. The *shari'a* is the door and the *haqiqa* is the house of the Presence. The Almighty says: '*Come to houses by their doors.*' (2:188)" Then Imam al-Junayd said, "There is no entry to the *haqiqa* except by the door of the *shari'a*." How excellent is what Sidi 'Abdullah al-Hibti az-Zajali said in his poem:

> There is no reaching of the goal except by the *shari'a*,
> like achieving *baqa* after your *fana*.
> Anyone who thinks that good lies in other than it,
> by Allah, has never experienced it!

So persevere in the recitation of the *wird*. It truly is your watering-hole, the well containing the water that will bring your heart to life. By reciting it you are letting down the bucket to lift that water to the surface and irrigate your being with illumination from the very source of guidance from which it comes. May Allah give us success in benefitting from the blessing He has given us and sharing it generously in every way we can with those we come into contact with.

# Derse 44

$$\text{اَلْغَافِلُ إِذَا أَصْبَحَ يَنْظُرُ مَاذَا يَفْعَلُ،}$$
$$\text{وَالْعَاقِلُ يَنْظُرُ مَاذَا يَفْعَلُ اللَّهُ بِهِ.}$$

**114: When he wakes up in the morning
the heedless person
looks to what he is going to do,
the person of intellect
looks to what Allah is going to do with him.**

Heedless people are ignorant of Allah, even if they do a lot of *dhikr* with the tongue. People of intellect have knowledge of Allah, even if they do less *dhikr* of the tongue, because what is important is the *dhikr* of the heart. The selves of heedless people are persistent in their desires and their hopes are far-reaching. In the morning they look to what they are going to do and try to manage their affair and are subject to much wishful thinking. They put faith in their own actions and rely on their state and their own strength. When the decree cancels out what they have decided on and destroys what they have hoped for, they become angry or annoyed, sad or despondent. By acting in this way what they are actually doing is competing with their Lord and showing bad *adab* towards Him. So they inevitably distance themselves from Allah and alienate their hearts from Him, unless they turn back to Him and continue to stand at His door until the veil is lifted from them. Then they will be united with the lovers.

People of intellect, on the other hand, demonstrate their true knowledge of the Divine Reality. They realise in their hearts the incomparable vastness of their Lord and concentrate on Him with all their being. The fruit of true knowledge of Allah shines in their hearts and the existence of other created beings does not distract them from Him. Their activity is by Allah, from Allah, and for Allah. In the morning they look to see what Allah will do with them and meet all that comes to them with equanimity, happiness, delight and joy since they are filled with certainty and serenity by the Lord of the worlds. Sayyiduna 'Umar ibn 'Abdu'l-'Aziz said, "I find no joy in my days except in the fulfilment of the decree." Abu 'Uthman said, "In forty years Allah has never put me in a state which I disliked nor moved to another which annoyed me."

If the *fuqara* want their actions to be by Allah, they should relinquish their feeling of entitlement and their lower aspirations. When they want to do something, they should act without haste and be patient, listening out for the invisible voice. Then Allah Almighty will enable them to hear what He desires them to turn to, whether that involves action or non-action. This has happened to us both when travelling and at home. We would only move by specific permission. Praise belongs to Allah. The possessor of true prudence is like that, acting with deep care and attention. Echoing the words of the *hadith*: "Deliberateness is from Allah and haste is from *shaytan*," Shaykh al-Majdhub, the *wali* and gnostic, Sidi Ahmad Abu Silham, used to often recite this verse:

> Take your time
> and do not try to hasten any matter you desire.
> Be merciful to creation.
> You are tested by One who is merciful.

So, O *murid*, you must concern yourself with this matter and seek understanding from Allah in all your affairs. He wrote to himself:

> Surrender to Salma and go wherever she goes.
> Follow the winds of the decree
> and move wherever they move.

Seek help in this matter by using the supplications left to us by the Prophet ﷺ such as his words: "O Allah, in the morning I possess no power to bring myself either harm or benefit or life or death or resurrection. I can obtain nothing except what You endow me with and can only avoid what You protect me from. So, O Allah, grant me success in saying and doing whatever words and actions make me pleasing to You, and grant me well-being and protection. You have power over all things." And there are other such supplications which bring about true resignation and submission to the will of Allah. The object of these supplications lies in their meaning not just their words.

All this is summed up in the advice of the shaykh of our Path, the Qutb Moulay Abdassalam Ibn Mashish, to a man who said to him, "Please assign to me some duties (*waza'if*) and *wirds* to perform." He became angry and said to him, "Am I then a Messenger so that I should impose obligations on people? The obligations are well-known and the acts of disobedience are well-known. Carry out the obligations and avoid any acts of disobedience. Guard your heart from desire for this world and love of rank and giving free rein to your appetites. In all of that be content with what Allah has allotted to you. When that results in what pleases you, which in that case is a manifestation of Allah's Beauty, thank Allah for it. When it results in hardship, which is then a manifestation of His Majesty, be steadfast in it. Love of Allah is the axis about which all blessings revolve. It conveys and embraces all good in this world and the Next. The fortress guarding all that has four towers: true scrupulousness, good intention, sincere action, and love of knowledge. And it can only be achieved through keeping the company of a right-acting brother or shaykh of good counsel."

# Derse 45

إِنَّمَا اسْتَوْحَشَ الْعُبَّادُ وَالزُّهَّادُ مِنْ كُلِّ شَيْءٍ لِغَيْبَتِهِمْ عَنِ اللَّهِ فِي كُلِّ شَيْءٍ، فَلَوْ شَهِدُوهُ فِي كُلِّ شَيْءٍ لَمْ يَسْتَوْحِشُوا مِنْ شَيْءٍ.

**115: The worshippers and the abstinent
are alienated from everything
since they have withdrawn from Allah in everything.
Had they witnessed Him in everything,
they would not be alienated from anything.**

The "worshippers" are those who are dominated by action and so they are absorbed in sensory worship. They stand in prayer in the night and fast in the day. The sweetness of worship has distracted them from the sweetness of witnessing the One Who is worshipped. So they are veiled by their worship from the One they worship. The "abstinent" are the ones who are dominated by non-action. They flee from this world and its people. They taste the sweetness of abstinence and stop with it and so are veiled from Allah by it. If they had recognised Allah in everything, they would not be alienated from anything and would be intimate with everything and would have shown *adab* with everything. Because of the acute discernment of their inner eye, the *'arifin* witness things as the places where the Real is manifest. At first they are veiled by the Real from creation, by the meaning from the sensory, and by Power from Wisdom. Then they return to witnessing the Real in creation and Power in Wisdom, recognising Him in everything. They are intimate with everything and have *adab* with everything. They esteem everything.

Sidi 'Ali, commenting on the statement of Shaykh Abu'l-Hasan ash-Shadhili regarding created beings: "I see them like dust in the air. If you examine them, you would not find them to be anything," said, "If you were to investigate them, you would find them to be something, and that thing is *'There is nothing like Him*. (42:11)'" In other words you would find them to be sites of manifestations of the Real from the lights of the *Malakut*, overflowing from the sea of the *Jabarut*.

In short, the *'arifin* have withdrawn from witnessing creation by witnessing the Real. So they are with creation by bodily form and with the Real by spirit. They have died and been resurrected and their rising has taken place. For them, the earth has been changed to *'other than the earth and heavens'* (14:48). They have been provided for by Allah, the One, the Conqueror, so they see lights while other people remain in the darkness of otherness. In this world, the secrets of His beings have been revealed to them which are covered by His veils of Divine force. In the Next World the secrets of His Essence are disclosed to them without the veil of Wisdom which is the effect of His Attributes, as he indicates in his next maxim:

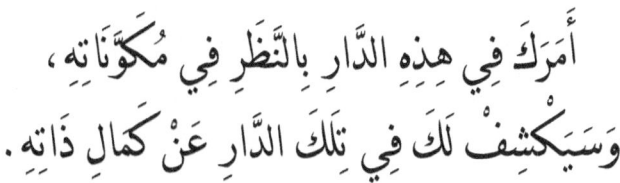

### 116: In this world He commanded you to look into the things He brought into being and in that world He will unveil for you the perfection of His Essence.

He commanded you to look at this world through the medium of the things He brought into existence, because here you will not be able to look at the reality of His Essence in the immensity of the primal Jabarut without any intermediary on account of the weakness of your structure, even if that is logically permissible, as is indicated by Sayyiduna Musa ﷺ asking for it. The wisdom of the All-Wise, however, demands that the secrets of Lordship be covered by the lights of the glories of Divine Wisdom since beauty must have a veil and the sun must have clouds. If He had appeared without the cloak of pride, perception would have occurred. Then there would not remain any rising. Rising occurs in the secrets of the Essence by looking at the lights of the Attributes. It never ends in either abode. So the Essence is never seen at all without a locus of manifestation. The meaning is only held by the sensory. This is the position of the people of realisation among the people of meanings.

If you were to ask why the Shaykh made a distinction between the two visions in respect of the two abodes when it is actually one vision because the manifestation is unified, the answer is that it is because in the manifestation of this world, the sensory dominates the meaning and Wisdom is evident and Power hidden. The reverse is the case in the Next World where the meaning will dominate the sensory and Power will be manifest and unveiled. There the reality of the Essence is unveiled more than it is unveiled here. This is the meaning of the distinction between the two visions. It is as what Shaykh Abu'l-Hasan said in his *Great Hizb*: "The might of this world is by faith and knowledge and the might of the Next World is by encounter and direct witnessing." This is for the elite. As for the common people, they only see the sensory both in this world and the Next. As for the vision which they obtain on the Day of Increase, it is possible that one of the lights of His Purity will appear to them. Or He may annihilate them to their sensory at that moment so that they witness the meanings of the Essence, and they enjoy their vision, and then He returns them to the sensory.

In short, the *tajalli* of the Essence falls into two categories. One category is by dense means. Their outward is darkness and their inward light, their outward is Wisdom and inward is Power, their outward is sensory and their inward meaning. That is the *tajalli* in this abode. The other category is by subtle luminous means, whose outward is light and inward is light, whose outward is Power and whose inward is Wisdom, whose outward is meaning and inward sensory.

That is the *tajalli* of the Next World. So the *'arifin* obtain witnessing and direct knowledge of Allah in this world and in the Next World are not veiled from Allah by houris or palaces. Rather they are always in vision, happiness, radiance and joy. Since they have gained direct knowledge of Him here, they are not veiled there. A man dies on what he lived and will be raised up on what he died on. This is not the case with the common people. Since they are veiled here by witnessing themselves, they will be veiled there from the vision of the One they worship except at a specific time in a specific manner. That is why Ibn al-'Arabi al-Hatimi wrote to Imam ar-Razi, "Come and we will acquaint you with Allah today before you die. Otherwise when Allah manifests Himself to His slaves, you will deny him and not recognise Him."

Shaykh Abu Muhammad 'Abdu'l-Qadir al-Jilani was asked about a man who claimed that he saw Allah with his physical eyesight (*basar*). He summoned him and asked him about that and he said, "Yes." So he rebuked him and forbade him to say that. Then he was asked, "Is he telling the truth or uttering a falsehood?" He replied, "He is confused and saying what he thinks is true." That was because he had witnessed the light of Divine Beauty with his inner eye (*basîra*). Then it crossed from his inner eye to his normal sight (*basar*) and affected it. So his eye saw his inner light while the rays of his inner eye were connected to the light of His witnessing and so what he thought he saw was what his inner eye witnessed. His outer eye only saw his inner eye." In short he saw Him with his inner eye and thought that he saw Him with his outer eye. The meaning behind that is that as long as the *ruh* remains veiled by human physicality, seeing is only accomplished by the physical eye and it only sees the physical. When *ruhaniyya* overpowers human physicality, the sight of the outer eye is reflected to the inner eye and then the outer eye sees the meanings which the inner eye sees. That is the meaning of the words of our shaykh al-Majdhub:

> My sight vanished in His sight,
> and I was annihilated to everything ephemeral.
> I realised that I did not find other
> and became delighted immediately,

Allah Almighty knows best. Your command in this abode is to see Him in the things He has brought into existence to console you for lack of witnessing His Essence since the lover cannot endure being without his beloved.

# Derse 46

لَمَّا عَلِمَ الْحَقُّ مِنْكَ وُجُودَ الْمَلَلِ، لَوَّنَ لَكَ الطَّاعَاتِ.

**118a: Since He knows that you easily become bored, He has varied acts of obedience for you.**

One aspect of Allah's boundless generosity is that since He knew that some of His slaves would certainly become bored with just one form of worship, He varied the acts of obedience He imposed upon us. This is because an aspect of the nature of the *nafs* is to become bored with repetition of the same thing. So when, for instance, you become bored with the prayer, you can move to doing *dhikr*. When you are bored with *dhikr*, You can move to recitation of Allah's Book, and so on. Moving in this way generates energy. Worship done with energy, even if it is only a little, is greater than worship done with lethargy, even if there is a lot of it. It is not the physical action that is important, even if there is a lot of it. What is important is the inner meaning. Shaykh Zarruq said, "Acts of obedience are varied for three reasons. One is out of mercy so that we will be refreshed by moving from one type to another. The second is to establish a methodology for us so that we will have no excuse for abandoning obedience. The third is to establish an ascription of the actions to us by the fact that we choose to do them. So the generosity is complete and obedience becomes easy for us."

One of the things that leads to boredom is people's tendency to overdo things, which can paradoxically result in failure to act at all. That is why obedience is limited to certain times as Shaykh ibn Ata'illah points out by saying:

وَعَلِمَ مَا فِيكَ مِنْ وُجُودِ الشَّرَهِ
فَحَجَرَهَا عَلَيْكَ فِي بَعْضِ الْأَوْقَاتِ

**118b: And He knows you are prone to overdoing things, so He has forbidden you to do them at certain times.**

The human tendency to overdo things – our over-eagerness – is a defect of the self which leads to over-hastiness in action and produces three calamities. The first of them is its opposite, inaction, the reaction of the self to gain relief after excessive action. The second is lethargy, which results in sluggishness, even if it is not complete inaction. The third is failing to complete one's duties due to over-hastiness. Being barred from actions at certain times has three benefits. The first is preventing over-eagerness. If there was no restriction, the self would rush to action in an overeager manner. The second is the prevention of procrastination. If there were no specific time for actions, the *nafs* would defer them to another time and that would lead to negligence. The third is that it enables us to remain constant in them.

If actions had not been at particular times they would have become subject to our moods and desires and we would not be able to maintain them consistently. Then Shaykh ibn Ata'illah explains the reason for these time restrictions with direct reference to the prayer and says:

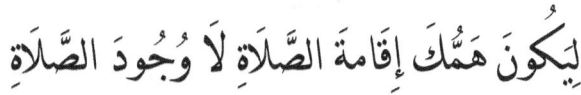

**118c: This is so that your aspiration will be to establish the prayer, not just for the prayer to be there.**

The secret in restricting the prayer to certain times is so that the *nafs* will yearn for it and take pleasure in it. Because of that it will have humility, presence and delight in it, which would not be the case if it was doing it all the time. If that were the case, it would not desire it. Indeed, it would be bored and perform it imperfectly. What is desired of you is the movement of your heart, not the movement of your body. As the hadith says: "Allah does not look at your forms or your actions. He looks at your hearts." So it is not a question of physical movement, it is about spiritual humility. The prayer is, therefore, restricted to certain times so that your concern is to establish and perfect it, both inwardly and outwardly. The mere doing of the prayer without it being established in this way means that it is dead and empty.

Imam al-Qushayri said that the establishment of the prayer certainly entails firstly the implementation of its outward pillars and *sunnas* but it is then necessary to disengage from them and devote yourself to the One to whom you are praying. Your body must be facing the *qibla* but your heart should be completely with your Lord. Shaykh ibn Ata'illah then elaborates further on why establishment of the prayer is so important, saying:

فَمَا كُلُّ مُصَلٍّ مُقِيمٌ.

## 118d: For not everyone who does the prayer establishes it.

Linguistically to "establish" (*iqama*) a thing means to perfect it and accomplish it completely. For instance, if you say "So-and-so has established his house," it means he has finished building it and put inside it everything it needs to make it completely habitable. So establishment of the prayer entails completely fulfilling both its outward and inward conditions. The opposite of establishment is to have gaps and deficiencies in execution. So not everyone who does the prayer establishes it. Many who pray get nothing but fatigue from their prayer. A hadith states, "If the prayer does not prevent someone from fornication and wrongdoing, then it has only increased them in distance from Allah." In another hadith, the Prophet  said, "Those who do the prayer are many but those who establish it are few." Shaykh Abu'l-'Abbas al-Mursi said that everywhere in the Qur'an that those who pray are mentioned in a praiseworthy way, establishment of it is always also mentioned. But when

Allah talks of those who pray with heedlessness, He says: '*Woe to those who pray and are forgetful of their prayer,*' (107:4) without mentioning its establishment.

You should know that, according to the Sufis, a prayer which is not accompanied inwardly by true humility and presence is defective and, according to scholars, it is not accepted. They say that you only have that part of your prayer in which your heart is present. The great aid to true humility is lack of attachment to this world. If you have this world – the daughter of Iblis – in your heart, her father is, of course, bound to visit her. So freedom from distracting thoughts is impossible as long as attachment to this world remains in the heart.

It's a little like having a tree in your garden where starlings congregate and endlessly pester you with their raucous twittering. You can chase them away but in no time they are back again. The only way to get rid of them is to cut down that tree. Once it's gone, the nuisance disappears. It is the same with this world. As long as you have it in your heart, you will always be plagued by it. Once you've expelled it, you will be free from its harassment, and Allah knows best. Another thing which will assist you to gain true humility in the prayer is a lot of *dhikru'llah*, both with the heart and the tongue, and also constant purity, because the outward is connected to the inward and when the outward is pure, the inward will also be pure. Success is by Allah.

# Derse 47

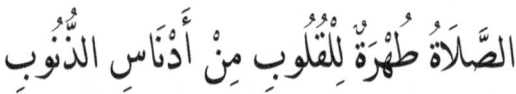

**119a: The prayer is purification for the hearts from the sins which have soiled them…**

The prayer is purification for the hearts from evils and defects through the humility, contrition, poverty, abasement and utter need inherent in it. When the heart is humbled by awe at the utter Majesty of Allah it is purified of all faults because the source and basis of all its defects is its craving for pre-eminence and high standing. An integral element in the nature of the *nafs* is a desire for height, elevation, pride, glory, and praise. It emerged from the World of Might and because of that feels entitled to honour on account of its illustrious origin. When, however, it was placed into the physical container of a body, the inexorable force of Divine Power reduced it to slavehood. However, at the same time, Allah allocated a door for it by which it would be able return to the glorious presence of Lordship from which it came. All that is needed for it to return to its radiant source is contrition and abasement. That is why Shaykh 'Abdu'l-Qadir al-Jilani said, "I went to every door and found a dense crowd at all of them. But when I went to the door of abasement and contrition I found there was no one there at all and so I entered by it. I say: 'Take the quick way to your Lord.'"

So if the *nafs* is contrite and abased, it is able to return to its source and achieve arrival. But if it is characterized by self-importance and pride, as is usually the case, it is veiled and driven away. When it is driven away, it finds itself far from Allah and when it is far from the Divine Presence physical appetites and satanic qualities become ingrained in it and it becomes the home of every base quality and estranged from every radiant quality. When, however, in His Compassion, Allah Almighty desires to show us Mercy and bring us near to His Presence, He takes us to the door He has allocated for us and inspires us to pray and makes us love the prayer. Then when, by that, we become purified from wrong actions and our evils and defects are washed away, we can draw near to the Presence of Allah and knock on the door and ask for the veil to be raised. This is what the shaykh is referring to when he continues:

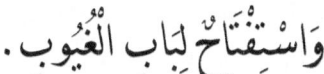

**119b: …a way of opening the door to the unseen worlds.**

This is the second fruit of the prayer. What is meant by the "unseen worlds" are the secrets of the *Malakut* and the secrets of the *Jabarut*. The prayer is a means of opening the door to the unseen worlds since it entails the purification of both the outward and inward. Muhammad ibn 'Ali at-Tirmidhi, al-Hakim, said, "Allah has summoned those who affirm His unity to these five prayers as a mercy to them and prepared for them hospitality of different kinds so that His slaves will receive gifts for every word they speak and action they make. Actions becoming delicious foods and words refreshing drinks. It is the bathing pool that the Lord of the Worlds has prepared for the people of His mercy five times every day so that no dirtiness remains on them. When the outward is purified by physical purification and the inward by spiritual purification, then the worshipper is ready to enter the Divine Presence."

So the first fruit of the prayer is purification and the second access to this door to the Unseen. On the other side of it is the conversation of the lovers beyond the veil which Shaykh ibn Ata'illah now alludes to by saying:

$$\text{الصَّلَاةُ مَحَلُّ الْمُنَاجَاةِ}$$

### 120a: Prayer is the place of intimate exchange

This is the third fruit of the prayer. *Munajat* – intimate exchange – is a term alluding to the words that lovers exchange with one another in the depths of the night. The slave's share in this intimate exchange with his Lord takes the form of the recitation and *dhikr* he addresses to Him. The Lord's share with his slave is the deep understanding, openings and removing of veils He grants to him in return. In a sound hadith we find: "The one who prays speaks intimately with his Lord." The Prophet ﷺ also said, "Allah Almighty said, 'I have divided the prayer into two halves between Me and My slave …and My slave will have what he asks for.' When the slave says, 'Praise be to Allah, the Lord of all the worlds,' Allah says, 'My slave has praised Me.' When he says, 'The All-Merciful, the Most Merciful,' the Lord says, 'My slave has lauded Me.' When the slave says, 'The King of the Day of Judgement,' Allah says, 'My slave has entrusted himself to Me.' When the slave says, 'You alone we worship. You alone we ask for help,' and Allah says, 'This is between Me and My slave.' When he says, 'Guide us on the Straight Path,' Allah says, 'This is for Me and My slave will have what He asks for.'"

In this way the one who prays continues to speak intimately with his Lord and seek His nearness until love and proximity to Allah are firmly established in his heart. So the lover is united with his Beloved in a pure place and this is expressed by Shaykh ibn Ata'illah in his words:

### 120b: …a mine of mirrored purity.

This is the fourth fruit of the prayer. A mine is the place where gold and silver are buried in the earth. It is used as a metaphor for the purity of the heart and spirit in this context because they have been purified from the blemish of any admixture with earthly materiality, meaning that this intimate conversation with Allah is free from any sensory confusion or interference. It is finer and purer than any other possible intimate exchange. As Ibn al-Farid said:

> I was alone with my Beloved, between us
> a secret finer than the softest wafting breeze.

The incomparable purity of this communication between the slave and his Lord is such that he will never want to leave Him for anything else. We read in a report: "When the slave stands for the prayer, Allah removes the veil between Himself and him and turns His face towards him." This generates a love within the being of the one who prays, a love that is so profound, so overwhelming, that it defies any attempt at description.

What is in truth being experienced is an echo emanating from that direct encounter between the Messenger of Allah ﷺ and his Lord when the prayer was first prescribed, an event we commemorate in all our prayers when we do the *tashshahud* – something issuing from the very source of all existence. O Allah make us people who are really thankful for the great gift of the prayer we have been given and who give to it the immense value it truly deserves, and O Allah, make us people who more and more come to experience something of its inner reality and taste its hidden secret.

# Derse 48

$$\text{مَتَى طَلَبْتَ عِوَضاً عَنْ عَمَلٍ، طُولِبْتَ بِوُجُودِ الصِّدْقِ فِيهِ وَيَكْفِي الْمُرِيبَ وِجْدَانُ السَّلَامَةِ.}$$

**121: When you ask for recompense for an action, true sincerity in it will be asked of you. Enough for a suspect is a real feeling of safety.**

When a good action, such as the prayer, comes from you and you ask Allah to recompense you for it, your request of Allah is dependent on your sincerity in it – that secret and core of true sincerity, which entails divesting yourself of any strength and power and self-awareness. That means ceasing to see the action as emanating from yourself at all, after having achieved presence and freedom from whispering, passing thoughts and any kind of psychic interference. Then your prayer is by Allah and for Allah and in it you withdraw from other-than-Him, your heart being immersed in the immensity of Allah's Presence. If this is the case, if this is how you really are, then you are justified in seeking the various repayments and rewards with which Allah recompenses righteous actions. If this is not the case, if this is not how you are, then know that your action is defective, and you should be too embarrassed to ask Allah to recompense you for a defective action.

In that case enough of a recompense for you, and indeed achievement of the goal you are hoping for, is security from destruction and perdition. The knowledge that you are safe from Allah's punishment and retribution should be sufficient to spare you from even thinking about any further reward. When someone is a suspect in a crime, the knowledge that they are safe from being punished for what they are suspected of is enough for them. If someone is suspected by a king and is imprisoned awaiting punishment for what he is accused of and is then told, "The King will give you such-and-such a gift," he will certainly say, "Security from his punishment is all I want from him."

We are instructed to perform actions, to be sincere in them, to do them correctly and to fulfil them completely. Then we produce acts of obedience that are filled with distracting thoughts and whisperings and, even if they are free of that, our asking for recompense inevitably involves seeing ourselves as doing them and attributing our actions to our own efforts. This is in fact a kind of hidden *shirk* that in itself merits punishment. So enough for us is that Allah gives us, through our actions, a feeling of being safe from His punishment.

Al-Wasiti said, "Worship in order to seek pardon is better than seeking reward." Khayr an-Nassaj said, "The outcome of your actions will be what is in keeping with them. So seek the legacy of Allah's bounty. It is more complete and better for you. Allah Almighty says: *'Say: "It is in the favour of Allah and His mercy that they should rejoice. That is better than anything they accumulate."'* (10:58) The meaning of his words is that the repayment for your necessarily defective actions will be what is in keeping with their inevitable imperfection and the repayment of the imperfect is bound to be imperfect. Therefore, it is far better to ask Allah for His favour. Allah's favour is perfect in every way and so it will be much more rewarding for you than anything that could possibly result from your actions. Allah knows best.

And anyway, how can you seek recompense for an action, which in reality was not yours in the first place, as the Shaykh's next words point out:

لَا تَطْلُبْ عِوَضاً عَلَى عَمَلٍ لَسْتَ لَهُ فَاعِلاً،
يَكْفِي مِنَ الْجَزَاءِ لَكَ عَلَى الْعَمَلِ أَنْ كَانَ لَهُ قَابِلاً.

### 122: Do not seek a recompense for an action of which you are not the doer. Enough recompense for the action is His acceptance of it.

It is confirmed among the people of the Truth that human beings are under the force of compulsion in a chosen container and they themselves have in reality neither action nor choice. The Doer is in every case the One, the All-Compelling. The Almighty says: *"Your Lord creates and chooses whatever He wills."* (28:68) And He says: *"Allah created you and what you do."* (37:96) And He says: *"But you *will not will unless Allah wills."* (76:30) And there are many other *ayahs* indicating the same thing. The Prophet ﷺ said, "Everything is by the decree and decision (of Allah), even lack of power and energy." He also said ﷺ, "Everyone is eased to that for which they were created. Someone who is one of the people of happiness will be eased to the actions of the people of happiness. Someone who is one of the people of wretchedness will be eased to the actions of the people of wretchedness." Then he recited: *"As for him who gives out and has taqwa and confirms the Good, We will pave his way to ease."* (92:5)

Since this is an established truth, how can we seek a recompense for an action we have in reality not done when that recompense is in fact dependent on the fact of its being ascribed to us and recompense for it is, in any case, contingent on it being accepted. How do we know whether an action has or has not been accepted? When Allah does grant us acceptance, in spite of the imperfection and defects inherent in our action, this acceptance alone is enough of a recompense for us for that action. It is only His beautiful veiling of our failings that makes any action we do worthy of acceptance. If it were not for the Pardon and Forbearance of Allah, no action would ever be accepted since, as we saw earlier, true purity of action is virtually impossible.

Allah says: *"No indeed! He has not done what He ordered him,"* (80:23), meaning that the human being has not done what his Lord commanded him to do in the manner in which He commanded him to do it. Corroborating this Allah tells us: *"Those are people the best of whose actions*

# 48

*will be accepted from them...*" (46:16). In this phrase the word used for "from" is not the usual preposition *"min"*, because that would necessarily imply that the actions were perfect and in themselves worthy of acceptance. Instead, here, Allah uses the preposition *"'an"*, which conveys the idea of overlooking something. This is made explicit in the following words when Allah continues: "*...and whose bad actions will be overlooked.*" If it had not been for that overlooking in respect of those actions, they would not have been accepted from them. The All-Generous, however, out of the vastness of His matchless Generosity and Bounty, does not apportion any blame whatsoever, but accepts from us the actions that He Himself has vouchsafed to us, despite the many defects in our performance of them. Praise be to Allah unceasingly for creating actions in us and then by them, in spite of our failings, fulfilling our highest desires and aspirations.

# Derse 49

**123: When He wants to manifest His overflowing favour to you, He creates a good action for you and then ascribes it to you.**

Allah Almighty has divided His slaves into three groups. He has made one group for His Retribution and manifested His Names the Exactor of Retribution and the All-Conquering on them. The form of disobedience is given to them by His Wisdom and is ascribed to them by His Justice and inexorable Power. Allah says: *"If your Lord had willed, they would not have done it."* (6:113) And: *"If Allah had willed, they would not have attributed partners to Him."* (6:108) So the proof against them is established in respect of ascription and the manifestation of Wisdom, as Allah makes clear in His words: *"Your Lord does not wrong His slaves."* (41:45) And: *"We did not wrong them; rather they wronged themselves."* (16:118) and many other similar *ayahs*.

Allah has made another group for His Forbearance in order to manifest on them His Names, the All-Forbearing and the

Most Merciful. They have their share of disobedience but then He adorns them with belief. They merit punishment for their disobedience but then Allah shows forbearance to them, pardons them, and admits them to the Garden.

He has made a third group for His Generosity in order to manifest on them His Names, the Generous and the Most Merciful. He created obedience and benevolence in them and adorned them with Islam and *iman*, sometimes adding to them the excellence of *ihsan*. He will admit them to vast Gardens and allow them to enjoy the vision of the Face of the All-Merciful. When Allah desires someone to join this company, He opens the way for them to different acts of obedience and creates in them the capacity to do good deeds. Then He ascribes those actions to them. He says, "My slave, you did such-and-such good and I will repay you for it. Enter the Garden by My permission and rise to your station by your actions. Your station will be according to the extent of your actions." Allah says: *"Enter the Garden for what you did."* (16:32)

The Prophet ﷺ said, "Everyone is eased to that for which they were created. Someone who is one of the people of happiness will be eased to the actions of the people of happiness. Someone who is one of the people of wretchedness will be eased to the actions of the people of wretchedness." Then he recited: *"As for him who gives out and has taqwa and confirms the Good, We will pave his way to ease."* (92:5) So it is vital for us to show correct *adab* towards Allah, the King and Judge, and not ascribe any of our imperfections or disobedience to Him. It is our *nafs* or *shaytan* that has made us err. As He says in two places: *"So do not let the life of this world delude you and do not let the Deluder delude you concerning Allah."* (31:32; 35:5) This means *shaytan*. So attribute any imperfection to the *nafs* and *shaytan*.

Nor should we ascribe our acts of obedience to ourselves. Sahl ibn 'Abdullah said, "When someone performs a good action and says, 'O Lord, I have been made to act by Your bounty and You have helped me and made it easy for me,' they thereby thank Allah for it and attribute it to Him and Allah says, 'No, rather you obeyed and therefore drew near.' If he looks at himself, however, and says, 'I acted, obeyed and because of that drew near,' Allah turns from him and says, 'No, I gave you success, helped you and made it easy for you.' When someone commits an evil action and says, 'O Lord, you decreed it for me and determined what I did,' then Allah becomes angry and says, 'No, it was you who did wrong, acted ignorantly and rebelled.' When he says, 'O Lord, I did wrong, I acted badly, and I acted ignorantly,' Allah turns to him and says, 'No, I decreed and determined it, and I have forgiven you, showed forbearance for it and veiled it.'" So this ascription of action to us by Allah makes us subject to either praise or blame as Shaykh Ibn Ata'illah elucidates in his next sentence:

لَا نِهَايَةَ لِمَذَامِّكَ إِنْ أَرْجَعَكَ إِلَيْكَ،

وَلَا تَفْرُغُ مَدَائِحُكَ إِنْ أَظْهَرَ جُودَهُ عَلَيْكَ.

## 124: There is no end of reasons to blame you if He sends you back to yourself. There is no end of reasons to praise you if He manifests His generosity on you.

When Allah wants to humiliate and abase someone, He returns them to their *nafs* and lower desires and delivers them up to them to them and hands them over to what they are turning to. Allah tells us: *"But if anyone opposes the Messenger after the guidance has become clear to him, and follows other than the path of the believers, We will hand him over to whatever he has turned to, and We will roast him in Hell. What an evil destination!"* (4:114) When someone's lower desires overcome them, it makes them deaf and blind to the dangers of the terrible downfall that brings in its wake. As the poet says:

> Do not follow the *nafs* in its lower desires.
> Following them brings terrible abasement with it.

When, on the other hand, Allah wants to exalt someone and show concern for them, He manifests His Generosity and Benevolence on them and takes care of them, protects them, and does not abandon them to their *nafs* and lower desires.

So there is no end to your blameworthiness if He returns you to your *nafs*, gives it authority over you, and abandons you to your lower desires. That is a sign of disfavour from Allah. We seek refuge with Allah from every loss and bad influence! And there is no end to your praiseworthiness if His Generosity is manifest on you and He protects you, shows His concern for you, isolates you from your *nafs* and comes between you and your management and speculation. The Prophet ﷺ said in one of his *du'as*: "If You leave me to myself, You leave me to weakness and exposure, wrong action and error. I put my trust in Your mercy alone."

In short, if you act by your Lord, He will take charge of your affair and there will be no end of reasons to praise you but if you act by your *nafs* and your own desires, you will be abandoned to them and there will be no end of reasons to blame you. That is because this world is simply a manifestation of the Names and Attributes of Allah. If He abandons someone to their *nafs*, He is manifesting His Majesty on them. If He does the opposite of that, He is manifesting His Beauty on them. And just as there is no end to His Majesty so also there is no end to His Beauty, and Allah knows best.

# Derse 50

$$\text{كَيْفَ تُخْرَقُ لَكَ الْعَوَائِدُ}$$
$$\text{وَأَنْتَ لَمْ تَخْرِقْ مِنْ نَفْسِكَ الْعَوَائِدَ.}$$

**127: How can normal patterns be broken for you when you have not broken the normal patterns in yourself?**

"Normal patterns" are what the *nafs*, the lower self, is used to and familiar with and with which it persists until it becomes difficult for it to break with them, whether they are dark ones or luminous ones, such as pursuing virtues and doing a lot of *nawafil*. There are two categories of pattern. There are outward physical ones and inward spiritual ones. The outward physical patterns are such things as eating and drinking too much, sleeping to excess, being over-concerned with clothing, socialising with people too much, putting faith in secondary means, engaging in a lot of talking and argumentation, criticising others, and also things like overindulging in physical acts of worship or book-knowledge and the like. Adverse inward spiritual patterns are things like love of rank and leadership, seeking elevation, love of this world and being praised, and also envy, pride, arrogance, showing-off, coveting creation, fear of poverty, worry about provision, coarseness, hardness of heart and other things which have been discussed previously.

If someone breaks these ingrained patterns of their *nafs*, the normal patterns of human experience will also be broken for them. All the things that normally stand between them and direct knowledge of their Lord will be cleared away and they will rise to the station of *ihsan*. So any aspiration we have to advance on the path of Allah is dependent on our breaking the habitual patterns of our *nafs* and if we have not broken these embedded patterns our hopes of advancing on the path, of growing in true knowledge of our *deen*, are in fact just wishful thinking.

We already mentioned the story of the man who accompanied Abu Yazid for thirty years without tasting any spiritual enlightenment. Abu Yazid told him, "Even if you prayed for three hundred years, you would not taste anything because you are veiled by your *nafs*." When the man asked him what he could do about this, the shaykh said to him, "Go immediately to the barber and shave your hair and beard off. Remove these fine clothes and put on a coarse woollen robe. Hang a nosebag round your neck and fill it with sweets. Then gather some children around you and say in your loudest voice, 'Children! I will give a sweet to whoever gives me a slap!' Then go like this into the market where you are known and respected until everyone who knows you has had a good look at you." When the man said this would be impossible for him, Abu Yazid told him,

"No one will have any access to the secrets of the Unseen, which are veiled from ordinary people, until they kill their *nafs* and break its natural patterning. If, and only if you do that, great blessings will open themselves up to you."

No one still subject to the embedded patterns of their *nafs* can expect to enjoy the presence of purity. Shaykh Abu'l-Mawahib said, "If someone claims to witness Beauty before disciplining himself with Majesty, reject him. He is a charlatan." There is no Majesty more difficult for the *nafs* than breaking its patterns. That might include exchanging might for abasement, wealth for poverty, rank for obscurity, and so forth. Abu'l-Hasan said, "O Allah, You have decided on abasement for the People so that they may become mighty and You have decided on loss for them so that they find gain. No one can have might by Allah until they have tasted abasement to Him, nor can they have wealth by Him until they have turned away from other than Him." Abu Hamza al-Baghdadi said, "The sign of the truthful Sufi is that he becomes poor after wealth, abased after might, and obscure after having fame." All these reports indicate that the breaking of the normal patterns of the *nafs* is a precondition for gaining true knowledge. If anyone claims to have it before he breaks them, he is a liar, as was stated by Shaykh Abu'l-Mawahib.

The breaking of patterns entails replacing them with their opposites, like replacing a lot of food and sleep with hunger and sleeplessness, and replacing a lot of fine clothing with a little of it or with coarse clothing, and like exchanging excessive socialising with retreat, overdependence on secondary means with *zuhd*, speech with silence and bad character with good character, exchanging love of rank and leadership for abasement, desire for reputation for loss of position in people's eyes, love of this world for abstinence in it and turning from it. In order for this to happen, for these inward patterns to be broken, you must have a perfect shaykh who joins the *haqiqa* and the *shari'a* and drives you forward by his *himma*. Then when you turn your hand to your *nafs* – moved by *himma* and helped by Power – you eradicate it completely. But if you have no shaykh, every time you quash it, it comes back larger than it was before. As our shaykh, Moulay al-'Arabi said, "A living *nafs* only dies at the hands of someone whose *nafs* is already dead."

# Derse 51

**131: If it were not for the beauty of His veiling, no action would be worthy of acceptance.**

In order for an action to be "worthy of acceptance" it must meet the conditions of acceptance. They are: absolute sincerity, complete presence, and true realisation of one's utter incapacity. This is extremely rare. So if Allah did not cover us with the beauty of His veiling and conceal our bad qualities with His overwhelming kindness and gentleness, no action we did would ever be worthy of acceptance. But the One Who grants us the gift of good actions also bestows on us the gift of acceptance. One of the people of Allah said, "There is only His favour, and we only live in His veiling. If the cover were removed, a calamitous state of affairs would be disclosed." Substantiating this, Allah says: *"Those are people whose best deeds We will accept from them,"* (46:16) The word used here for 'from' is *'an* rather than *min*. That conveys the sense of overlooking not just reception. It is as if Allah were saying, "Those are people whose actions We are indulgent about and so accept from them," and Allah knows best.

It is related that the Messenger of Allah ﷺ said, "Affliction, lower desires and appetites were baked into the clay of Adam." That is the meaning of the words of the Almighty: *"We created man from a mingled drop to test him,"* (76:2). Affliction, lower desires and appetites are mixed into the human form and cling to us as long as our physical structure and humanity persist. This means our actions are inevitably defective and would not be worthy of acceptance were it not for the beauty of Allah's veiling of their defects. For this reason we are more in need of Allah's generosity and pardon when we obey Him than when we disobey him, as the Shaykh goes on to say next.

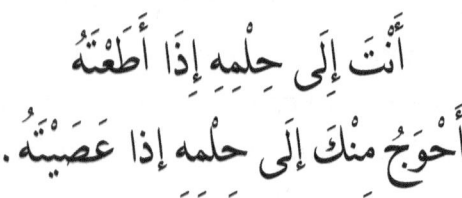

### 132: You are more in need of His forbearance when you obey Him than when you disobey Him.

That is because obedience is the carpet of light and elevation and so the *nafs* has desire for it and pleasure in it, and because people notice the one who has outward obedience and look at him with the eye of esteem and set out to serve and honour him. Whenever someone is elevated in the eyes of other people, they fall in Allah's eyes if they rejoice in that and are happy with it. That is not the case with disobedience, which is the carpet of abasement and contrition and incurs other people's contempt. Whoever diminishes in the eyes of creation becomes greater in the eyes of Allah. That is why when someone obeys his Lord, they are more in need of His forbearance and pardon than when they disobey Him, because obedience which brings about a feeling of self-importance and arrogance is far uglier than disobedience which brings about abasement and need.

In reality, of course, such obedience is not obedience at all because acts of obedience that distance you from Allah are not really obedience and disobedience which brings you closer to Him is not really disobedience. We read in a *hadith* that Allah Almighty says, "I am with those who have contrite hearts for My sake." And someone who has Allah with Him is far better than a thousand whose apparent obedience alienates them from Him. Shaykh Abu Yazid said, "Repentance for disobedience need only be done once but repentance for obedience must be done a thousand times." Returning to our need for veiling, Shaykh Ibn Ata'illah then says:

السَّتْرُ عَلَى قِسْمَيْنِ: سَتْرٌ عَنِ الْمَعْصِيَةِ، وَسَتْرٌ فِيهَا؛ فَالْعَامَّةُ يَطْلُبُونَ مِنَ اللَّهِ تَعَالَى السَّتْرَ فِيهَا خَشْيَةَ سُقُوطِ مَرْتَبَتِهِمْ عِنْدَ الْخَلْقِ، وَالْخَاصَّةُ يَطْلُبُونَ السَّتْرَ عَنْهَا خَشْيَةَ سُقُوطِهِمْ مِن نَظَرِ الْمَلِكِ الْحَقِّ.

**133: There are two sorts of veiling:
veiling from disobedience and veiling in it.
Common people seek the veil from Allah in it,
since they fear loss of rank in other people's sight.
The elite seek to be veiled from it,
since they fear they may fall from
the sight of Allah, the King, the Real.**

In relation to disobedience, Allah's veiling is of two kinds. One is when people seek to be veiled in their disobedience so as not to be disgraced by it. The other is when people seek to be veiled from it so as not to fall into it. So the common people seek to be veiled by Allah in their disobedience when it occurs so that they do not lose status in other people's eyes. They want to hide it from other people but not from Allah Who is always with them. It would be more fitting for them to pay greater heed to Allah and His Messenger if they are believers. However, they mind what other creatures see more than they mind what their Creator sees. That is due to the weakness of their faith, lack of certainty and the dullness of their insight. In one report Allah Almighty says, "My slave, if you do not know that I see you, your faith is defective. If you do know that I see you, do not then make Me the least of those who look at you."

As for the elite, they ask Allah to veil them from disobedience and protect them from it, fearing that they will fall from the sight of their Lord because disobedience on the part of a *faqir* is bad *adab* and if someone has bad *adab* with the lovers, they will be shown the door. If they do happen to disobey, they hasten to apologise, and show embarrassment and contrition. So they are serious in pursuing the Path and do not stop with themselves since, in their view, their selves have no real existence. Nor do they turn to creation since they only have eyes for the Creator. They withdraw from seeing the sensory by witnessing the meaning and from seeing creation by witnessing the Creator.

As for the elite of the elite, they do not seek anything or fear anything. All things with them are one thing and by their unified vision they are spared everything else. They see everything as emerging from the realm of Allah's Power and so they meet it with acceptance and pleasure. If it is obedience, they witness the blessing in it. If any disobedience should occur, they witness the element of force in it. They show *adab* with Allah in it by repentance, contrition, and establishing the *shari'a* of Allah and the *Sunna* of His Prophet ﷺ.

# Derse 52

مَنْ أَكْرَمَكَ إِنَّمَا أَكْرَمَ فِيكَ جَمِيلَ سَتْرِهِ،
فَالْحَمْدُ لِمَنْ سَتَرَكَ لَيْسَ الْحَمْدُ لِمَنْ أَكْرَمَكَ وَشَكَرَكَ.

**134: Anyone who honours you**
**only honours the beauty of His veil in you.**
**Praise is due to the One Who veiled you!**
**Not to the one who honoured you and thanked you!**

When Allah Almighty undertakes to preserve you by His concern for you and veils your bad qualities with the veil of His concern, He covers your quality with His quality and your attribute with His attribute. So when people turn to you with respect, esteem and admiration, they are, in fact, recognising Allah's favour to you, not seeing qualities belonging to you. Anyone who honours you, is in fact honouring the beauty of Allah's veiling in you. As He says in *Sura an-Nisa'*: "*If it were not for Allah's favour to you and His mercy, all but a very few of you would have followed Shaytan.*" (4:83) And again in *Sura an-Nur*: "*Were it not for Allah's favour to you and His mercy, not one of you would ever have been purified.*" (24:21)

So praise in reality only belongs to the One Who has veiled you, not to the one who has honoured you, since if any of your evil qualities had appeared to people, they would have disliked and despised you. Therefore, thank Allah for the generosity He has shown to you by veiling over your evil qualities which would otherwise provoke all kinds of insult and retaliation. Shaykh Zarruq said, "Were it not that He veiled me from acts of disobedience, I would not have obeyed Him. Were it not that He veiled me in my acts of disobedience, I would have been humiliated and singled out for dislike. Were it not for the blessing of my Lord, I would be among those who are summoned for punishment. So all people interact with one another, protected by their Lord's veiling of them. If He were to remove His veil from them, those who love them most would hate them, those kindest to them would harm them, and those who are gentlest with them would destroy them." How excellent is what the poet said:

> They think well of me but there is no good in me.
> I am a wrongdoing slave as You know.
> You have concealed all my faults from their eyes
> and clothed me in a beautiful garment of concealment,
> And so they began to love me and I am loved,
> but they have confused me with another.
> Do not disgrace me among them on the Day of Rising.
> Be for me, my Lord, in the Place of Gathering.

When you realise that the One Who honours you is in reality the One Who has veiled your faults and covered over your hidden bad qualities, even though He is totally aware of them, you should take Him to be your Companion, as the Shaykh goes on to say next:

$$\text{مَا صَحِبَكَ إِلَّا مَنْ صَحِبَكَ وَهُوَ بِعَيْبِكَ عَلِيمٌ،}$$
$$\text{وَلَيْسَ ذَلِكَ إِلَّا مَوْلَاكَ الْكَرِيمُ.}$$

### 135a: Your only true companion is the One Who keeps your company in full knowledge of your faults, and that is none other than your Generous Lord.

When you know that in reality your true Companion is your Lord, then you must recognise the reality of that company and maintain your *adab* towards Him outwardly and inwardly. You should be ashamed of Him seeing you anywhere He has forbidden you to be or not seeing you somewhere He has ordered you to be. In *hadith*, the Prophet ﷺ said, "Show proper modesty before Allah." Those with him said, "We are modest, *alhamdulillah*." He told them, "True modesty before Allah is that you guard your head and what is inside it and your belly and what it contains and that you remember the grave and its punishment. Whoever does that is showing true modesty before Allah."

Taking Allah, the One Who knows all your faults, as a companion in this way makes you safe from imposture, showing off and pretence because you know there is no point in trying to deceive the One Who always knows both your secrets and what you make public. Yet if you disobey Him, He veils you and if you apologise to Him, He accepts your excuse. It has been said that one aspect of the good news for the believers in the *ayah* in *Sura at-Tawba*: "Allah has bought from the believers their selves and their wealth in return for the Garden," (9:112) is that of their selves not being returned on account of their defectiveness, since, in this case, the buyer has prior awareness of it!

Know that there are two invaluable aspects of the love and friendship that characterise true companionship. One of them is the forbearance of your companion in disregarding your failings and flaws and the second is their love for you and desire for your presence without wanting anything from you. So Shaykh Ibn Ata'illah then says:

خَيْرُ مَنْ تَصْحَبُ مَنْ يَطْلُبُكَ لَكَ لَا لِشَيْءٍ يَعُودُ مِنْكَ إِلَيْهِ .

### 135b: The best companion is the One Who seeks you without wanting anything that comes from you to Him.

The only One this truly applies to is the Rich-beyond-need, the Praiseworthy, the One Who does what He wills and loves whomever He wills without reason or cause. He brings near whomever He wishes and distances from Himself whomever He wishes. He says: *"He will not be questioned about what He does, but they will be questioned."* (21:23) And: *"If your Lord had willed, they would not have done it."* (6:113) And: *"If Allah had wished, He could have guided all mankind."* (13:31)

It is clear then that the best companion is your Lord who seeks you for His presence and selects you for His love without any benefit accruing to Him from you. It is simply kindness and goodness from Him to you. So how could you leave Him and seek intimacy with someone else who is more likely to harm you than benefit you? One of the people of Allah said, "Put most people to the test and you will find them to be scorpions. When you seek company, then seek the company of people whose state elevates you and whose words direct you to Allah."

And the company of someone who connects you with Allah is, in reality, the company of Allah since there is nothing other than Him. Someone with direct knowledge of Allah has become a pure light from the light of Allah. The Prophet ﷺ said, "Allah has men such that whoever looks at them is happy with a happiness after which He will never be wretched." They exist and will never be cut off. They are manifest as the sun is manifest and are not hidden except from those for whom Allah desires expulsion and distance. May Allah bring us into such company and keep us there. And we seek refuge with Allah from being stripped after receiving, from an evil decree, from the gloating of our enemies, from debilitating illness, from the disappointment of our hopes and from the removal of blessings. Amin.

# Derse 53

النَّاسُ يَمْدَحُونَكَ لِمَا يَظُنُّونَهُ فِيكَ،
فَكُنْ أَنْتَ ذَامّاً لِنَفْسِكَ لِمَا تَعْلَمُهُ مِنْهَا.

**142: People praise you because of
what they suppose is in you,
but you must blame your self
because of what you know of it.**

When people praise you for something you know you do not possess, know that those are in fact voices originating from the Divine Reality urging you to improve your state. They are telling you not to be pleased with what you hear and not to rely on what is being said. Censure your self and do not be deluded by other people's praise. They only know what you outwardly show whereas you know the truth of your inward reality. One of the people of Allah said, "If someone delights in people's praise of them, that gives *shaytan* an open doorway into them." Another said, "O Allah, do not punish me for what they say and forgive me for the things they do not know."

It is clear that words of praise from people must emanate from the Divine since, in reality, there is nothing in existence except Allah. So the people of understanding of Allah listen to what is being said to them and if they hear praise, they look inside themselves. If they have what they are being praised for, they know they are being told to thank Allah for granting it to them. If they do not have it in them, they know that they are being told to make themselves worthy of it. This is why when Abu Hanifa heard people praising him for praying the entire night when he only prayed half of it, he began to pray the entire night.

Allah sharply reprimands those who like being praised for something they have not done. He says: *"They love to be praised for what they have not done. Do not suppose them to have escaped the punishment."* (3:188) Al-Muhasibi said, "The person who delights in undeserved praise is like someone who pretends to be sweet smelling when in reality they smell like a pile of dung." For this reason Shaykh Ibn Ata'illah then goes on to say in his next sentence:

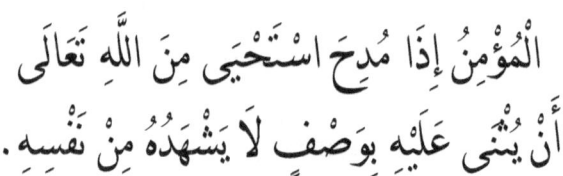

### 143: When the believer is praised, he is ashamed before Allah to be praised for a quality he does not see in himself.

It is confirmed that all good action is only the result of a prior decree. So part of Allah's complete blessing to you is that good is created for you and then ascribed to you. When praise is applied to you for something, then be modest before Him on account of being praised for something you know comes from other than yourself or because the praise is completely undeserved and is for something that has no basis in yourself at all. Then you must ask Allah for strength to increase in what will make you truly pleasing to Him. *"Your Lord is the Doer what He wills."* (11:107) Being praised for what you have not done will not harm you so long as you realise that Allah and not you is the only one actually worthy of praise. If someone is praised for what he does not have and is deluded by that, he is ignorant of his Lord, as Shaykh Ibn Ata'illah then indicates:

أَجْهَلُ النَّاسِ مَنْ تَرَكَ يَقِينَ مَا عِنْدَهُ لِظَنِّ مَا عِنْدَ النَّاسِ.

## 144: The most ignorant of people is someone who leaves something he is certain about for other people's opinion.

What we are certain of is our knowledge of our bad qualities and hidden faults and the imperfections and shortcomings that we have. What people see is the good qualities and lights of obedience that appear outwardly, not seeing the hidden faults and selfish desires that accompany them inwardly, and so they praise them. If people are content with that and rejoice in what they say, then they are the most ignorant and foolish of people, being satisfied with the good opinion of creatures and not fearing the displeasure of the Creator. The reverse of this is desired for the *faqir*. He should be contracted when praised and expanded when censured until they are the same for him. This is when the person praising them is one of the people of the *deen* and good. When it is someone ignorant or impious, there is no stupidity greater than being pleased with their praise and rejoicing in it.

It is related from one of the people of Allah that one of the common people praised him and he wept. His student said to him, "Are you weeping when you have been praised?" He told him, "He did not praise me until some of my character was in keeping with his character. That is why I wept." Yahya ibn Mu'adh said, "Evil people's attestation of your integrity a defect for you and their love for you is fault for you." Another was told that the common people praised him and he showed great dislike of it. He said, "Perhaps they saw something in me which they liked. There is no good in what they like and they harm me."

So the *faqir* should conceal his good qualities and acts for which he might be praised and display permissible behaviour that is likely to lower him in other people's eyes. The shaykh of our shaykhs, Moulay al-'Arabi, said, "The *faqir* should not have a reputation greater than that of his foot." You should have outward majesty and inward beauty and whatever majesty you display outwardly should be equalled by the amount of beauty entering you inwardly. Outward adornment ruins the inward whereas the ruin of the outward adorns the inward. So the flourishing of the inward is commensurate with what you ruin outwardly, and ruin in the inward is commensurate with how you make the outward flourish. How excellent is what Shaykh al-Majdhub said about the ignorant:

> They agree to abandon the *deen*
> and cling stubbornly to wealth and clothes.
> They wash their outer garments
> and leave their hearts empty.

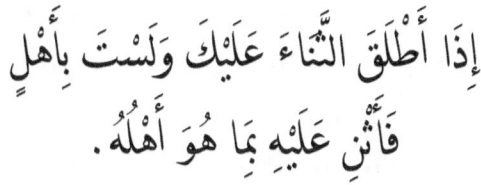

### 145: When He lets you be praised and you are not worthy of it, praise Him because He is worthy of it.

When Allah lets you be praised on the tongues on His creatures for what you do not know in yourself and you are not worthy of, then praise Allah as He truly does deserve to be praised. That is to thank Him for the blessing of allowing the tongues of others to praise you. He is the One Who concealed your evil qualities from them and showed them your good qualities. If He had showed an atom's weight of your bad qualities, they would hate and abhor you. The slave is the locus of all imperfection and the Real is the locus of all perfection. So any aspect of perfection which may appear is filtered from His perfection. All praise in reality belongs to Allah. When it comes to you, return it to its true Source. In reality, it is only directed to its Source, but when the objective differs the judgement differs. One of the masters was praised and was silent. He was asked about that and said, "I do not have any of that. I do not err about myself. I am in separation. The One Who makes things happen and transpire is Allah alone." Some of the people of Allah claim separation when they hear praise and cast dust on their heads in retreat.

In the matter of praise and blame people fall into three categories. One group rejoice in praise and dislike blame because their selves dominate them. There is no doubt that they delight in might and elevation and are constricted by blame and abasement. They are the negligent common people. Another group dislike praise and love blame because they are striving against themselves. So they welcome all that pains and kills their *nafs*, and they flee from all that revives them and strengthens them. They are the worshippers, ascetics and the travelling murids. The third group delight in praise since they witness it as coming from their Lord and are contracted at blame since through it they witness the Majesty of the One Who attends to them. They are the *'arifin*.

# Derse 54

إِذَا وَقَعَ مِنْكَ ذَنْبٌ فَلَا يَكُنْ سَبَبًا لِيَأْسِكَ مِنْ حُصُولِ الاِسْتِقَامَةِ مَعَ رَبِّكَ، فَقَدْ يَكُونُ ذَلِكَ آخِرَ ذَنْبٍ قُدِّرَ عَلَيْكَ.

**148: When a wrong action issues from you, don't let that be the cause of your despairing of putting things right with your Lord. It might well be the last wrong action decreed for you.**

The truthful wayfarer travels like a cavalryman on the attack. He goes so swiftly that he almost flies. When he has a tumble or fall, or a stumble or misstep, he gets back up on his steed and continues on his forward charge, heading for his goal. However if, when he falls, he starts to dwell on his fall, making him reluctant to get up and go on, that puts him in grave danger of failing to reach his goal. So, *faqir*, when a wrong action comes from you, do not let it be reason for your being cut off from Allah or despairing of going straight with Him; that will just multiply the evil effects of what you have done. Then your disobedience and wrongdoing will overwhelm you. Wrong action can and should act as a kind of mercy to you and serve as notification to you of your need to improve your situation. So when you fall over, get up and when you've got up, go on. It might be the last wrong action Allah has decreed for you.

Reflect on what happened with many of the *awliya* who started out as thieves and villains and then became great men of Allah, such as al-Fudayl, Abu Ya'za and many others. We have an excellent example in them of the benefit of having a good opinion of Allah. Allah says: *"Say: 'O My slaves who have transgressed against yourselves do not despair of the mercy of Allah…'"* (39:53) and He says: *"Who despairs of the mercy of his Lord except for misguided people?"* (15:56) and He also says: *"No one despairs of solace from Allah exception for people who are unbelievers."* (12:87) The Messenger of Allah ﷺ said, "Every son of Adam makes mistakes, and the best of those who make mistakes are those who repent." Allah says: *"Allah loves those who turn back from wrongdoing and He loves those who purify themselves."* (2:220) These *ayahs* bolster hope and encourage moderation and correctness. Then Shaykh Ibn Ata'illah explains the basis of hope and fear and their source with his words:

إِذَا أَرَدْتَ أَنْ يَفْتَحَ لَكَ بَابَ الرَّجَاءِ فَاشْهَدْ مَا مِنْهُ إِلَيْكَ،

وَإِذَا أَرَدْتَ أَنْ يَفْتَحَ لَكَ بَابَ الْخَوْفِ فَاشْهَدْ مَا مِنْكَ إِلَيْهِ.

## 149: If you want the door of hope to open for you look at what comes from Him to you.
## If you want the door of sorrow to open for you look at what goes from you to Him.

If you want to increase your hope in the All-Gracious, All-Generous, just look at the goodness, kindness, gentleness, and favour that flows continually from Him to you. Has He accustomed you to anything but His favour? Has He given you anything but good? He has expanded His grace to you and prepared His Garden for you. He has blessed you in this abode with the complete blessing of His guidance and has prepared for you timeless, endless delight in the Abode of Peace and, on top of that, He has given you the promise of the supreme vision of His Glorious Face.

But if you want to have the door of sorrow and fear to open up for you, you need only look at the shortcomings, failures, acts of self-indulgence and heedlessness that go from you to Him. If that is what you are looking at, your sorrow will inevitably continue and your fear increase. It might well even become the cause of your developing a bad opinion of your Lord and then your foot might slip from the right path after having been firmly planted on it.

The Prophet ﷺ said, "By the One in whose hand my life is, if you had not been people prone to wrong action, Allah would have removed you and brought other people who did commit wrong actions and ask for the forgiveness of Allah Almighty so that He could forgive them. He is the All-Pardoning, Most Merciful." This hadith indicates that it is better in the sight of Allah for people to look to His generosity and forgiveness than to anticipate His retribution and punishment.

There is nothing better than two qualities: good opinion of Allah and good opinion of the slaves of Allah. There is nothing worse than two other qualities: bad opinion of Allah and bad opinion of the slaves of Allah, as it states in hadith. There remains a higher third possibility, which is withdrawing from experiencing either hope and fear by witnessing what comes directly from Allah. That is the station of the people of witnessing. That is why they achieve balance in all their states. May Allah benefit us by them. Amin.

The fruit and result of hope is expansion. The fruit and result of fear is contraction. That is why the shaykh next says:

رُبَّمَا أَفَادَكَ فِي لَيْلِ الْقَبْضِ مَا لَمْ تَسْتَفِدْهُ فِي إِشْرَاقِ نَهَارِ الْبَسْطِ ﴿ لاَ تَدْرُونَ أَيُّهُمْ أَقْرَبُ لَكُمْ نَفْعاً ﴾ .

### 150: He might teach you during the night of contraction what you did not learn in the luminosity of the day of expansion.
### "You do not know which of them is of more benefit to you."

Contraction and expansion are states which alternate for a person, like the alternation of night and day. The

## 54

*nafs* has no share in contraction whereas the *nafs* does have a share in expansion. What the *nafs* has no share in is more conducive to safety and likely to be of greater benefit. Contraction is like the night, and the night is the time of intimate conversation, true friendship, lovers meetings and removal of the veil. He might teach you in a night of contraction, of confinement of the self, of sensory deprivation and of constriction things you do not learn in the day of expansion through gaining knowledge, doing lots of *'ibada*, and generally feeling good about yourself. Contraction has benefits and expansion has benefits. The slave does not know which of them will profit him more. We must be happy with whatever Allah directs towards us and face it with acceptance and *adab*.

So do not seek expansion when He confronts with contraction, and do not seek contraction when He confronts you with expansion. You might learn from one of them what you cannot learn from the other. You do not know which of them is more beneficial or more harmful to you. The evidence for that is the *ayah* which was revealed about the inheritance of the father in relation to that of the son: *"With regard to your fathers and your sons, you do not know which of them is going to benefit you more."* (4:11) Expansion is like the father because it comes from witnessing what comes from Allah to you and that is the act of Allah which is the source of existence. Contraction is like the son because it comes from witnessing what goes from you to Him and is therefore contingent and dependent. Our ignorance of which one – contraction or expansion – is more beneficial to us, is analogous to our ignorance of whether fathers or sons are of more benefit to us.

The essential thing is to obey Allah by concentrating on doing what is pleasing to Him and unhesitatingly accepting the condition in which he places us, without rebelling against it or thinking something different would be better for us. If we truly succeed in doing that our hearts will be illuminated, our secrets and inner core purified, and the veils and coverings removed from us, opening us up to the lights and secrets we sing about during nights of dhikr and long to experience for ourselves.

# Derse 55

$$\text{مَطَالِعُ الأَنْوَارِ الْقُلُوبُ وَالأَسْرَارُ.}$$

## 151: The rising-places of lights are the hearts and secrets

"Rising-places" are the points on the horizon where the sun and other heavenly bodies rise. "Lights" here refer to the *waridat* and unveilings which remove the veils that cover the normal manifestation of created beings. We have already mentioned that, according to many Sufis, the lower self (*nafs*), intellect (*'aql*), heart (*qalb*), spirit (*ruh*) and secret (*sirr*) are one thing. So there is in reality nothing but the spirit which changes its state according to its purification and the stages of development it passes through.

As long as it is only preoccupied with its worldly portions and appetites, it is called "lower self" and its light is eclipsed. When it is kept in check and hobbled with the hobble of the *shari'a*, although it still inclines to acts of disobedience and wrong actions, it repents after its disobedience and in that stage takes the name of "intellect". Its light is faint because it is still confined inside the prison of created being and fettered by intellectual proofs and evidence. When it desists from acts of disobedience, moving between distraction and wakefulness and concern about obedience and disobedience, it is called "heart". At that point it becomes open to the first of the rising of inward lights and the lights of turning towards Allah begin to shine on it.

The *waridat*, which are the lights of turning, continue to fluctuate on it until it begins to truly rely on Allah and find tranquillity in the remembrance of Allah. Then it is called "spirit" and experiences the first rising of the light of direct encounter with the Real. This leads to the removal of the veil and the opening of the door allowing it to enter into the Presence of the lovers. When it is completely purified of the darkness of the sensory and cleansed from the impurity of everything other-than-Allah, it is called the "secret" and experiences the first rising of the lights of direct witnessing of the Divine Presence. As for rising ixn knowledges and the fruits direct vision, there is no end to them ever.

In short, as long as individuals remain confined within the ambit of the lower self and intellect, they are dominated by darkness because in that state they are submerged in the senses and annihilated in darkness and retrogression. So they do not have any lights rise for them because they fail to turn to their Ever-Generous, Ever-Forgiving Creator. As for the heart, spirit, and secret, they are the places where lights do rise: the heart being where the first lights of turning rise, and the spirit and the secret being where the lights of direct encounter with Allah have their rising place. Then Shaykh Ibn Ata'illah makes clear the source of this light, which rises in the heart and then shines on the spirit and then the secret. He says:

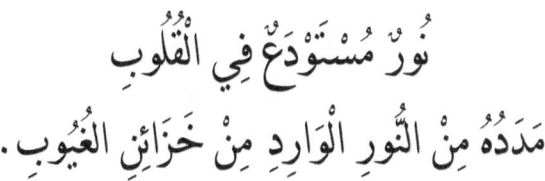

## 152: There is a light lodged in the heart – it is aided by the light emanating from the treasuries of the Unseen Worlds.

The "light lodged in the heart" is the light of certainty. It is weak at first, like the light of the stars, and is the light of Islam. Then it increases in strength, fed by the light coming from the "treasuries of the Unseen Worlds", until it becomes like the light of the moon. It is then the light of *iman*. It continues to grow brighter and brighter through obedience, *dhikr* and good company until it is like the light of the sun. It is then the light of *ihsan*. The treasuries of the Unseen Worlds referred to are the lights of the Divine Attributes and the secrets of the Divine Essence. They are what help to increase the lights of Islam and the lights of *iman*, and then the lights of *ihsan* shine out and overwhelm the existence of created beings.

Know that in the technical usage of the Sufis there is a reason why the three elements of the *deen* are placed in this order: first Islam, then *iman*, then *ihsan*. So long as a person's actions are restricted to the outward sensory world, they are said to be occupying the station of Islam. When their zone of action becomes the heart and they start to purify it, divest it of attachment to this world, adorn it with good qualities and fill it with sincerity, the person concerned is said to be occupying the station of *iman*. When their zone of action is the spirit and the secret, in which case it takes the form of reflection and contemplative vision, the person concerned is said to be occupying the station of *ihsan*. This is not the same order the *fuqaha* give them. They put *iman* before Islam, and say that nothing can be valid without it.

One of those who achieved realisation said, "Know that the realm of the *mulk*, which is the visible world, is the domain of outward lights whereas the realm of the *malakut*, which is the world of the Unseen, is the domain of inward lights. The best known lights in the realm of the *mulk* are three: the light of the sun, the light of the moon, and the lights of the stars. Their equivalents in the world of the *malakut* are the light of direct vision, the light of understanding and the light of knowledge. When the star of knowledge rises in the night of ignorance, the Next World and unseen matters appear. When the moon of understanding rises on the horizon of *tawhid*, the nearness of the Real becomes apparent. When the sun of direct vision rises on the horizon of absolute singularity (*tafrid*), certainty is strengthened and the Face of witnessing shines forth. The first light that penetrates the breast is the light of Islam. When the heart is expanded with it, the light of *iman* shines in it. When it is strong, then it turns into direct witnessing of the Divine Presence."

So by means of this light the heart has the potential of expanding to the point that it encompasses direct knowledge of the Divine Reality and this is borne out by Allah's words on the tongue of His Messenger in the *hadith qudsi*: "Neither My earth nor My heaven contain me, but the heart of My believing slave contains me." Look at this wondrous organ that is the human heart, a created thing that is capable of encompassing direct knowledge of the Lord of the worlds – glory be to Him. What an immense and majestic thing it is! So, my companions, show love for those hearts which have indeed actually come to encompass the Knower of the Unseen Worlds so that they may in turn convey you to the knowledge of the Unseen Worlds that they themselves have gained. Success is by Allah.

# Derse 56

سُبْحَانَ مَنْ لَمْ يَجْعَلِ الدَّلِيلَ عَلَى أَوْلِيَاؤِهِ إِلَّا مِنْ حَيْثُ الدَّلِيلِ عَلَيْهِ وَلَمْ يُوصِلْ إِلَيْهِمْ إِلَّا مَنْ أَرَادَ أَنْ يُوصِلَهُ إِلَيْهِ.

**156: Glory be to Him Who makes guidance to His *awliya* nothing other than a means of guidance to Himself. And only brings a person to them when He wants to bring them to Himself.**

"Guidance" is what advances someone on the Path and takes them to the Goal. So when Allah takes you to a *wali* and directs you to him, He is taking you to knowledge of Him and directing you to it. If He guides you to one of His *awliya* and acquaints you with his secret, He is taking you by the hand and conveying you swiftly to His presence. Allah only guides to His *awliya* those he wants to guide to Himself. No one reaches them unless Allah wants them to reach Him. So esteem for the Shaykh is based on this mutual dependence. Our shaykh said about the words of Shaykh Ibn Ata'illah: "Reaching Allah is reaching knowledge of Him", "Your reaching Him is reaching the one with direct knowledge of Him." In other words when Allah conveys you to such a person and acquaints you with them, He has in fact conveyed you to Himself. To the extent that if He veils you from such people, He has actually veiled you from Himself. There is no way to direct knowledge of Allah except by means of their direct knowledge of Him.

And just as the Real has veiled His pure Essence with His might and force, He veils His *awliya* with the attributes of humanness they display, so the only people who really recognise them are those that Allah, in his prior concern for them, has chosen to do so. Or, you might say, only the elite recognise the elite. We read in *Lata'if al-Minan*: "The people of Allah among the elite of His slaves are the brides of existence, and brides are veiled from wrongdoers. They are the people of the Cave of Refuge. Few are those who truly recognise them. Shaykh Abu'l-'Abbas al-Mursi said, 'Recognition of the *wali* is more difficult than knowledge of Allah. Allah is known by His perfection and beauty. How do you recognise a creature like yourself who eats as you eat and drinks as you drink?'" Then he said, "When He wants to acquaint you with one of His *awliya*, He hides his humanness from you and opens up to you the secret of his election."

So the *awliya* cannot be recognised by their outward form; they can only be recognised by perception of their inward state. As has been said: "How many a dusty, dishevelled person with tattered garments is such that if they were to swear an oath by Allah, Allah would fulfil it." Anyone who thinks the outward form is what matters will not recognise the *wali* and will only see a mortal who eats food and walks in the market-place. Normal eyesight only sees dense forms and does not recognise the subtle meanings and the noble secrets those forms contain. If Allah desires happiness for a person, he first endows them with belief and affirmation and then gives them guidance and success. So affirmation of the secrets of *wilaya* is the beginning of knowledge of Allah. This is why Shaykh Abu'l-Hasan said, "Affirmation of this Path of ours is *wilaya*."

One of them said, "Allah has men whom only the elite recognise. Allah has men whom the elite and common recognise. Allah has men whom neither the elite nor the common recognise. Allah has men whom He displays in the beginning and veils in the end. Allah has men whom He veils in the beginning and displays in the end. Allah has men, whom only He knows, and only the noble Guardians who are entrusted with guarding the secrets are aware of what is between Him and them. Allah has men He has singled out for His gnosis and He does not disclose the reality of what is between Him and them to the Guardians or anyone else until they meet Him. They are the witnesses of the highest secrets of the Unseen and they are the ones brought near. They are those whose spirits Allah takes with His own hand. They are those whose bodies are beautiful due to the beauty of their spirits. As soon as the earth covers them, they are resurrected, shining with the lights of the immortality placed within them, as they go on with the One Who Goes On (*al-Baqi*). They are hidden under the veil of intimacy, immersed in the sea of love and purity. The are those whom Allah Himself takes in hand. Allah says: '*And those who make Allah their friend, and His Messenger and those who believe: it is the party of Allah Who are the victorious!'"* (5:58)

# Derse 57

$$\text{حَظُّ النَّفْسِ فِي الْمَعْصِيَةِ ظَاهِرٌ جَلِيٌّ،}$$
$$\text{وَحَظُّهَا فِي الطَّاعَةِ بَاطِنٌ خَفِيٌّ،}$$

**159a: The portion of the self in disobedience is loud and clear. The portion of the self in obedience is secret and hidden.**

The portion of the lower self in disobedience lies in the gratification of forbidden appetites and other sensory pleasures, which are forbidden, that are openly evident. The portion of the lower self in obedience, however, lies in pride in spiritual experiences, seeking information about unseen matters, and desire for reputation, and this is not at all easy to detect. Treating this second hidden sickness is far more difficult than treating the first open one. The first can be treated by withdrawal, avoidance of the places where such things occur, holding to good company, and increasing in acts of obedience and *dhikr*. This is not the case with the second kind of sickness. In its case, acts of obedience merely increase it and make it worse since they are what foster it and give it growth.

The only treatment for this inner sickness is unsettling fear, intense yearning, or keeping the company of a true man of Allah with love and affirmation. One of the people of Allah said, "If someone's *nafs* is difficult for him, he should surrender it to a teaching shaykh. Allah says: *'But if you make things difficult for one another, another woman should do the suckling for you.'* (65:6) If your selves are difficult for you, then ask another self to suckle it until the time of weaning is complete. If this doesn't happen, you will die in a state of sickness and not meet Allah with a sound heart." So we are under an obligation to keep a close watch over our hearts. When the *nafs* latches on to, and starts to relish, particular acts of obedience, we should introduce it to something else, even if it is something lesser outwardly. We should go to our shaykh if we are confused about this and find out which actions are going to be heavier on our *nafs*, because that is a sign of them being truly beneficial to us.

Shaykh Ahmad ibn Arqam said, "My *nafs* told me to go out to fight jihad and I said, 'Glory be to Allah Almighty! Allah tells us that the *nafs* commands to evil and this one is commanding me to do good? That can't be. It is just that it is lonely and wants to meet people, and for people to talk about it and show respect towards it.' I told it, 'Alright but I will not go to anywhere where people know me.' It happily agreed to that so I thought that's not good either. Allah speaks the truth. I then asked it, 'Will you fight the enemy without hesitation and be ready to be the first to be killed?'

It agreed again so I said, 'O Lord, tell me what is going on. I suspect my *nafs* and Your words are certainly true.' Then it was as if my *nafs* addressed me and said, 'You kill me every day many times by opposing me and denying my appetites without anyone being aware of that. If you fight and are killed, I will be saved from you once and for all and people will say to one another, "Ahmad is a martyr," and so I will have nobility and renown among people.' So I stayed behind and did not go out that year."

Imam al-Junayd was asked, "When does the sickness of the *nafs* become its cure." He said, "When its passion is opposed, its sickness becomes it its cure." Then Shaykh Ibn Ata'illah clarifies probably the greatest of the sicknesses hidden in obedience by saying:

وَمُدَاوَاةُ مَا يَخْفَى صَعْبٌ عِلَاجُهُ.

رُبَّمَا دَخَلَ الرِّيَاءُ عَلَيْكَ مِنْ حَيْثُ لَا يَنْظُرُ الْخَلْقُ إِلَيْكَ.

**159b: It is very hard to cure what is hidden.**

**160: You might show off in such a way that no one needs to look at you.**

"Showing off" in this context is seeking people's admiration and doing that by performing righteous actions, whether those actions are apparent to people or hidden from them. Showing off can happen even when no one sees what you do and this is more difficult than the first because, as the hadith says, it is more hidden than the movement of an ant. One man of knowledge used to say, "I struggled to remove showing-off from my heart by every means. But as soon as I removed one aspect of it, it sprang up in another way which I had not thought of." Another said, "One of the greatest forms of showing off is seeing giving and withholding, harm and benefit, as coming from the creation." Yet another said that there are different categories of showing off, all of which are a defect in the *deen*. One, which the worst, is that someone intends other people to see their action and they would not have done it otherwise. A second is to act to gain the admiration of other people. A third, more hidden type, is to show off to oneself so that one's actions become the cause of one feeling good about oneself – "What a good boy am I" – and all too often superior to other people and this is very difficult to eradicate.

People who show off have signs which are not hidden. They are energetic in public but lazy when alone, or their actions are perfect in places where people can see them and slipshod where only Allah sees them. Another thing is that they seek the esteem and respect of other people and expect them to hasten to look after their needs. If anyone fails to fulfill what they feel entitled to, they are upset about that. They make a difference between the respect they feel is due to them and the respect they owe to others, and between the disrespect shown to them and that they show to others.

If someone discovers any of these symptoms in themselves, they should know that they are showing off in their actions, even if those actions are hidden from other people's eyes. In a hadith we find that such people will be told that they have no reward on the Last Day because they have already received it from those for whom their actions were done. And that is the kind of showing off which great people of Allah fear and count themselves as being prone to. For instance, al-Fudayl ibn Iyad said, pointing at himself, "Whoever wants to look at a hypocrite, should look at this one." Malik ibn Dinar heard a woman saying to him, instead of *imra'i* – my man – *mura'i* – which means my show-off. He said, "This woman has rediscovered my name which the people of Basra have forgotten." There are many other examples of this.

Only those with direct knowledge of their Lord, the people of true *tawhid*, are safe from open and hidden showing off because Allah has purified them from every kind of *shirk* and made them withdraw from looking at creation by the lights of certainty and gnosis He has illuminated them with. They do not hope to obtain benefit from people and they do not fear suffering harm from them. The actions of such people are sincere even if there are people all around them. But, as Shaykh Ibn 'Abbad said, everyone other than them, people whose eyes are on the creation and who see the benefits and harm that come to them as stemming from it, are showing off in their actions, even if they are worshipping Allah away from everything else on the very top of a mountain.

# Derse 58

رُبَّمَا وَجَدْتَ مِنَ الْمَزِيدِ فِي الْفَاقَاتِ مَا لَا تَجِدُهُ فِي الصَّوْمِ وَالصَّلَاةِ .

الْفَاقَاتُ بُسُطُ الْمَوَاهِبِ .

إِنْ أَرَدْتَ وُرُودَ الْمَوَاهِبِ عَلَيْكَ صَحِّحِ الْفَقْرَ وَالْفَاقَةَ لَدَيْكَ ﴿ إِنَّمَا الصَّدَقَاتُ لِلْفُقَرَاءِ ﴾ .

**175: You might find a gain in states of need that you do not find in fasting or the prayer.**

**176: States of need are carpet loads of gifts.**

**177: If you want gifts to come to you establish poverty and need in yourself.**
**"Zakat is for the poor and destitute..." (9:60)**

People find that they gain from states of need what they do not gain from fasting and the prayer. That is because need is an action of the heart whereas fasting and prayer are actions of the limbs and an atom's weight of the actions of the heart is better than mountains of the actions of the limbs. States of need are nourishment for the spirit and fasting and prayer are nourishment for the heart. The spirit is the locus of direct witnessing and the heart is the locus of watchfulness and the distance between those two is well known.

One of the people of Allah said, "Know that Divine openings only occur in hearts which are empty of attachments and preoccupations. People may do a lot of prayer and fasting but the door of their hearts is kept shut by their preoccupation with the affairs of this world. This applies to the majority of people. Others may only do a little prayer and fasting and yet the door of their hearts is opened to inner knowledges and the descent of luminous understanding. Such people, however, are few in number. Outward acts of worship are all too often affected by showing off; but the *nafs* has no part in true humility."

It is said that Allah Almighty says to His slave, "I refine you in the furnace of need so that you will turn into pure gold." We read in *at-Tanwir*, "Know that there are subtle secrets in affliction and need which are only understood by those with insight. If it were only for the fact that the *nafs* is humbled, abased and cut off from its portions by those things, that would be a more than sufficient result. It is said that whenever abasement occurs, help comes along with it. Allah Almighty says: *'Allah helped you at Badr when you were abased.'* (3:123)"

*Faqir*, if you desire inner gifts and for them to come to you, then establish genuine poverty and need in yourself. When you have genuinely established them in yourself, then prepare yourself for a long list of gifts, for clouds of them will come to you. What is meant by gifts in this context are Divine knowledges, unveiling, tranquillity, wisdom, and secrets which come to the purified heart from the treasuries of the unseen worlds. The purest that the heart can be is when the lower self departs, and the departure of the lower self is achieved by abandoning its appetites and desires, something that, in most cases, is only achieved in the state of need and poverty.

That is why people of Allah rejoice in need and tend to grieve over wealth. Something of this world was given to one of them and he said, "This is a punishment. I do not know what the reason for it is." Al-Harawi said, "Need is an attribute of *zuhd* and is the greatest pleasure of the seeker of Allah since it brings him to Allah and enables him to sit before Him. It is the greatest of stations because by it attachments are cut out and stripped away and the heart is occupied with Allah alone. It is said that the true *faqir* does not own anything and is not owned by anything."

Sahl was asked, "When can a *faqir* find rest?" He replied, "When he does not see anything other than Allah." Ash-Shibli said, "The faqir does not see wealth in anything except Allah." In *'Awarif al-Ma'arif*, as-Suhrawardi says: "Poverty is the basis of *tasawwuf* and its support." One of them said, "The end of poverty is the beginning of *tasawwuf* because *tasawwuf* is a comprehensive name for the acquisition of all radiant good qualities and the abandonment of every base characteristic." They all agree that there is no entry to the presence of Allah except by the door of poverty. Anyone who does not achieve poverty will not realise anything of that which the People call them to. With true poverty gifts come one after another and inner knowledges expand in the *faqir* until he is the wealthiest of the wealthy.

One of *salihun* said, "I had some money and I saw a poor person in the Haram sitting for some days without eating or drinking. He was wearing old rags. I said to myself, 'I will enrich him with this money I have.' So I put it in his lap, saying, 'Use this to help yourself with your needs in this world.' He tipped it out onto the ground and said to me, 'I bought this seat with my Lord in return for all that I owned and now you want to ruin it for me!' Then he went off and left me picking up what I had given him. By Allah, I have not seen anyone mightier than him when he cast that money aside nor anyone more abased than me when I picked it up." This is the sound establishment of poverty and need inwardly and outwardly.

When something came to one of them, in the morning he was saddened. When morning found him with nothing, he was happy. He was told, "This is the opposite of the way most people behave." He said, "When I do not have anything in the morning, I have a good example in the Messenger of Allah. When I have something, I cannot say that the Messenger of Allah is my model." This is the state of our shaykhs according to what we have read about them. I heard that the shaykh of our shaykh, Moulay al-'Arabi ؒ, used to light a candle before retiring and look in the corners of his house. When he found something, he brought it out and gave it away as *sadaqa* and spent the night in need. That was his state in his condition of *tajrid*.

Shaykh Ibn Ata'illah then finishes by citing the noble *ayah*: *"Zakat is for: the poor and destitute..."* (9:60) as evidence for the fact that in reality the gifts and knowledges Allah gives a person are pure favour and not in any sense a repayment for actions they may have done or states they may have had. This is because *zakat* is not given as a recompense for any action. Allah Himself says about this matter: *"Mankind! You are the poor, in need of Allah, whereas Allah is the Rich beyond need, the Praiseworthy."* (15:35) May Allah enable us, whatever our circumstances, to truly recognise our own state of need and poverty and total dependence on Him and to see Him, in every instance, as the one and only source of all wealth and power.

# Derse 59

$$\text{الْعِبَارَاتُ قُوتٌ لِعَائِلَةِ الْمُسْتَمِعِينَ}$$
$$\text{وَلَيْسَ لَكَ إِلَّا مَا أَنْتَ لَهُ آكِلٌ.}$$

**187: Expressions are nourishment for needy listeners. You only get from them what you are able to digest.**

The expressions of the people of Allah are nourishment for the hearts of the *fuqara* who are seeking to increase the certainty in their hearts and to directly witness the presence of their Beloved. They continue in the care of their shaykh and are dependent on him until their certainty is complete and their states are rightly guided. Then they become independent in themselves. The sign of their right guidance is that they take inward provision from everything and nothing diminishes their state. They understand Allah in everything and they recognise everything for what it is and they drink from everything. When they are like that, they are independent in themselves and are ready to guide others.

One of the people of knowledge said, "Whoever does not understand the squeaking of the door, the buzzing of flies or the barking of dogs, is not one of those with true intelligence. As for the one who has not reached this station, he must remain in the nest in the care of the one who provides for him and feeds him. If a bird flies from the nest before its wings are strong, dogs and falcons will catch it, and women and children will play with it. When a *faqir* is in the nest of the shaykh and he feeds him along with all the others there, he is given no food except what he is able to eat. Anything other than that would destroy him. The food of an infant is not the same as the food of an adult person. The same applies to the teaching conveyed by shaykhs to their *murids*. Each of them is given what befits their state.

So the shaykhs remind in general terms, referring in what they say to the states of the beginning, the middle and the end, and everyone takes what is conducive to their state. As Allah tells us twice in His Book: *"All the people knew their drinking place."* (2:59) So the beginner on the Path is not exposed to the reminder of the one at the end of the Path for that would corrupt his state. If infants eat adult food, it sticks in their throat and chokes them. If adults eat the food of infants, it does not sustain them. This is the meaning of the words of shaykh, "You only get from them what you are able to digest," in other words you will only be nourished by the expression according to the amount of it that you are able to inwardly digest. Otherwise you would choke on it. Allah knows best.

One of the brothers asked about the nature of spiritual and physical nourishment. I replied that physical nourishment is well-known and spiritual nourishment plays a similar role in the being to that of physical nourishment. The body of an infant cannot tolerate adult food until it has matured and grown up. Similarly, the spirit also has to be nurtured little by little. At first it can only manage *dhikr* of the tongue; then it progresses to *dhikr* of the heart together with the tongue; then its food is *dhikr* of the heart alone; then its nourishment becomes *dhikr* of the spirit, which is reflection; and then its final sustenance is *dhikr* of the secret, which is pure vision. Then it is able to eat and drink anything it desires to the point that it is able to swallow up all existence. If reflection or vision, which is the food of the people of Allah, were to be given to someone at the beginning of their Path, while they were still, as it were, at an infant stage, they would spit it out and cast it aside. But when the spirit is fully developed, it can digest everything and drink from everything. Then it is proper for it to fly in the highest *malakut* and to go wherever it wishes.

So what is gained from a drink by a group, who are drinking from the same cup, often varies considerably due to the difference in their degree of understanding, to the stage they have reached on the spiritual path. An illustration of this is the case of some people who heard someone saying, *"Ya Sam'tar Bara!"* This happened when a man standing at Safa in Makka called out, *"Ya Sam'tar Bara"* to another man whose name it was. Three people heard him and each of them understood it in a way that was appropriate to their state. One heard, *"as-sa'a tara bara"* – "In an hour you will see dust,"; the second heard, *"as'a tara bara"* – "Strive and you will see dust"; and the third heard, *"ma awsa' bara"* –

"Dust does not encompass." So the first was looking ahead, the second was beginning and the third had arrived.

It was the same in the case of Ibn al-Jawzi. He was studying twelve sciences in Baghdad and one day he went out on some errand and heard someone singing:

> When the twentieth of Sha'ban has passed,
> drink your night's drink during the daytime hours.
> And do not use small tankards when you drink.
> The time is too short for small ones to be used.

He immediately departed, in rapturous state, heading for Makka, where he stayed devoting himself to the worship of Allah until the day he died. What he had understood from the poet's words was that this life is soon going to end and that our time in this world is very brief.

Shaykh Ibn Ata'illah says in *Lata'if al-Minan*: "Know that in the case of this kind of understanding of meanings, which are beyond the normally understood meaning of the words used, the expression does not in itself convey what is understood from it. Rather what is gained through it is an additional understanding, which Allah gives to this group of the masters of hearts, beyond the common understanding conveyed by the words themselves. This understanding derives from an inward wisdom that is hidden in the outward form in much the same way that plants are hidden in the seeds from which they eventually emerge. That is because the luminous help and openings that come to such people from Allah have an ineffable inward connection to the outward form of what is expressed. It may be that the outward meaning of the expression coincides with the inward understanding gained from it or it may be that the inward understanding is quite different from the outward form of the expression used."

May Allah open our understanding to inward meanings of this kind in such a way that our hearts will be brought to life and that this will transform us into people whose central purpose in life is to see Allah's *deen* implemented in every way open to us and made available to many more people than at present have access to it.

# Derse 60

$$\text{إِذَا الْتَبَسَ عَلَيْكَ أَمْرَانِ، فَانْظُرْ إِلَى أَثْقَلِهِمَا عَلَى النَّفْسِ فَاتَّبِعْهُ، فَإِنَّهُ لَا يَثْقُلُ عَلَيْهَا إِلَّا مَا كَانَ حَقًّا}$$

**192: When two matters are unclear to you, see which is heavier on the self and follow that! For only what is true is heavy on the self.**

This is the sound criterion for travellers on the Path who are busy with the greater jihad. Allah says in *Surah al-Hajj*: "*Do jihad for Allah with the jihad due to Him*" (22:76) and He says in *Surah al-'Ankabut*: "*As for those who do jihad in Our Way, We will guide them to Our Paths.*" (29:68) So all that is heavy on the *nafs* of the murid, and to which they are averse, is true and it is essential that the murid should follow it. They should avoid things that are easy on the *nafs*, for that indicates that they are false and will reinforce it, making it stronger.

This matter varies greatly with different people. Something may be heavy for one self but not heavy for another. For instance, some people find silence hard and some find speech hard. Some find being alone hard and others find being with other people hard. Some find fasting hard and some find not fasting hard. Some find begging hard, and the *nafs* will die in a single hour of it, and some of them find begging easy, as they are accustomed to it before being asked to do it. So the *fuqara* should have insight into their own *nafs* and proceed with it on the basis of denying it what it wants and giving it its opposite. That is how the *fuqara* should be with themselves if they want to progress on the Path; oppose their *nafs* in what it demands and suspect anything it recommends.

When the heart is purified and the *nafs* is subdued and nothing of it remains, only then should it be agreed with, since then only the Real is manifested in it. As Allah says: *"Truth has come and falsehood has vanished."* (17:81) Whereas the traveller on the Path is harmed by management and choice, the one who has arrived benefits from it. The traveller on the Path is harmed by too much socialising, whereas that has no adverse effect on the one who has arrived. The traveller on the Path is harmed by this world and flees from it but the one who has arrived is free from attachment to it and it does not harm them; indeed, it may help them. The result is that the one who has arrived is the reverse of the traveller on the Path in all his affairs, and success is by Allah.

All who want to strive against their *nafs*, its wiles and subterfuges still being unclear to them, must hand it over to a shaykh of instruction. They must submit to his insight into it and follow his indication of how they can best oppose it and gain the upper hand over those defects in it that are holding them back on the Path. This is the *Sunna* of Allah with His slaves. Your *nafs* does not want to abandon its ingrained habits and desires; that is its nature; so it must be surrendered to someone who will help you against it, if you are serious in your desire to purify your heart and to truly be able implement Allah's *deen*. Only those who are willing and able to recognise and oppose the hidden desires and inner appetites of their own selves will be able to advance on the Path and reach the goal which is the ultimate aim and purpose of all human aspiration, direct knowledge of Allah, their Creator and Lord. And Allah knows best.

There is no doubt that, for many people, one of the major inner obstacles to be overcome is fear of poverty and anxiety about provision. The Prophet ﷺ said, "I am amazed at a person who works for this world, when he will be provided for in it without work, and does not work for the Next World, when he will only be provided for there by the work he did for it." The Prophet ﷺ also said, "If someone is concerned with the Next World, Allah puts wealth in his heart and this world comes to him in spite of itself. If someone's concern is this world, Allah puts his poverty before him and only what is decreed for him of this world comes to him. Provision seeks the person as he seeks it." Yahya ibn Mu'adh used to swear that wisdom cannot exist in a heart which has three defects: concern for provision, envy of creatures, and love of rank.

Habib al-'Ajami used to serve Hasan al-Basri and one day made food for their fast-breaking. A beggar came and Habib gave it all to him. Hasan said, "Habib, you have a lot of certainty, but little knowledge. Why didn't you give him half and feed yourself with the other half?" He said, "Sidi, its reward is yours and I ask forgiveness of Allah." When night came, there was a knock at the door and Habib went out and found a slave with a lot of food. It was raining and the lad was weeping. He asked him, "What is this?" He replied, "This is food. My master told me: 'If Hasan al-Basri accepts it from you, then you are free for the sake of Allah.' I have been a slave a long time." Habib said, "There is no god but Allah! Freeing a slave and feeding the hungry!" Then he took it to Hasan and said, "Sidi, you have a lot of knowledge and little certainty." He said, "Habib, we came before you but you have outstripped us!"

One of the rich said, "While I was asleep I dreamt that a man stood over me in the world of sleep and rebuked me and told me, 'Respond to the grieved!' I woke up and was alarmed, not knowing what to do. Allah put it in my heart to take a bag containing a hundred dinars, mount my animal and let go of its reins. It took me out of the town to a ruined mosque and halted. I dismounted, went into the mosque and found a poor man who was calling on Allah, asking Him for some of his bounty. I asked him about his state and he said, 'I have a family, and my daughters have not eaten for three days, so I am asking Allah for some of His bounty.' I gave him the hundred dinars and said to him, 'When they're gone, come and ask me and I'll give you more. I am so-and-so.' He said, 'No, by Allah, I only ask Allah.' Then I left amazed at his trust in Allah."

# Derse 61

فَيَّدَ الطَّاعَاتِ بِأَعْيَانِ الأَوْقَاتِ
لِئَلَّا يَمْنَعَكَ عَنْهَا وُجُودُ التَّسْوِيفِ،
وَوَسَّعَ عَلَيْكَ الوَقْتَ لِتَبْقَى لَكَ حِصَّةُ الِاخْتِيَارِ.

**194: He specified particular times
for acts of obedience
so that procrastination would not
keep you from doing them.
But He made the time for them wide
so that you would have a share in
choosing when to do them.**

Two characteristics of the *nafs* are putting things off until later and hoping beyond hope. If it were left to its own choice, the *nafs* would never turn to its Lord. Knowing that His slaves would not be impelled to Him by love nor propelled to Him by pure desire, Allah drove them to Him in the chains of anxiety at the fear of the Fire or in the trap of greed for the bliss of the Garden. He obliged on them acts of obedience to Him. He then specified particular times for them because if that had been left to the choice of His slaves, only a few of the people of His love would have turned to Him with them. He expanded the time for doing them so that we would have a share in choosing to do them and to give us some leeway in respect of them. If the time for them had been made narrow, it would have made things extremely difficult and constricting for us. Praise belongs to Allah for His favour and the vastness of His mercy! There is a saying: "Whoever asks is answered. Whoever is diffident is disappointed." Look at how Allah has coupled guidance with striving and has obliged on Himself what is not obliged for Him. He says – and He is the truest in speech – *"As for those who do jihad in Our Way, We will guide them to Our Paths. Truly Allah is with the good-doers."* (29:68)

Ar-Rabi' ibn Khaytham used to repeat the following *ayah* and weep: *"Do those who perpetrate evil deeds suppose that We will make them like those who believe and do right actions."* (45:20) He would cry out, "O self of mine, would that I knew which of the two groups you are in!" This *ayah* is called "The one that makes the worshippers weep". Sahl said about it: "The people of good action are not like the people of bad action. The people of good action will be in *'on seats of honour in the Presence of an All-powerful king,'* whereas the people of bad action will be *'in the punishment of the Blaze'.*"

عَلِمَ قِلَّةَ نُهُوضِ الْعِبَادِ إِلَى مُعَامَلَتِهِ، فَأَوْجَبَ عَلَيْهِمْ وُجُودَ طَاعَتِهِ، فَسَاقَهُمْ إِلَيْهِ بِسَلَاسِلِ الإِيجَابِ

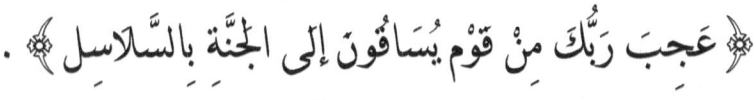

### 195: He knows of His slaves lack of enthusiasm in their dealings with Him, so He has made obedience obligatory for them and drives them to it by the chains of obligation. "Your Lord is amazed at a people who have to be driven to the Garden in chains."

Allah's knowledge of this lack of enthusiasm on the part of His slaves is clear from His words: *"But very few of My slaves show thanks!"* (34:16) and: *"How few they are!"* (38:23) Because of this, He has made it obligatory for them to obey Him and threatened to punish them for not doing so. So He drives them to Himself by the chains of obligation. The Shaykh then quotes the famous hadith referring to the captives of Badr in which the Prophet ﷺ said about them: "Your Lord is amazed at a people who have to be driven to the Garden in chains." The amazement is because Allah has told us that every possible good thing that a human being can hope for will be there for them in the Garden and people of true intelligence who hear this are prepared to expend every effort and undergo all kinds of difficulties in order to attain it. Yet these people are averse to it and run from it so that they must be dragged to it – that place in which lies the fulfilment of all their desires – in chains, as if it was the worst thing that could happen to them.

Allah has no need of anything whatsoever. So He only commands us to do this and forbids us from doing that for the sake of the benefit it will bring us and the harm it will avert from us. He has obliged us to do actions that make us pleasing to Him, and are therefore entirely for own benefit, and has forbidden us to do things that would make us displeasing to Him, and which would therefore be entirely to our own detriment. One of the people of knowledge said, "People fall into three categories. First, there are slaves who obey Allah out of pure worship, thankfulness, and simple obedience. Their fulfilment of their obligations increases them in honour and high rank. Then there are slaves who obey Allah out of respect for His Commandments. Their fulfilment of their obligations is to make them known and manifest Wisdom through them. Then there are slaves who obey Allah out of fear of His punishment and hope for His reward and if it were not for that, they would not worship Him. So in their case the obligation is a kindness to them. There is good in all of them, but what a difference there is between them!"

In reality there are two categories. The people of the veil obey out fear and desire and the people of direct vision obey out of love and thankfulness. That is the station of the Prophets and the great people of Allah. The Prophet ﷺ said, "Should I not be a thankful slave?" Lordship without slavehood is imperfect and slavehood without Lordship is impossible and inconceivable. When the knowers of Allah realise this secret, which is that slavehood has no existence in itself and that its only existence lies in the secret of

Lordship manifest in the ordinances of slavehood, and they recognise that reality in state and tasting, then their worship is nothing but gratitude. Their actions are by Allah for Allah. The worship of such people is great in meaning even if it is little in the sensory. It can never be little since everything they do is worship. Their sleep is worship. Their eating is worship. Their walking is worship. It is about those like this that the hadith is reported, "The sleep of the people of knowledge is worship." The bounty of Allah is absolutely without limit.

All this is eloquently summed up in Shaykh Ibn Ata'illah's next sentence:

أَوْجَبَ عَلَيْكَ وُجُودَ طَاعَتِهِ،
وَمَا أَوْجَبَ عَلَيْكَ إِلَّا دُخُولَ جَنَّتِهِ .

**196: He has made service of Him obligatory for you. But in reality, He has only made entry into the Garden obligatory for you.**

# Derse 62

مَنِ اسْتَغْرَبَ أَنْ يُنْقِذَهُ اللَّهُ مِنْ شَهْوَتِهِ،
وَأَنْ يُخْرِجَهُ مِنْ وُجُودِ غَفْلَتِهِ فَقَدِ اسْتَعْجَزَ الْقُدْرَةَ الإِلَهِيَّةَ ﴿ وَكَانَ اللَّهُ عَلَى كُلِّ شَيْءٍ مُقْتَدِراً ﴾.

**197: Anyone who finds it strange that Allah should rescue him from his appetites and bring him out of his heedlessness thinks that Divine Power is powerless. But *"Allah has power over all things."***

There is no doubt that Allah Almighty is not lacking the power to do anything whatsoever He wills. His command is overwhelming and the hearts of His slaves are in His hand and He turns them over in whatever way He wishes. People who are immersed in heedlessness and drowned in the oceans of their appetites should not consider it strange that Allah might rescue them from that heedlessness and bring them out of the clutches of their appetites. That would make their *iman* defective. How could they think it strange when our Lord says: *"Allah has power over all things"* ﷺ We are one of those things. The Almighty says: *"O My slaves who have transgressed against yourselves, do not despair of the mercy of Allah. Truly Allah forgives all wrong actions."* (39:50) He also says: *"But if anyone repents after his wrongdoing and puts things right, Allah will turn towards Him"* (5:41) and there are other *ayahs* that say the same.

The Prophet ﷺ said, "If you were to commit wrong actions until your mistakes reached up to the clouds of heaven and were then to repent, Allah would turn to you." We should remember those before us among the people of heedlessness and disobedience who then became great people of Allah. Some, like al-Fudayl ibn 'Iyad, Abu Ya'za and several others, were even thieves and robbers. At the beginning of his *Risala*, al-Qushayri mentions some of these and he put them first to strengthen the hope of the wrongdoers. He mentioned the man who killed ninety-nine men and then asked a monk about repentance. The monk told him, "Repentance is not possible in your case," so he made it a full hundred. Then he asked a scholar, who directed him to repentance and told him to go to a town where there were people worshipping Allah. He set off for them but died on the way. The angels of mercy took him. The full story is to be found in *Sahih Bukhari*. There is also the story of the thief who asked a scholar if repentance was possible for him. Mocking him, the scholar picked up a dry stalk and said, "Take this. When it turns green, your repentance will be accepted." He took it with that intention and began to worship Allah. One day he looked at it and it had become pliant and green.

I have met people who were drowned in heedlessness, had abandoned the prayer and knew almost nothing about the *deen* who then became transformed and turned into men of great knowledge. And I have met people who were immersed in wrong actions and wronging others and then became people of great right action. As a general rule this blessing occurs to those who stumble into the company of men of Allah who possess the elixir, and they exist in every age. This is something well-known and does not require any substantiation. Anyone who doubts it is more extraordinary than someone who denies the light of the sun after it rises or the light of the moon after it appears, as the author of the *Burda* makes clear:

> Eyes with ophthalmia may deny the light of the sun
> and a mouth, due to illness,
> may deny the sweet taste of water.

Yet there are those who deny the existence of shaykhs of instruction and claim that there is no such thing as people of spiritual transmission. *"It is not the eyes which are blind, but the hearts in the breasts which are blind."* (22:44) They are blind to the Path of the people of Allah and only able to see the path of the outward, like bats which can see in the darkness but not in the light. No, Allah may allow His slaves to be overcome by their lower appetites and incarcerate them in the prison of heedlessness and wrongdoing, and then grant them true repentance, so they awaken from their heedlessness. Then He admits them among His lovers so that they come to know the true extent of the innumerable blessings Allah has bestowed on them.

رُبَّمَا وَرَدَتِ الظُّلَمُ عَلَيْكَ، لِيُعَرِّفَكَ قَدْرَ مَا مَنَّ بِهِ عَلَيْكَ

## 198: Sometimes darkness may come over you to make you recognise the measure of His favour to you.

There is no doubt that obtaining a thing after striving for it is more pleasurable and precious than getting it without expending any effort. Love after separation is sweeter than love without having been separated. Serenity after upheaval is more relieving than serenity without that upheaval having taken place. Weaning the *nafs* from the things with which it is familiar and from its habits gives a greater sense of achievement than that gained by a *nafs* that is pliable and submissive, which has not had to put in the effort. So the reward or the value of something is commensurate with the energy expended on it. This explains the wisdom of sending distraction and appetite to a person: when they overcome them and escape from them they are truly able to recognise the immense value of the blessing Allah has granted to them.

Allah may well make darkness overwhelm you. That darkness may take the form of adversity, sorrows, love of appetites or debts, so that you find yourself drowning in the murky depths of these difficulties and locked up in the prison of their darkness. And then out of nowhere He may suddenly bring you out from them. That is so that after this opening you will recognise the preciousness of what Allah has blessed you with, increase in love and thankfulness to Him and truly value the secret He has placed in you. This is why Allah has made the Garden a zone encircled by hated things so that, after they enter it, its people will better recognise the true value of the blessing which Allah has bestowed on them. And the same applies to the Garden of direct knowledge of Allah: it too is encircled with hated things so that the people of Allah will recognise the immense value of the secret which has been unveiled to them and the great good which Allah has granted them.

Know, therefore, that this darkness which descends on people's hearts and veils them from their Lord is brought about by Divine Wisdom through the means of this world, the *nafs* and *shaytan*. If someone is abstinent in respect of this world, frees themselves from the domination of their *nafs* and remembers Allah to the point that *shaytan* burns up and melts away, they will enter into the company of the lovers and the door to knowledge of the unseen worlds will be opened up to them. One of the men of knowledge said, "Know that when the Creator created the heart, He made it a treasury for His secrets, a mine for His lights and a locus through which He has access to His slave. Allah did not create anything in existence nobler than the human heart. Then he posted at the door of the heart the basest and worst of things, since His Wisdom stipulates the joining of opposites which no one else has power over. He thrust before the door of the heart a dead body and a barking dog: they are this world and *shaytan*. Whoever wants the secret of Allah to enter the treasury must stop looking at the putrid corpse and turn away from the yapping dog, because it has no way to get at the one who turns away from it. Anyone who turns to them prevents the light, which Allah desires to place there, from entering the house of the heart. He has put those odious things there as a protective shield in front of the treasure in order to protect it."

It is said that this world is the daughter of *Shaytan* and so anyone who is married to this world becomes the son-in-law of Iblis. He loves his daughter dearly so as long as someone is married to her, he will find *Shaytan* to be his constant companion. The Messenger of Allah ﷺ said, "When Allah desires good for His slave, He makes him abstinent in this world and desirous of the Next World and shows him his own faults." He was asked, "Messenger of Allah, which people are the worst?" He replied, "The rich," meaning the miserly. Then he said ﷺ, "If anyone esteems a wealthy person for his wealth, in the sight of Allah he is like someone who worships an idol. If anyone is sad about forfeiting anything of this world, he draws closer to the Fire by the distance of a year."

Allah revealed to Musa ﷺ, "I do not choose the one who loves wealth. I do not choose the one who loves this world. There is never room in the same heart for both love of Me and love of it. O Musa, the one who fears creation does not fear Me, and the one who fears he will fail to receive his provision does trust in Me. By My Might and My Majesty, no one places his trust in Me without My giving him enough for his needs. The keys of the *mulk* and the *malakut* are in My hand. No one takes refuge in Me without My admitting him to the Garden and sparing him hardship. If anyone clings to other than Me, means are cut off from above his head, I make the earth slip from under his feet, and do not care how I destroy him.

"O Musa, I have sealed the Torah with five principles for you. If you act by them, all knowledge will benefit you; otherwise, none of it will. The first is to trust in My provision which is guaranteed to you as long as my treasuries are full, and My treasuries are always full and will never run out. The second is not to fear anyone with power as long as My Power continues, and My Power will always continue and remain forever. The third is not to see the faults of other people as long any fault remains in you and everyone will always have a fault. The fourth is not to cease to fight *shaytan* as long as your *ruh* remains in your body for he will certainly never stop fighting you. The fifth is to never feel safe from My devising, even when you find yourselves in the Garden, for it was in the Garden that what happened to Adam happened, and so you are never safe from My devising."

May Allah give us success in recognising His Wisdom and Mercy in the darkness of any inward or outward difficulties He places in our way and grant us the knowledge and courage we need to overcome them and discover the priceless treasures that lie hidden on the other side.

مَنْ لَمْ يَعْرِفْ قَدْرَ النِّعَمِ بِوِجْدَانِهَا عَرَفَهَا بِوُجُودِ فِقْدَانِهَا .

### 199: Anyone who fails to recognise the value of blessings by the fact of their presence

## will certainly come to recognise it by the fact of their absence.

What the shaykh says here is a sound and tested truth. When blessings and well-being come to a person one after another, they often do not recognise their worth or give the them value they deserve. But when those blessings are removed and they are stricken with affliction, pains and hardship, they then recognise to the full the value of their previous well-being. The same applies to the *fuqara*. When they are given the gifts of concentration, reflection and knowledge they all too often do not esteem their true value. Then when they are afflicted by heedlessness, worldly distractions and dead hearts, they recognise the true value of what they had. Because of this they are impelled to turn with renewed energy, almost desperation, to Allah, and He returns to them what had been removed from them.

It is said that Allah Almighty says to Jibril, "Jibril, withdraw the sweetness of My love from the heart of My slave to test him," and Jibril withdraws the sweetness of love from the heart of that slave. When he is put under pressure in this way and entreats, seeks refuge and weeps, Allah says to Jibril, "Return to him the sweetness of My love. I have found him truthful." If the sweetness of love is withdrawn from the heart of a *faqir* and they do not entreat and plead, nothing will be returned to them, and that sweetness will be permanently removed. We seek refuge with Allah from that ever happening!

The way we can actively acknowledge the value of the blessings we have been given is by reflecting on them and by reflecting on our state before they existed. So when you are rich, physically or spiritually, remember your previous poverty. When you are healthy, remember the time you were ill. When you obey Allah remember your former disobedience. When you do *dhikr*, remember your earlier heedlessness. When you have a shaykh, remember the time when you had no guidance. It is the same with every blessing. You should look to its opposite which existed in you before you got it. If you do that you will not fail to recognise its value and be thankful for it and so it will remain with you. If, however, we do not reflect on the blessings we have received and do not recognise their true value and neglect to be grateful for them, they will be stripped away from us without our realising it. One of the people of Allah said, "Thanking Allah with the tongue is humble acknowledgement of His blessing to you; thanking Allah with the hand is by serving Him and His people with sincerity; and thanking Allah with the heart is by witnessing His favour to you." Al-Junayd said, "Do not see yourself as meriting a blessing, for if you do you will be disobeying Allah by means of the very blessing he has given you!"

# Derse 63

لَا تُدْهِشْكَ وَارِدَاتُ النِّعَمِ عَنِ الْقِيَامِ بِحُقُوقِ شُكْرِكَ،
فَإِنَّ ذَلِكَ مِمَّا يَحُطُّ مِنْ وُجُودِ قَدْرِكَ.

**200: Do not let the inflow from your blessings dazzle you so much
that you fail to fulfil your duty of gratitude for them.
That is something that will certainly lower your rank.**

If someone reflects on himself and the blessings he has, he finds himself immersed in blessings, both physical and spiritual. He realises he has the blessing of sight, the blessing of hearing, the blessing of smell, the blessing of taste, the blessing of speech, the blessing of the intellect, the blessing of two hands, the blessing of two feet, the blessing of health and well-being, the blessing of sufficiency, the blessing of family, and the blessing of children. Then he looks at the blessing of guidance to Islam, the blessing of belief, the blessing of obedience, the blessing of knowledge, the blessing of those of his brothers who help him, and then the greatest blessing of all, the blessing of a shaykh to guide him to what Allah has prepared for him after death a blessing which has no end. Finding himself immersed in these abundant blessings, he should not be so dazzled by them that he fails to be grateful for them. The expression: "Praise be to Allah, Lord of the worlds" is enough for the thankfulness of the tongue. Do you not see that the Garden is one of the greatest of all blessings and the gratitude of the people of the Garden in it is expressed in the words, "Praise be to Allah, the Lord of the worlds." Allah says of them: *"The end of their call is: 'Praise be to Allah, the Lord of all the worlds!'"* (10:9)

It has come in one of the reports that Da'ud ﷺ said, 'Lord, how shall I thank you when I am unable to thank You except with one of the blessings you have given me? Your blessing obliges me to be grateful and gratitude is itself a blessing which demands gratitude!" One of them wrote:

> Since thankfulness to Allah is a blessing for the slave
> from Allah which obliges thankfulness,
> How can he give sufficient thanks
> for the blessing of thankfulness
> Even if he does so all the time and life went on forever?

Another said:

> Praise be to You, our Master, for every blessing,
> and part of the sum of blessings is my words,
> "Praise belongs to You."
> There is no praise which is not a granted blessing.
> Glory be to You! The slave is not strong enough
> to praise You!

In another transmission, Da'ud ﷺ said, "My God, every hair of the son of Adam has a blessing under it and a blessing on top of it. How can he thank you enough?" Allah revealed to Him, "Da'ud, I give a lot and am pleased with a little. Enough thankfulness is that you know that whatever blessing you have is from Me." Allah also revealed to him: "When you recognise that all blessings are from Me, then you have thanked Me and I am pleased with that in you."

One of the governors of 'Umar ibn 'Abdu'l-'Aziz wrote to him, "I am in a land in which there are many blessings and I fear my heart will be lacking in gratitude!" 'Umar wrote to him, "I used to think you had more knowledge of Allah than that! Allah Almighty does not give a slave a blessing for which he praises Him but that his praise for it is better for him than the blessing he has received. If you do not realise that, just look in the Book of Allah. Allah says: *'We gave knowledge to Da'ud and Sulayman who said, "Praise be to Allah Who has favoured us over many of His believing slaves."'* (27:15) And Allah says: *'And those who had taqwa of their Lord will be driven to the Garden in companies...'* (39:70) And then He says: *'They will say, "Praise be to Allah Who has fulfilled His promise to us,"'* (39:71) and what blessing could be greater than entering the Garden?"

The key to this blessing is the prior blessing of the cure and healing of the heart from the sickness of desire for this world which confines it in the prison of heedlessness and exposes it to Divine anger. The Shaykh then points that out so that the slave will recognise the value of this blessing when Allah has cured them of it, or ask Allah to grant them that blessing when Allah has not yet cured them of it. He says:

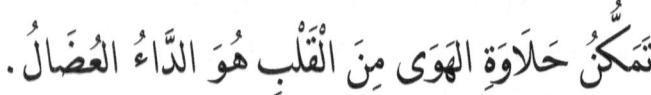

## 201: The sweetness of desire ingrained in the heart: that is the incurable sickness.

The sweetness of desire falls into two categories: the desire of the *nafs* and the desire of the heart. The desire of the *nafs* refers to its physical appetites, such as its desire for food and drink, clothes, mounts (and expensive cars), sexual pleasure and fine houses. The desire of the heart refers to appetites of a more abstract kind, such as love of rank, leadership, power, praise, and reputation and also, in the case of worshippers and ascetics, the sweetness of physical acts of obedience and, in the case of scholars, the sweetness of the knowledge of texts and book learning.

The desire of the *nafs* is comparatively simple to take care of. It can be quickly treated by its turning away from the objects of that desire, abstention from them, and keeping good company. But the desires of the heart, when they are deeply embedded, are far more difficult to deal with. They represent an incurable illness which doctors are unable to treat and cannot cure. It can only be removed by Divine gift through foreordained Divine concern, with or without means being employed, as Shaykh Ibn Ata'illah then indicates by saying:

لَا يُخْرِجُ الشَّهْوَةَ مِنَ القَلْبِ إِلَّا خَوْفٌ مُزْعِجٌ أَوْ شَوْقٌ مُقْلِقٌ

## 202: Appetite only leaves the heart through an unsettling fear or restless yearning.

When subtle appetites are firmly rooted in the heart, it is extremely difficult to treat it and so they can generally only be driven out by a forceful manifestation of Majesty or Beauty. Majesty usually manifests in the form of an unsettling fear which rouses you from your appetites and detaches you from your normal comfort zone and family ties. Beauty manifests in the form of a kind of restless yearning which liberates you from your lower desires and makes you forget yourself and direct yourself to your Lord. When fear or yearning of this kind enters the heart, it expels from it all the distractions that occupy it and it is filled with pure knowledge and lights. Then a person's actions become truly sincere and the Lord of Immensity and Majesty turns towards him. However, because this illness is so intractable, it constitutes the densest of the veils that lie between Allah and many scholars and worshippers. This is because the cause of it is a hidden appetite they themselves are often not aware of. Allah describes those who suffer from it in the ayah: *"People whose efforts in the life of this world are misguided while they suppose that they are doing good."* (18:99) They have been misguided from the path of the elite and remain on the path of those veiled from the truth.

The scholars of outward knowledge believe that there is nothing superior to what they have and I have even heard some of them say that gives them the station of *ihsan*. They say they are acting by the outward meaning of the Book and the *Sunna* and there can be nothing higher than that. How can such a person be delivered from that delusion except by divine concern? The worshippers say that their intense activity is the ultimate expression of love and obedience but they are, in fact, increased in distance from Allah by their belief in the innate effectiveness of their actions. So the veil between them and their Lord is made denser and they are further entrenched in their state.

The common people and the people of distraction are actually the most likely people to be guided and to reach their Lord. In a hadith, the Messenger of Allah ﷺ said, "Most of the people of the Garden are simple-minded," in other words prone to ordinary distractions. One clear illustration that the appetite of the heart is worse than the appetite of the *nafs* is the story of Adam and *Shaytan*. Adam's appetite, causing him to eat what was forbidden, was a physical one and so he was easily put right by Allah's gift of *tawba*. *Shaytan's* appetite, however, was in his heart. He said, "*I am better than him.*" So he was consigned to the Fire forever.

Know that there are two kinds of fear: the fear of the common people and the fear of the elite. The fear of the common people is fear of punishment and disgrace, whereas the fear of the elite is of fear of being cut off and veiled from their Lord. There are also two kinds of yearning. The yearning of the common people is for *houris* and palaces, and the yearning of the elite is for witnessing and presence. The yearning of the common people is for physical delight and the yearning of the elite is for spiritual delight. The yearning of the common people relates to Allah's words: *"Allah has promised the men and women of the believers Gardens with rivers flowing under them, remaining in them timelessly, for ever, and fine dwellings in the Gardens of Eden."* (9:73) The yearning of the elite relates to His words: *"And Allah's good pleasure is greater still. That is the great victory."* (9:73) May Allah place us among the best of such people by His infinite grace and generosity! Amin.

# Derse 64

كَمَا لَا يُحِبُّ العَمَلَ المُشْتَرَكَ، لَا يُحِبُّ الْقَلْبَ الْمُشْتَرَكَ، العَمَلُ المُشْتَرَكُ لَا يَقْبَلُهُ، وَالْقَلْبُ المُشْتَرَكُ لَا يُقْبِلُ عَلَيْهِ.

**203: As He does not love a shared action,
nor does He love a shared heart.
He does not accept the shared action,
He does not draw near to the shared heart.**

A shared action is one that is accompanied by the desire of the *nafs* for this world and the shared heart is one in which there is love for something other than Allah. Actions that are accompanied by such desires are corrupted and what is corrupted is not accepted. Allah Almighty says in a *hadith qudsi*: "Of all those to whom association is attributed, I am the furthest removed from what is associated with Me. If anyone does an action in which he associates other than Me with Me, I abandon him and what he associates with Me." A heart in which there is love for some other is sullied by lower desires and not fit for the presence of the Lord. How excellent is what ash-Shushtari said:

> I have a Lover who is very jealous,
> remaining alert over my heart like a bird.
> If it sees anything there, it refuses to visit.

Anyone who safeguards their actions with true sincerity is worthy of acceptance and one of the elite. Anyone who guards their heart against the intrusion of created beings, finds it filled with knowledges and light, and it becomes a spring of direct vision and secrets.

Know that a shared action is one that is corrupted by one of three defects: showing-off, pride or seeking repayment for it. As we know the Prophet ﷺ said of showing-off, that it is hidden *shirk*. And there is a hadith in *Sahih Muslim* in which he ﷺ talks of three who will be the first to enter the Fire on the Day of Rising. They are a man of knowledge who recites seeking the acclamation of other than Allah, a man who displays courage fighting seeking the acclamation of other than Allah, and a man of wealth who gives *sadaqa* seeking the acclamation of other than Allah.

Pride entails having too much regard for the self, ascribing action to it and claiming to be superior to other people. Allah says: "*So do not claim purity for yourselves. He knows best those who have fear of Him.*" (53:31) It is said that this means: "When you perform an action, do not say, 'I did it', attributing it to yourself, and do not display it to those around you to shore up your reputation with them. The Messenger of Allah ﷺ said, 'There are three great dangers: greed which is gratified, appetite which is indulged, and self-admiration.'" The Messenger of Allah ﷺ also said, "Even if you do not commit wrong actions, I fear for you something that is worse than wrong actions and that is pride." Zayd ibn Aslam said that the words: *"Do not claim purity for yourselves"* mean "Do not believe that you are virtuous." Another of the *Salaf* said, "I prefer to spend the night asleep and the morning regretting that than to spend the night in prayer and then the morning feeling self-righteous." 'A'isha was asked, "When is a man a wrongdoer?" She replied, "When he thinks that he is a good-doer."

It is said that a proud person is one who is blind to the evils in themselves and their actions. Some degree of self-examination is essential for anyone travelling on the path of Allah. If someone does not examine the wellspring of their actions, they are lost. The person who examines their actions is the one who has true fear of Allah and proper fear of acting wrongly. Such people do not desire any praise for themselves nor do they claim to be virtuous on account of what they do. They are not like those who are over-sure of their own opinions and intellect and disdain to ask and do not listen to good counsel from other people because they see them as being somehow less than themselves. We ask Allah for protection from that and for well-being and right thinking.

As for seeking compensation and repayment, we have already mentioned that several times. The nub of it is that if you ask Him for the reward, He will ask you for the secret of sincerity. It is enough for anyone who is concerned about the soundness of their actions for them to know that any action which contains any of these defects is not accepted by Allah with the acceptance granted to the elite. So a shared heart is a heart that is subject to one of three defects: desire for this world, desire for spiritual reputation, or desire for the blessings of the Next World. All of them detract from sincerity and remove those subject to them from the degree of the elect. Success is by Allah.

أَنْوَارٌ أُذِنَ لَهَا فِي الْوُصُولِ، وَأَنْوَارٌ أُذِنَ لَهَا فِي الدُّخُولِ.

## 204: There are lights that are allowed to arrive. And there are lights that are allowed to enter.

The "lights that are allowed to arrive" are the lights of *iman*, and they belong to the people of evidence and proof. Because their hearts have not been emptied of desire for other-than-Allah, and the forms of created things are still present in them, when lights arrive from Allah, they find their hearts filled with these forms and so they halt outside and do not come in. "The lights that are allowed to enter" are the lights of *ihsan* – the lights of direct witnessing and vision. That is because when they reach those whose hearts have been freed from other than their Lord and Creator, the lights are able to flow into them unimpeded, find room there and settle in their very core.

The difference between the light that arrives and the light that enters is that in the case of the person whose heart the light merely arrives at, you see them sometimes with this world and sometimes with the Next World, sometimes with the portion of their *nafs* and sometimes devoted to the right of their Lord, sometimes with distraction and sometimes with awareness. Those who have light enter the core of their hearts, on the other hand, are not distracted either by the things of this world nor the delights of the Next World. They are absent from themselves, present with their Lord.

One of people of knowledge said, "When faith is in the outward part of the heart, the slave loves both the Next World and this world and so such a person is sometimes with his Lord and sometimes left to himself. The firmness of the light in someone's heart and how much enters it is directly proportional to the amount they turn their back on this world and abandon their lower desires." Corroborating this the Messenger of Allah ﷺ said, "When light enters the heart, it is opened and expanded." He was asked, "Does that have a sign, Messenger of Allah?" He said, "Yes, aversion to the Abode of Delusion, turning to the Abode of Eternity, taking provision for your time in the grave, and preparation for the Day of Gathering."

Know that lights which are allowed to arrive are universal to all Muslims. We already mentioned what Shaykh Abu'l-Hasan as-Shadhili said: "If the light of the disobedient Muslim were to be disclosed, it would illuminate everything between heaven and the earth." As for the lights which are allowed to enter the heart, however, they are only for the elite – for the people who have, by Allah's generosity and mercy, freed themselves from concern for other than their Lord and from everything that might make that light diminish in brightness and power. May Allah keep us in their company and count us among them.

# Derse 65

حُقُوقٌ فِي الأَوْقَاتِ يُمْكِنُ قَضَاؤُهَا،
وَحُقُوقُ الأَوْقَاتِ لَا يُمْكِنُ قَضَاؤُهَا،

**208a: There are rights of some times
that can be made up for
and rights of other times
that cannot be made up for.**

The rights of the first of the times referred to are acts of obedience for which Allah has specified a particular time, such as the five prayers and confirmed *sunnas*, and *zakat*, fasting and hajj also have a specified time in the year. Even when the time for them has passed, it is still possible to make them up, although the person concerned is then accused of neglect. However, the rights of the other times referred to are connected with awareness of Allah or witnessing Him in them – each one according to his capacity – and, mitigating this, Allah says: *"Allah does not burden any self with more than He has given it."* (65:7) If the rights of these times are missed, it is not possible to make them up because each subsequent moment also has a specific right attached to it which leaves no room for the previous one. There is no instant in which you are not obliged to act for Allah and to occupy yourself with what will bring you nearer to Him and earn His good pleasure. Emphasising this the shaykh continues:

مَا مِنْ وَقْتٍ يَرِدُ إِلَّا وَلِلَّهِ عَلَيْكَ فِيهِ حَقٌّ جَدِيدٌ، وَ أَمْرٌ أَكِيدٌ، فَكَيْفَ تَقْضِي فِيهِ حَقَّ غَيْرِهِ وَأَنْتَ لَمْ تَقْضِ حَقَّ اللَّهِ فِيهِ.

**208b: For no moment arrives in which you do not owe Allah a new duty and a definite transaction. How can you, then, in it, fulfil the right of someone else when you have as yet failed to fulfil the right of Allah?**

There is no moment or instant which comes to you without Allah having a new right over you in it. It might take the form of *dhikr*, reflection, awareness, witnessing, or physical or spiritual service. Acknowledging this is part of realising true slavehood and carrying out what is truly owed to your Lord. If you neglect what is owed to Allah in any moment and the next moment comes, there is no possibility of making that previous moment up. You cannot make up the right of one moment in any subsequent moment. If the right of Allah over you in any moment is missed, that's it.

Shaykh Abu'l-'Abbas said, "There are four times for the slave and there is no fifth: blessing, affliction, obedience or disobedience. In each of them Allah is due a right from His slave: thankfulness in times of blessing, steadfastness in times of affliction, witnessing the favour in times of obedience, and shame and regret in times of disobedience. Corroborating this the Prophet ﷺ said, 'Whoever is given to should be thankful; whoever is afflicted should be steadfast; whoever is wronged should forgive; and whoever commits a wrong action should ask forgiveness.' Then he was silent ﷺ. They asked, 'What is it, Messenger of Allah?' He then quoted the *ayah*: '*They are the ones who are safe, it is they who are guided,*' (6:82) in other words they will be safe on the Day of Rising and they are guided in this world. It is also said that they are safe in both the worlds and are guided to Allah's presence in both realms of being."

It is clear that completely fulfilling the rights Allah has over us in every moment is basically impossible for any human being. Allah Almighty tells us: "*They do not measure Allah with His true measure.*" (6:92) meaning that we cannot worship Him as He should be worshipped nor know Him as He should be known. We cannot, in the case of most of us, even do that during the prayer itself, so how on earth are we going to do it in every moment? However, Allah says about some people: "*He singles out whomever He will for His mercy.*" And we should know that there are human beings who do fulfil Allah's right over them in this way. One of them said, "For twenty years nothing has occurred to my heart except Allah Almighty." Shaykh Abu'l-Hasan said, "Anyone who truly loves Allah does not employ His limbs except in what is acceptable to His Beloved, and all his breaths are breathed in obedience to Him. If something were to come between him and obedience, he would immediately leave this world because for such people obedience has become the very nourishment of their selves. If they were to abandon it, they would die. May Allah give us their benefit. Amin."

Neglecting the rights of each moment is in a way wasting the time we've been given, which the shaykh then points out by saying:

$$\text{مَا فَاتَ مِنْ عُمُرِكَ لَا عِوَضَ لَهُ،}$$
$$\text{وَمَا حَصَلَ لَكَ مِنْهُ لَا قِيمَةَ لَهُ.}$$

### 209: You cannot bring back any of your life which has gone and what you have gained from it is beyond any price.

The life of the believer is his capital in which lies his profit or loss. Whoever holds on firmly to it is one of the successful. Whoever wastes it in triviality and negligence is one of the losers. There is no replacement for what you have wasted since what has gone will never return. What you have truly won from it is inestimably precious. A single hour is worth more than all the gold on the earth. An hour in which you have truly remembered Allah will result in a realm without any borders and everlasting delight. This world and everything in it doesn't amount to even the tiniest fraction of it. This is why the early Muslims were so rigorous with their time and so determined to take every advantage of it, allowing themselves very little rest and inactivity.

In a hadith the Messenger of Allah ﷺ is reported as saying, "An hour does not pass for the slave during which he fails to remember Allah without that being a cause of regret for him on the Day of Rising." Al-Hasan al-Basri said, "I have met people who were fiercer and more solicitous about watching over their breaths and their moments than you are about watching over your dinars and dirhams. Just as one of you only spends a dinar or dirham that will earn him a profit or make more money for him, so those people never waste a single breath in anything other than obedience to Allah." Imam al-Junayd said, "When the moment is missed, it cannot be recaptured, and nothing could be more precious than the moment." It is said that the hours of the night and day being twenty-four, when the Day of Rising comes, twenty-four chests will be set up in a row. Those who filled them with obedience to Allah in this world will see them as treasure-chests filled with luminous jewels. Whoever wasted them will see them as just empty boxes and will feel regretful about it.

We read in a report that while the people of the Garden are enjoying their wonderful delights, a light will shine from above them which will illuminate their palaces, just as the sun illuminates things in this world. They will look up and see those above them, the people of 'Illiyun, who will appear like brilliant stars on the horizon. They will surpass them in respect of light, beauty and delight the way the moon outshines the rest of the stars. They will see them travelling on fine mounts which are bearing them through the air to visit the Master of Majesty and Generosity. They will call out: "Our brothers! This isn't fair! We used to pray as you prayed and fast as you fasted. Why have you been preferred to us?" A voice will come from Allah: "They were hungry when you were full, thirsty when you were satisfied, and naked when you were clothed. They remembered when you forgot. They wept when you laughed. They got up when you were asleep. They felt fear when you felt safe. That is why they are preferred over you today." That is the meaning of the words of Allah: *"No self knows the delight that is hidden away for it in recompense for what it used to do."* (32:17)

# Derse 66

مَا أَحْبَبْتَ شَيْئاً إِلَّا كُنْتَ لَهُ عَبْداً،
وَهُوَ لَا يُحِبُّ أَنْ تَكُونَ لِغَيْرِهِ عَبْداً.

**210: You do not love anything
without becoming its slave.
But He does not want you to be
a slave to other-than-Himself.**

When the heart loves something, it turns to it and is humble to it and obeys it in all that it commands. The lover obeys the one he loves. This is the reality of slavehood – humbleness and obedience. The heart has only one face. Whenever it turns towards its Master, it turns away from other than Him and is His slave in reality. When someone turns to their desires, they turn away from their Master and are a slave to other-than-Him. Allah – glory be to Him! – is not pleased for His slave to be a slave to other than Him. Allah Almighty says about this, censuring someone who is a slave to his passion: *"Have you seen him who takes his whims and desires to be his god whom Allah has misguided knowingly, sealing up his hearing and his heart and placing a blindfold over his eyes? Who then will guide him after Allah?"* (45:22) This *ayah* is a text censuring someone who loves his lower desires rather than his Master.

As for the interpretation of the people of the inward, it is actually an indication (*ishara*), not commentary (*tafsir*). We read in a hadith that the Qur'an has an outward and an inward, a measure and something beyond it. The hadith, which is not in any of the major collections, reads: "Not an *ayah* has been revealed of the Qur'an but that it has an outward and an inward, and every letter has a frontier (*hadd*) and every frontier has something beyond it." And it is reported that the shaykh of our shaykh, Sidi Muhammad ibn 'Abdullah, said about what is indicated by this *ayah*, "It is possible that it is, in fact, an *ayah* of praise and means: 'Have you seen the one who takes his God, who created him, as the object of his desire and does not love other than Him? He makes him wander astray in His love with knowledge and a clear sign from his Lord and He has sealed up his hearing and heart with His love. He has put a covering on his sight, preventing him from looking at other than Him. Anyone who has been given this immense guidance, has no guide after Allah except Him.'"

Conveying this meaning is outside of the literal understanding of the *ayah* and gives us an inward meaning for it. It is not valid as a *tafsir* of the *ayah*. You should know that the explanation of the words of Allah and the words of the Messenger of Allah ﷺ, which the People of the Inward sometimes give to them and which runs counter to the ordinary meaning, is not considered by them to be the same as the normative understanding of the texts concerned. Such people always confirm the orthodox understanding of the *ayah* or the *hadith* but then they point out the subtle indications, fine points, and secrets which may lie beyond what is demanded by a literal interpretation of the words. Allah has selected them and enabled them to do this it by the purity of their secrets. This is mentioned by the author in *Lata'if al-Minan*.

To return to the topic of seeking true slavehood to Allah and freedom from being a slave to anything else, the Prophet ﷺ said, "Ruined and lost is the slave of this world and the slave of the dirham and the slave of the garment. May he be disappointed and fail! May he be pierced with a thorn and not extract it." Imam al-Junayd was asked, "Who is really a slave?" He replied, "The one in whose heart there remains the slightest attachment to other than Allah because the *mukatib* remains a slave as long as he still owes a single dirham." He was asked, "Who is then is a free man?" He replied, "The one who is rescued from the bondage of his nature and whose heart is delivered from the appetites of his *nafs*."

Shaykh ash-Shibli had a follower. One day someone gave him nice *jelaba* to wear and he put it on and went to visit the shaykh. Ash-Shibli was wearing a tall hat on his head and desire for that hat entered the heart of that *faqir*. He thought to himself that it would go very nicely with his new *jelaba*. The shaykh saw this and so he stripped the man of the *jelaba*, took off his own hat and threw them both into the fire, saying to him, "There should not remain in your heart any turning to other than Allah." One of the people of the outward, who was present and rigid in his outward adherence to the *shari'a*, was appalled at the shaykh's action and angrily voiced his objection to it. He was unable to understand what lay behind the shaykh's behaviour and that sometimes what the Sufis do is based on the reality of what is in people's hearts.

Know that whoever is saved from the bondage of his animal nature and rescued from the captivity of his *nafs* will truly realise love of his Lord. Love has a beginning, a middle and an end. The beginning and first stage of love is holding steadfastly to obeying Allah's commands and avoiding His prohibitions. The Almighty says: *"If you love Allah, then follow me and Allah will love you."* (3:31) The middle stage of love is shown by the tongue extolling Him with *dhikr* and the attachment of the heart to witnessing the Beloved. Its end cannot be grasped by expression or captured by allusion. A poet said of it:

> Only Allah remains. There is no Lord but Him,
> the Beloved of the heart, withdrawn from every goal.
> Congratulations to the one who obtains
> the love of His Beloved
> and plunges into the noblest source by leaving every other.
> A blessing without end for him, renewed
> in every moment by the number of his breaths.

# Derse 67

لَا تَيْأَسْ مِنْ قَبُولِ عَمَلٍ لَا تَجِدُ فِيهِ وُجُودَ الْحُضُورِ، فَرُبَّمَا قَبِلَ مِنَ الْعَمَلِ مَا لَمْ تُدْرِكْ ثَمَرَتُهُ عَاجِلًا.

**219: Don't despair of His accepting an action when you do not find any presence in it. He may accept the action even if you do not perceive its fruits immediately.**

We already mentioned the words of the shaykh: "If you find the fruit of your deeds quickly, that is a proof of their acceptance!" This does not mean, however, that if you do not find that fruit, they are not accepted. He is silent about that. If the conditions of acceptance exist for them from the *shari'a* point of view, in other words if they are accompanied by sincerity, *taqwa* and legal correctness, then they are accepted by Allah, Allah willing, whether or not any fruit from them appears.

So if you fear Allah outwardly and inwardly as much as you can, and do your actions sincerely for the sake of Allah, but do not experience sweetness in them or the presence of your heart in them and do not find their fruit in terms of experiencing inward expansion or greater awareness of Allah, do not despair of Allah's acceptance of them. Lack of the existence of such states and the experience of sweetness does not necessarily mean that our actions are not accepted. On the contrary it is very possible for actions to be accepted whose fruits are not immediately perceived. Allah may give you the reward for them later. So you must never think little of your actions or abandon them on account of your lack of presence in them or failure to experience any sweetness from them. Rather you must continue doing them until you pluck their fruits. If someone persists in knocking on the door, that door will certainly be opened for him. Listen to what the poet says:

> Seek and do not worry about attainment.
> The bane of the seeker is to become frustrated.
> Do you not see that by constant dripping,
> water wears away the hardest stone.

Remember the story of the worshipper who remained in Makka for forty years, saying, "At Your service, O Allah. At Your service!" while all the time an unseen voice was saying, "Not at Your service! Your hajj is rejected." He continued, not leaving his place or stopping his action. A man came to sit with him and when the worshipper said, "At Your service," and the voice said, "Not at your service!" he got up and left him, saying to himself, "This is a man who has been rejected!" The worshipper called to him, "Why are you leaving?" He replied, "Sidi, you said, 'At Your service' and a voice replied to you, 'Not at your service'!" He told him,

"I have been hearing this voice for forty years. But is there any other door I can go and stand at? If Allah were to drive me away a million times, I still would not leave His door." So Allah Almighty accepted him and the next time he said, "At Your service," a voice came back, "My slave, at your service and assistance!" See how the one who clings to the door is joined to the lovers and the door is opened to him. That is why the Prophet ﷺ said, "The action which Allah loves most is the most constant, even if it is only little." And he said ﷺ, "Allah does not grow weary [of giving rewards] until you grow weary [of asking]."

The purpose of our action is to carry out the duties of slavehood and to honour the rights of Allah's Lordship. Its purpose not to seek states and stations. According to the people who have true knowledge of *tawhid,* doing that detracts from sincerity. In fact a state may well become an obstacle for someone who stops at it and finds it sweet. That is why one of the people of Allah said, "Fear the sweetness of obedience. It is a deadly poison for the one who stops with it. How many people are prevented by it from witnessing the One Who is Worshipped!" Therefore do not be the slave of the state; be the slave of the Maker of states. Explaining this further the author says:

لَا تُزَكِّيَنَّ وَارِداً لَا تَعْلَمُ ثَمَرَتَهُ، فَلَيْسَ الْمُرَادُ مِنَ السَّحَابَةِ الْإِمْطَارَ، وَإِنَّمَا الْمُرَادُ مِنْهَا وُجُودُ الْأَثْمَارِ الْإِثْمَار.

## 220: Do not claim true reality for any spiritual state until you know its fruits.
## It is not rain that is desired from the clouds.
## It is the production of fruit that is desired from them.

The real fruit of a spiritual state is genuine inner transformation, in other words the elimination of harmful characteristics within your being and the acquisition of beneficial ones, the eradication of vices and attainment of virtues. If you wish, you could say that the fruit of the genuine spiritual state is true repentance, humility, serenity, forbearance, *zuhd*, generosity, and selflessness. It brings about freedom from the domination of physical appetites and defects of the *nafs* and enables you to escape from the prison of outward existence and ascend to the open space of inward witnessing and vision.

The Shaykh has mentioned all these things in different places. He said at the beginning of the book: "He only sent a spiritual state to you so that it would bring you to Him. He sent a spiritual state to you to deliver you from the control of other than Him and to free you from being a slave to outward appearances. He sent a spiritual state to you to release you from the prison of your worldly existence and bring you to the open space of inner witnessing." And he said later: "When a true spiritual state comes to you from Allah it tears your bad habits to pieces." If a spiritual state comes upon you and does not have this result – does not leave you with the qualities we have mentioned – do not regard it as being genuine. Be very much on your guard concerning it in case it has a satanic origin. A divinely inspired spiritual state is followed by coolness, stillness, abstinence, and serenity. A satanically inspired spiritual state is followed by fervour, arrogance, aggressiveness and self-affirmation.

What is desired of any such state is not its joy, lightness and ecstasy, in other words its feelgood factor. What is desired of it is the true fruit we mentioned earlier, things that truly do ensure your advancement on the Path of Allah. So rainclouds are indeed an accurate metaphor for spiritual states. What is actually desired from rainclouds is not in fact the rain that comes down from them. What is really desired from them is the coming into being of the fruits that the rain produces out of the soil it mixes with.

# Derse 68

$$\text{لَا تَطْلُبَنَّ بَقَاءَ الْوَارِدَاتِ بَعْدَ أَنْ بَسَطَتْ أَنْوَارُهَا وَأَوْدَعَتْ أَسْرَارَهَا، فَلَكَ فِي اللَّهِ غِنًى عَنْ كُلِّ شَيْءٍ، وَلَيْسَ يُغْنِيكَ عَنْهُ شَيْءٌ.}$$

**221: Do not desire a spiritual state to remain
after its lights have expanded
and its secrets have been deposited.
In Allah you have richness
beyond need of anything else.
But nothing makes you rich beyond need of Him.**

Seeking for a thing indicates love of it and when you love a thing you are enslaved by it. Allah Almighty does not like you being a slave to anything except Him. Therefore do not seek to have a state or station with Him. If states, which are of divine origin, come upon you and then they dissolve and depart, do not seek to make them last after their lights have expanded in your heart and the darkness of other than Allah and created forms have been expelled from it and its secrets of increased certainty and direct witnessing are lodged in it. You could say, "Do not seek for spiritual states to continue after their lights have expanded, freeing you from the bondage of physical appetites and habits of the self, ridding you of your bad qualities and adorning you with good ones." For this is what results from the lights of true spiritual states. When their secrets are lodged in your heart they take the form of certainty, peace of mind and knowledge, or doing without, contentment and submission, or humility, abasement and contrition. This is the sign of the authenticity of the spiritual state and the reaping of its harvest. When that happens, you have no need of anything else. In Allah you have wealth beyond need of everything and have no need of anything. Nothing will enrich you beyond your need for Him. As the shaykh will say, "What has the one who lacks You found? What does one who has found You lack?" A poet said:

> For everything that leaves you there is recompense.
> But if Allah leaves you, there is no recompense.

It is indicated from Allah: "Do not rely on anything except Me. It will bring you misfortune and kill you. If you rely on knowledge, We will pursue you in it. If you take refuge in action, We will return it to you. If you trust in a state, We will make you stop with it. If you feel at home with ecstasy, We will lead you on in it. If you look to creatures, We will entrust you to them. If you are deluded by gnosis, We will disguise it for you. So what device and what strength do you have with Me? Be pleased with Us as a Lord so that We are pleased with you as a slave." Abu Sulayman ad-Darani was asked about the best with which one can draw near to Allah and said, "The best way to draw near to Allah is to look at your heart and not to desire other than Him in this world and the next." It is said about that:

> Whoever recognises Allah and is not sufficed by direct knowledge of Allah,
> that is the one who is wretched.
> The slave does not act by the might of wealth,
> and all might belongs to the godfearing.

If you obtain wealth by Allah, you have no need of anything other than Him. So do not hope to make the state continue, or at any *warid* or station other than witnessing the All-Knowing King. Your hoping to make the state or *warid* continue is evidence that you are not enriched by Him, as the shaykh explains:

تَطَلُّعُكَ إِلَى بَقَاءِ غَيْرِهِ دَلِيلٌ عَلَى عَدَمِ وِجْدَانِكَ لَهُ

### 222a: A proof that you have not found Him: you are waiting and hoping for other-than-Him to continue.

If you find Him, then you will not be looking for anything else and will not need anything at all. So anyone who delights in the *warid* and state has not achieved union. Anyone who is in need of other than Allah is not someone with direct knowledge of Allah. Anyone who needs something, or relies on something other than Allah, has nothing to do with us and does not have anything. I often say to the *fuqara*, "Anyone you see visiting anyone other than the Shaykh after taking the *wird* remains one of the common people and shows by his lack of true sincerity that he has not entered the land of the elite. If he had entered the land of the elite, then his *himma* would be concentrated and his heart gathered and he would not need the water of other than him. His thirst for other than his shaykh is proof that he had not drunk from his water. How excellent is what the speaker, who I think is al-Ghazali, said:

My heart had disparate desires,
but since my eye saw You, My desires are concentrated.
So those whom I had envied began to envy me,
and I became a master of mankind since You are my Master.
I left people their *deen* and this world,
being busy with Your *dhikr*, O my *deen* and my world!

One of the signs of wealth in Allah is also intimacy with Him and alienation from other than Him. Allah has no need of anything but nothing is free of need of Him. When someone wants a state or station other than witnessing his Lord and then does not achieve it, he is far from the Divine Presence, as the Shaykh then explains:

وَاسْتِيحَاشُكَ بِفِقْدَانِ مَا سِوَاهُ
دَلِيلٌ عَلَى عَدَمِ وُصْلَتِكَ بِهِ .

**222b: A proof that you have not reached Him:
you are grieved when you do not have other-than-Him.**

Your grief at failing to achieve states and *waridat* is proof that you have not arrived since, if you had reached Allah, you would not be grieved by lack of anything. In reality, you do not lack anything. The sign of wealth in Allah is that when someone loses something, whose loss normally causes pain, like that of a child, for instance, or a relative, or pleasure in physical worship, or anything like that, he resorts to his direct knowledge of Allah and has no need of anything. That is what is desired of the slave. The Almighty says: *"That is so that you will not be grieved about the things that pass you by or exult about the things that come to you."* (57:22)

We read in *at-Tanwir*: "Know that Allah Almighty makes you enter a state so that you can gain by it, not so that it diminishes you. It comes bearing the gift of Allah's recognition of you. He brings it about by His Name, the One Who Begins, and initiates it and makes it last until it has conveyed to you what it contains. When it has conveyed its trust, He turns to it with His Name, the Returner, and makes it return and takes it back. So do not seek to make the messenger remain after he has conveyed his message nor to make the trustee remain after he has handed over his trust. False claimants are disgraced by the removal of states and they are dismissed from the ranks of position. So the fault appears and the veils are imposed. How many a person lays claim to being enriched by Allah when in fact he is only being enriched by his obedience, its light and opening! How many a person lays claim to might in Allah when he is only being strengthened by his position and antipathy towards creation, relying on what his appearance of knowledge establishes with them! So be the slave of Allah, not the slave of causes. Since you have in reality a Lord and not a cause, be for Him as He is for you."

# Derse 69

مِنْ تَمَامِ النِّعْمَةِ عَلَيْكَ أَنْ يَرْزُقَكَ
مَا يَكْفِيكَ وَيَمْنَعُكَ مَا يُطْغِيكَ .

## 225: An aspect of perfect happiness is that He provides you with what is enough for you and prevents you from overstepping the limits

An aspect of Allah's granting perfect happiness to His slave is that he directs his aspiration to Himself alone and frees his heart from any attachment whatsoever to other than Him. So He provides him with sufficient to prevent him from being attached to other than Him. That is wealth by Allah and there is no greater blessing than wealth by Allah and withdrawal from other than Him. And Allah protects His slave from anything that might lead him to overstep the limits and therefore from being distracted by that from his Lord. When Allah provides someone with what is enough to support them physically, by way of food, drink and shelter, and spiritually, in terms of knowledge, action, and direct experience, and protects them from anything that might make them overstep, and so prevent them from being present with their Lord, then His blessing to them is complete. So thank Him for all He has given you, turn to Him alone in your difficulties and reject anything that prevents your heart from rising to Him.

Allah says: *"Allah will defend those who believe,"* (22:36) and He says: *"Allah is with those who show fear of Him and with those who are good-doers."* (16:128) The Prophet ﷺ sought refuge from all that distracts the heart and makes a person forget their Lord, be that poverty or wealth. He used to seek refuge from poverty which makes you forget and wealth which makes you overstep. He said ﷺ, "O Allah, make the provision of the family of Muhammad adequate!" And he said ﷺ, "The best *dhikr* is the hidden one," in other words *dhikr* of the heart, which is reflection, "and the best provision is that which is adequate." The Prophet ﷺ said, "The sun does not rise without two angels accompanying it who are heard by all creatures except jinn and men. They say, 'O people, hasten to your Lord! What is little and adequate is better than what is abundant and diverting.'" And in another hadith the Prophet ﷺ said, "Wealth is not having a lot of goods. Wealth is self-sufficiency." Commenting on that a poet said:

> The wealth of the self is what suffices it
> > and satisfies its needs.
> > If it has more than that,
> > then that wealth turns into loss.

'Abdu'l-Wahid ibn Zayd ؓ said, "I heard that there was a mad girl in the ruins of Ayla saying wise things. I searched for her until I found her. Her head was shaved and she was wearing a woollen robe. When she saw me, she said, 'Welcome to you, 'Abdu'l-Wahid.' I was amazed that she knew my name me when she had never met me before. I replied, 'May Allah welcome you.' Then she asked, 'What has brought you here?' I said, 'Counsel me.' She said, 'Astonishing! A counsellor seeking counsel! Know, 'Abdu'l-Wahid, that when a slave of Allah has what is adequate for him and then inclines to something more of this world, Allah strips from him the sweetness of abstinence and he will find himself bewildered and distracted. If he is favoured by Allah, he will be inspired in his secret by the words, "My slave, I wanted to magnify your worth with My angels, make you an example for My *awliya* and a guide for the people who obey Me, but then you inclined to the goods of this world and forsook Me. So I alienated you after your intimacy with Me, abased after your might, and impoverished you after your wealth. Return to the way you were before and I will return to you what you used to know yourself to be."' Then she left me and the regret remained in my heart."

It says in one of the revealed Books, "The least that a scholar will suffer when he inclines to this world is that he will be stripped of the sweetness of intimate conversation with Me." Having what is enough for you is a blessing but having more than that can be a punishment, as the shaykh said, because the *nafs* is naturally disposed to love gifts and hate loss. When it receives gifts, it feels delight. If they are taken away, it is distressed. If someone wants his joy to continue, he should not take more than what is enough to suffice him and then he will not be distressed at losing it as the shaykh makes clear when he says:

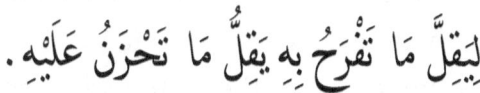

## 226: If you are happy with little, there's very little that will make you sad.

If you want your happiness to last, do not seek to possess anything whose loss would cause you grief. Your sorrow over its loss is evidence of your love for it. If you confine yourself to what you have no choice about where property, rank, authority or anything else are concerned, losing what you have is unlikely to be a cause of distress to you. One of the people of Allah was asked, "Why are you never sad?" He replied, "Because I do not acquire anything whose loss would make me sad." A poet said about that:

> Whoever does not want see what will cause him grief
> should not acquire anything which he fears to lose.

It is reported that a king was once presented with a turquoise goblet inlaid with gems, unique in its craftmanship and beauty. He was extremely delighted by it. He asked one of wise counsellors with him "What do you think of this?" The man replied, "I see it as a source of affliction and deprivation." The king asked, "How is that?" He answered, "If it is broken, it will be a great misfortune. If it is stolen, you will miss it badly and you will not be able to find anything like it to replace it. Before it was brought to you, you were safe from either of these tribulations." It happened that the goblet did get broken and the king was indeed intensely distressed about it. He said, "My wise counsellor spoke the truth. If only it had never been brought to us and we had never set eyes on it!"

There is another aspect of the matter which is better than this. It is that if you are free from your *nafs* and then it becomes a target for the arrows of fate, you will not oppose your Lord in what He does to you. When that is the case there is no doubt that you will be tranquil and your joy will persist because that means you will always be happy with whatever comes from your Lord and you will welcome it with pleasure, experiencing the sweetness of the coolness of submission to His will.

# Derse 70

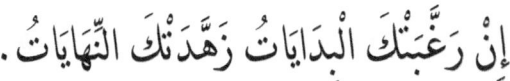

**228a: If you find the beginning of things attractive,
You will find that their endings repel you.**

A high position that is ephemeral, such as one based on wealth, connections, family or whatever it may be of worldly prestige, begins with the sweetness of the self's enjoyment of it and its share in it; but then its end is made bitter by the loss of that high position and by the abasement and humiliation which follows it. If this high position, whose initial sweetness will vanish, seems attractive to you at first, the bitterness of its ending will certainly repel you. Do not let your delusion at the outward glamour of things of this world, deceive you regarding the inevitable, eventual regret hidden within them. A poet has written:

> If someone praises this world for something
> that delights them in it,
> by my life, they will soon be blaming it.
> When it is taken away, they feel nothing but regret,
> and when it increases, they are overwhelmed by its cares.

'Ali wrote to Salman al-Farisi, "The metaphor of this world is that of a snake. It is soft to the touch but its venom is deadly. Turn away from all that you like in it because it will only be with you for a short time. Do not let it worry you too much because you know for certain you will leave it. The happier you are in it, the sadder you will be about leaving it." It is said that Allah has linked this world to calamities and disasters and revealed to it: "Be harsh to My friends and gentle and sweet to My enemies!"

If someone looks at this world objectively, they will be content with a bare minimum of it since there is nothing good in it that does not have a most unpleasant opposite: like wealth and penury, youth and senility, health and illness, joy and sorrow, worldly power and humiliating abasement, and finally life and death. It is related about the righteous wali, Sidi Qasim ibn Sabih, that a governor wanted to harm him and so he fled to the tomb of Imam al-Ghazali. He sat there, in his troubled state. A branch of basil stretched out to him from the grave with a paper on which these two verses were written in ink that had not yet dried:

> When time casts upon you a disaster one day,
> welcome it with patience and expand your breast to it.
> For the vicissitudes of time are many and varied.
> One day you see hardship and another day ease.

When someone halts at the outward appearance of something of this world, unseen voices call to him from inside it: "This is just an outward allurement, so do not be deluded." This is the meaning of the shaykh's next words:

إِنْ دَعَاكَ إِلَيْهَا ظَاهِرٌ نَهَاكَ عَنْهَا بَاطِنٌ .

## 228b: If the outward of something invites you to it, its inward should hold you back from it.

The outward of this world appears sweet and verdant but its inward is actually foul and bitter. It has been compared to salty water which drowns and does not quench. The one who possesses this world drowns in their love of it and dies thirsting for it. It has also been compared to a dream in which a sleeper experiences great happiness only to wake up to the ongoing difficulties of their daily life. Some else said that it is like honey mixed with a deadly poison; it is consumed with relish but then afflicts and kills the one who eats it. Yet another compared this world to a will-o'-the-wisp which, if followed, leads you to destruction but if turned away from has no damaging effect on you at all.

As the Prophet ﷺ told us, the Fire is surrounded by indulgence of the lower appetites and the Garden by patience in adversity, so Allah *ta'ala* makes this world difficult for the believers, in order to encourage them to turn from it. This is so that they will advance towards Him with their whole being and make Him their aspiration and so that they will turn away from this world and turn towards the Next World. Thus Allah Almighty constricts this lower world for the believers so that they will rise from it to the world above. Only people of true insight are able to appreciate that independently; most of us need help to enable us to reach that understanding. The shaykh indicates this by saying:

عَلِمَ أَنَّكَ لَا تَقْبَلُ النُّصْحَ الْمُجَرَّدَ لِمُجَرَّدِ الْقَوْلِ،
فَذَوَّقَكَ مِنْ ذَوَاقِهَا مَا سَهَّلَ عَلَيْكَ فِرَاقَهَا.

## 230: He knew that you would not accept simple good advice, so He let you taste this world a bit so that it would be easy for you to part with it.

Allah knew that some of His slaves would not accept simple good advice and would not turn from this world simply by virtue of being warned about it. How many – even people of knowledge – listen to the Qur'an alerting them to its dangers and warning them about its delusory nature and yet still ignore that reminder. So when Allah desires to choose for His presence those of His slaves He wishes, He disturbs things for them in this world and imposes afflictions and trials on them. All of that is from their Lord's concern for them so that they will taste the bitterness of its inward reality and not be deluded by the sweetness of its outward appearance. The Prophet ﷺ was asked, "Who are the friends of Allah who will feel no fear and know no sorrow?" He replied, "Those who look at the inward reality of this world when most people look at its outward appearance, and are concerned with the end result when most people are only concerned with the here and now."

So all these manifestations of Majesty, these difficulties that change the self and subdue it, are immensely beneficial. It is said that trials come according to a person's ability to withstand them and that every trial they go through increases their standing with Allah. It may be that something of love for something of this world remains in someone's heart, or reliance on something in it, and so Allah gives power over them to someone or something that will give them trouble and make things difficult for them. All of that is out of concern for them so that they will travel eagerly from this world to the world of light. Then sweetness and bitterness, might and abasement, wealth and poverty are all the same for them because they realise that all is from Allah and there is nothing but Him in existence. This is true knowledge, the only knowledge which is really useful.

## Detailed Contents

| | |
|---|---|
| **Foreword** | **1** |
| **Derse 1** | **3** |
| 1: A sure sign of reliance on action | 3 |
| **Derse 2** | **10** |
| 2: Your desire for divestment | 10 |
| **Derse 3** | **17** |
| 4: Give yourself a rest from management: | 17 |
| **Derse 4** | **22** |
| 5: Your earnest striving for what has already been guaranteed to you | 22 |
| 6: Do not make a delay in His giving you something you have fervently prayed for, | 25 |
| **Derse 5** | **28** |
| 7: Do not let the fact that something promised does not happen, | 28 |
| **Derse 6** | **34** |
| 8: If He opens up a way of making Himself known to you, | 34 |

## Detailed Contents

| | |
|---|---|
| **Derse 7** | **40** |
| 10: Actions are simply set-up images. | 40 |
| **Derse 8** | **44** |
| 11: Bury your existence in the earth of obscurity. | 44 |
| **Derse 9** | **50** |
| 13a: How can a heart be illuminated | 50 |
| 13b: And how can it travel to Allah | 53 |
| **Derse 10** | **55** |
| 17: Anyone who wants something | 55 |
| **Derse 11** | **59** |
| 18: Putting off action until you have free time | 59 |
| **Derse 12** | **62** |
| 19: Don't ask Him to remove you from one state | 62 |
| **Derse 13** | **65** |
| 24: Do not be surprised at the appearance of worry and sorrow | 65 |
| **Derse 14** | **70** |
| 25: There is no stopping a goal | 70 |
| 26: A sign of success in the end: | 72 |
| 27: Whoever has a radiant beginning | 74 |
| **Derse 15** | **75** |
| 28: What is stored away in the unseen dimension of the secrets | 75 |
| 29: What a difference there is between someone guided by Him, | 76 |
| 30: As for those who have reached Him: | 80 |

### Derse 16 — 82
- 31: Those travelling to Him — 82

### Derse 17 — 85
- 32: Better to look at the defects hidden inside you — 85
- 33: The Real is not veiled — 87

### Derse 18 — 90
- 34: From the qualities of your humanness, — 90
- 35a: The root of every act of rebellion, every appetite — 93
- 35b: The root of every act of obedience and self-restraint — 93

### Derse 19 — 95
- 38: Do not let the intention of your *himma* veer to other-than-Him. — 95
- 39a: Do not ask other-than-Him to relieve you of a need — 96
- 39b: How can anyone relieve it other than the One — 97
- 39c: If someone is incapable of relieving their own need — 98

### Derse 20 — 100
- 40: If you cannot think well of Him — 100
- 41: What could be more astonishing than that — 103

### Derse 21 — 105
- 42a: Do not travel from created being to created being. — 105
- 42b: Look at the words of the Prophet ﷺ: — 108

## Detailed Contents

**Derse 22** — **111**
    45: No amount of action stemming from the heart of a *zahid* can ever be called small. — 111

**Derse 23** — **115**
    47: Do not give up *dhikr* of Allah — 115

**Derse 24** — **120**
    48: A sign of the death of the heart: — 120
    49: Do not become so overwhelmed by your wrong action — 121
    50: There is no minor wrong action when you are confronted by His justice. — 125

**Derse 25** — **127**
    60: It is only their growth from the seed of covetousness — 127

**Derse 26** — **131**
    63: Whoever does not advance to Allah — 131

**Derse 27** — **135**
    64: Whoever is not grateful for blessings — 135
    65: Have fear that the fact that He remains good to you — 138

**Derse 28** — **141**
    66: It is ignorance on the part of a *murid* with bad *adab* — 141

**Derse 29** — **146**
    73: If you want to know your worth with Him — 146
    74: When He gives you obedience — 149

**Derse 30** — **151**
    75: The best thing you can ask for from Him — 151
    76: Sorrow over loss of obedience — 153

## Derse 31 — 156
    78: Hope goes hand in hand with action. — 156

## Derse 32 — 160
    80: He expands you so as not to keep you in contraction. — 160

## Derse 33 — 165
    83: It may be that in giving to you He deprives you, — 165
    84: When He opens for you the door of understanding what deprivation really is, — 167

## Derse 34 — 170
    85a: Material existence: Its outward is deception; — 170
    85b: The *nafs* looks at their outward deception, — 173

## Derse 35 — 175
    86: If you want the kind of might that will never vanish — 175

## Derse 36 — 179
    88: A gift from a creature is really deprivation — 179

## Derse 37 — 183
    89: Our Lord is far too majestic, when a slave deals with Him in cash, — 183
    90: It is enough repayment for your obedience — 185
    91: Enough of a reward for the actively obedient — 185

## Derse 38 — 188
    92: Whoever worships Him for something they hope for from Him — 188

# Detailed Contents

**Derse 39**     **192**
     93: When He gives to you,
     He is showing you His goodness.     192

**Derse 40**     **196**
     95a: He may well open the door of obedience for you     196
     95b: He may well decree wrong action for you     197
     96: Disobedience that instils abasement
     and utter poverty is better than obedience     198

**Derse 41**     **201**
     105: Let the pain of affliction be lessened for you by     201
     106: Anyone who thinks that His pervading gentleness
     is in any way separate from His Decree     203

**Derse 42**     **205**
     107: What is feared for you is not that
     the Path will be unclear to you.     205

**Derse 43**     **208**
     112: Only an ignorant man disparages the *wird*.     208

**Derse 44**     **213**
     114: When he wakes up in the morning
     the heedless person     213

**Derse 45**     **217**
     115: The worshippers and the abstinent
     are alienated from everything     217
     116: In this world He commanded you
     to look into the things He brought into being     219

## Derse 46 — 223

    118a: Since He knows that you easily become bored,   223

    118b: And He knows you are prone to overdoing things, 224

    118c: This is so that your aspiration will be to establish the prayer,   225

    118d: For not everyone who does the prayer establishes it.   226

## Derse 47 — 228

    119a: The prayer is purification for the hearts   228

    119b: …a way of opening the door to the unseen worlds.   229

    120a: Prayer is the place of intimate exchange   230

    120b: …a mine of mirrored purity.   231

## Derse 48 — 233

    121: When you ask for recompense for an action,   233

    122: Do not seek a recompense for an action of which you are not the doer.   235

## Derse 49 — 238

    123: When He wants to manifest His overflowing favour to you,   238

    124: There is no end of reasons to blame you   241

## Derse 50 — 243

    127: How can normal patterns be broken for you   243

## Derse 51 — 247

    131: If it were not for the beauty of His veiling,   247

    132: You are more in need of His forbearance when you obey Him than when you disobey Him.   248

    133: There are two sorts of veiling:   249

# Detailed Contents

**Derse 52**                                      **252**

    134: Anyone who honours you             252

    135a: Your only true companion is the One Who keeps your company in full knowledge of your faults,     254

    135b: The best companion is the One Who seeks you    255

**Derse 53**                                      **257**

    142: People praise you because of what they suppose is in you,             257

    143: When the believer is praised, he is ashamed before Allah             258

    144: The most ignorant of people             259

    145: When He lets you be praised             261

**Derse 54**                                      **263**

    148: When a wrong action issues from you,             263

    149: If you want the door of hope to open for you             265

    150: He might teach you during the night of contraction 266

**Derse 55**                                      **269**

    151: The rising-places of lights are the hearts and secrets             269

    152: There is a light lodged in the heart             271

**Derse 56**                                      **274**

    156: Glory be to Him Who makes guidance to His *awliya*             *274*

**Derse 57**                                      **278**

    159a: The portion of the self in disobedience    278

    159b: It is very hard to cure what is hidden.    280

    160: You might show off in such a way             280

**Derse 58** — **283**
- 175: You might find a gain in states of need — 283
- 176: States of need are carpet loads of gifts. — 283
- 177: If you want gifts to come to you establish poverty and need in yourself. — 283

**Derse 59** — **288**
- 187: Expressions are nourishment for needy listeners. — 288

**Derse 60** — **293**
- 192: When two matters are unclear to you, see which is heavier on the self and follow that! — 293

**Derse 61** — **297**
- 194: He specified particular times for acts of obedience — 297
- 195: He knows of His slaves lack of enthusiasm — 299
- 196: He has made service of Him obligatory for you. — 301

**Derse 62** — **302**
- 197: Anyone who finds it strange that Allah should rescue him from his appetites — 302
- 198: Sometimes darkness may come over you — 305
- 199: Anyone who fails to recognise the value of blessings — 309

**Derse 63** — **311**
- 200: Do not let the inflow from your blessings dazzle you so much — 311
- 201: The sweetness of desire ingrained in the heart: — 314
- 202: Appetite only leaves the heart through an unsettling fear — 315

# Detailed Contents

**Derse 64**     **318**
    203: As He does not love a shared action,     318
    204: There are lights that are allowed to arrive.     321

**Derse 65**     **323**
    208a: There are rights of some times     323
    208b: For no moment arrives in which
    you do not owe Allah a new duty     324
    209: You cannot bring back
    any of your life which has gone     326

**Derse 66**     **329**
    210: You do not love anything
    without becoming its slave.     329

**Derse 67**     **333**
    219: Don't despair of His accepting an action     333
    220: Do not claim true reality for any spiritual state     336

**Derse 68**     **338**
    221: Do not desire a spiritual state to remain     338
    222a: A proof that you have not found Him:     340
    222b: A proof that you have not reached Him:     341

**Derse 69**     **344**
    225: An aspect of perfect happiness is that
    He provides you with what is enough for you     344
    226: If you are happy with little,     347

**Derse 70**     **349**
    228a: If you find the beginning of things attractive,     349
    228b: If the outward of something invites you to it,     351
    230: He knew that you would not accept
    simple good advice,     352

www.ingramcontent.com/pod-product-compliance
Lightning Source LLC
Chambersburg PA
CBHW021959160426
43197CB00007B/191